DISCARD

```
HD          The Courage to
5715.2      change
.C64
```

THE COURAGE TO CHANGE

THE COURAGE TO CHANGE

New Directions
for Career Education

Edited by
ROMAN C. PUCINSKI
and SHARLENE PEARLMAN HIRSCH

PRENTICE-HALL, INC., Englewood Cliffs, New Jersey

© 1971 by PRENTICE-HALL, INC., Englewood Cliffs, New Jersey

All rights reserved. No part of this book may be reproduced, in any form, by mimeograph or any other means, without permission in writing from the publisher.

13-184440-7

Library of Congress Catalog Card Number: 70-152862

Printed in the United States of America

Current printing (last digit):
10 9 8 7 6 5 4 3 2 1

PRENTICE-HALL INTERNATIONAL, INC., London
PRENTICE-HALL OF AUSTRALIA, PTY., LTD., Sydney
PRENTICE-HALL OF CANADA, LTD., Toronto
PRENTICE-HALL OF INDIA (PRIVATE) LIMITED, New Delhi
PRENTICE-HALL OF JAPAN, INC., Tokyo

CONTENTS

PREFACE ix

I
THE COURAGE TO CHANGE

PROLOGUE: A Prospectus for the Seventies
Roman C. Pucinski 3

II
POWER TO THE PEOPLE

INTRODUCTION 21
PAPER PASSPORTS TO EMPLOYMENT: A Challenge to Credentialism
Hugh Calkins 23
ACCOUNTABLE FOR WHAT? Measuring Up to the World of Work
Grant Venn 34

SCENE OF HOSTILITY AND HOPE: The City as Educator for Work
  Paul W. Briggs   43

BLACK MAN, WHITE WORLD: Necessary National Manpower Priorities
  Cleveland L. Dennard   52

THE NEW WOMANHOOD: Education for Viable Alternatives
  Elizabeth J. Simpson   59

III
TURNING AROUND THE SYSTEM

INTRODUCTION   83

WORKPOWER FOR THE SEVENTIES: Requirements for Talent, Knowledge, and Skills
  Garth L. Mangum   85

OPTING FOR CAREER EDUCATION: Emergence of the Community College
  Marvin J. Feldman   109

THE AGONY OF CHOICE: Guidance for Career Decisions
  David V. Tiedeman   121

TEACHING THE TEACHERS: New Dimensions for Instructional Roles
  Carl J. Schaefer   131

COLLABORATION AT THE CROSSROADS: Business and Education
  Samuel M. Burt   140

MARRIAGE OF VITAL SKILLS: Vocational Education and Manpower Training
  Lowell A. Burkett   150

SPARKING STATE INITIATIVE: An Education Bureaucracy Reorganizes
  Sherwood Dees   160

IV
THUNDER FROM ABOVE

CAPTAINS AT THE HELM: New Directions for Educational Leadership
Sharlene Pearlman Hirsch   171

V
THE COURAGE TO CHANGE RECONSIDERED

EPILOGUE: Prospects for the Future
Roman C. Pucinski   187

INDEX   197

PREFACE

Although neither of us knew it at the time, we probably first conceived this project at the end of 1967, when our professional association began —Roman C. Pucinski, as Chairman of the General Subcommittee on Education in the U.S. House of Representatives which led the fight for the Vocational Education Amendments (ultimately passed unanimously by the House and by a substantial majority in the Senate in 1968); and Sharlene P. Hirsch as Education Director on the Subcommittee staff assisting Congressman Pucinski with the vocational education legislation.

The contributors to this book were also instrumental in effecting those amendments in various ways. A number of them testified during the extensive hearings held by the Subcommittee on vocational education; others have been involved subsequently in evaluating or initiating programs funded under the legislation.

Since passage of the amendments, however, new questions have been raised regarding the place of career development programs in the schools. The term "vocational education" continues to conjure up stereotyped images and old prejudices, and in some school districts voc-ed programs have not quite met the expectations of those who framed the new legislation. Youth unemployment has been growing at an alarming rate. Even the students themselves have begun to question the values which underlie their entire educational experience.

Deeper consideration of the issues seems to indicate a need to turn around the entire educational system—with its insensitivities, bureaucracies, professional inbreeding, outdated standards, hesitant leadership, and lack of meaning for life and work in a complex adult world—and to refocus education on the problem of preparing young people for the world of work. This does not mean simply vocational education on a grander scale. It suggests a combination of a Deweyan view of education, one which speaks to the learner's attitudes and feelings as well as intellect, with a Gestalt perspective of the world of work—its values, social and political structures, economic orientations, etc.—as well as discrete job-skill training.

Attainment of such a monumental goal will require considerable courage—from the profession and the public. In education, as elsewhere, established institutions rapidly become entrenched in the status quo and highly resistant to pressure for change, no matter how altruistic and well-meaning their inner guard.

We were extremely fortunate in being able to attract a distinguished group of contributors whose wisdom has added significant dimensions to this volume. We express deep appreciation for their participation and patience, their commitment, and many valuable suggestions regarding the overall direction of the book.

Any undertaking of this nature obviously requires some division of labor. Each author prepared the particular chapter which bears his name. As the editors we assumed responsibility for integrating manuscripts into the overall format of the book as well as editing the papers, and any errors committed in the revision process are solely ours.

We also convey deepest thanks to the most significant people in our respective lives—Aurelia, Aurie, and Romie Pucinski, and Lee Hirsch—our best critics, most devoted supporters, and colleagues in every endeavor.

ROMAN C. PUCINSKI
SHARLENE PEARLMAN HIRSCH

THE COURAGE TO CHANGE

I

THE COURAGE TO CHANGE

PROLOGUE:
A Prospectus for the Seventies

ROMAN C. PUCINSKI

THE STATUS QUO REVISITED
Home of the Brave

Years ago philanthropist Andrew Carnegie liberally endowed a "heroes' fund" to honor average Americans who risk their lives to save others. Winners of the medals—many of which have been awarded posthumously—have swum into raging rapids, plunged into foreboding wells, flung themselves onto railroad tracks, and otherwise put their lives in jeopardy for fellow human beings.

American education has had its share of cutting-edge thinkers—Horace Mann, Henry Barnard, John Dewey, B. F. Skinner, and Jerome Bruner, to name a few—as well as the services of many other honest, dedicated professionals. But neither the public nor the profession really expects educators to be risk-takers—either in the Carnegian sense of heroes or simply as private citizens ready to sacrifice their professional careers for pedagogic principles.

Public education, for the most part, has been long on rhetoric and short on results. Many of the most stalwart, aggressive, inventive change agents have eventually found themselves "killed off" by the system—victims of bureaucratic freeze-outs as documented by David Rogers in *110 Livingston Street*,[1] scorn and apathy from colleagues and superiors, opposition from the public, or sheer exhaustion from the magnitude of

---

[1] David Rogers, *110 Livingston Street* (New York: Random House, 1968).

the task. Discouraged at expending so much energy with such disappointing results many have ended up modifying their dreams or retreating to other arenas. This tragic trend must be halted; we must develop the courage to change.

The question of personal fortitude arises here because it seems to have a direct bearing on educational quality. Indeed, ineffective leadership and educational mediocrity appear inextricably linked.

Ever since the debut of Sputnik, education has had a kind of "love-hate" relationship with the American people. In the past ten years, taxpayers have multiplied their investment in public schools. In 1963 the nation's education bill was $55.5 billion. According to U.S. Department of Health, Education, and Welfare projections, it will grow to $92.2 billion by 1980, an increase of 66 percent. Almost simultaneously, however, the education profession has been bombarded by accusations and complaints from growing segments of the public it serves.

Crossfire of Concern

Many articulate critics have commented on the contemporary education scene. This diverse group includes John Holt, Herbert Kohl, Jonathan Kozol, James Herndon, Peter Schrag, Vice-Admiral Hyman G. Rickover, Charles Silberman, Neil Postman, Edgar Friedenberg, Paul Goodman, Arthur Bestor, Ivan Illich, and Nat Hentoff. School people have been cursed by angry parent and community representatives, blessed with marvelous new technologies and curriculum developments, and, in many places, rewarded with splendid buildings that have flexible space, acoustical carpeting, and streamlined furnishings.

Nevertheless, for most of the nation's approximately 51 million elementary and secondary school students, education has survived virtually intact over the past half-century. A substantial proportion of the 20,000 American school districts persist as assembly-line organisms, with poorer quality control than any private enterprise could reasonably afford.

In a modern world of computerized information storage and retrieval, students are required to memorize facts instead of developing their intellectual strength to synthesize, relate, and critically analyze material. As former Secretary of Health, Education, and Welfare Robert H. Finch once said:

> All too often we are stuffing the heads of the young with products of earlier innovation rather than teaching them how to innovate. We treat their minds as storehouses to be filled rather than as instruments to be used.[2]

---

[2] Robert H. Finch, "That Question of Relevancy," *The School and the Democratic Environment,* The Danforth Foundation and The Ford Foundation (New York: Columbia University Press, 1970), p. 21.

Teachers bestow accolades almost exclusively for written accomplishments, although communication in a McLuhanesque world encompasses such media as film making, video taping, audio recording, television, and computers, as well as the performing and manual arts. Most serious of all, in a world where courage to change may be the key to survival, young people feel inhibited from using imagination or experimenting with new questions or answers that might be ridiculed as "wrong," "stupid," or "bad." And too often the creative teacher and imaginative school administrator find themselves shouted down by disciples of the status quo.

Every youngster is educable, according to psychologist Kenneth B. Clark, provided his teachers hold high expectations for him, and his spirit is uplifted rather than demoralized by the anger or neglect of the status quo. Students should be reading, writing, thinking, and creating at levels at least commensurate with their ages and aptitudes but, as standardized test results show, severe learning deficiencies exist in many systems, such as New York, Chicago, Los Angeles, and Washington, D.C. Herbert A. Ott estimates that man is using at maximum only 5 percent of his capacities and potentialities,[3] and the schools must share in the blame for this under-utilization of human energy.

Tyranny of Forgotten Promises

School systems share a problem in common with whales. The latter face possible extinction because of the greed of poachers and the poison of polluted waters. Furthermore, particular species of whales live in even greater danger from gigantism. Having grown so massive, these creatures hang precariously at the end of their evolutionary limb, with survival a real uncertainty.

School systems, likewise, have expanded into gross elephantine structures. In trying to serve many masters at once, they have become the "everyman" of social institutions.

The list of their obligations is lengthy. To cite a few, schools are held responsible for teaching morality; health and safety; physical development; respect for country and Constitution; appreciation of literature and the arts; proper dress and sexual attitudes; role expectations for men, women, and children; obedience of authority; reverence for free enterprise; esteem for thrift and diligence; skills in mathematics, foreign languages, English composition, and literacy; familiarity with history and geography of the world; belief in nonviolent, peaceful evolution; cooking, sewing, and child-rearing; shop, agriculture, and technical training;

---

[3] Herbert A. Ott, "New Light on the Human Potential," *Saturday Review* (December 20, 1969), pp. 14-17. Copyright 1969 Saturday Review, Inc.

driver education and office skills; decorum and deportment; leadership development; sportsmanship; and order. School systems are expected to nurture musical and artistic talents, to develop a concern for environment and drug abuse, and to guide and counsel students.

With this enormous burden and range of responsibilities, it is hardly surprising that schools so often accomplish so little. In the eyes of the public, their commitments have become the "tyranny of forgotten promises." And their response to overload has become dysfunction.

Leading the Resistance

What can the isolated teacher do with 35 to 135 students to instruct and little or no assistance, we are asked, and the question seems valid. School principals charge unresponsiveness from above; superintendents make the public the villain for not spending more; and managers in the central office downtown claim they just follow instructions. Where, then, can we begin to make changes?

Institutional resistance to reform has been dramatic and widespread in American education. As John Gardner has pointed out:

> No human organization wants to know the whole truth about the consequences of its operations. It tends to filter out the bad news and prevent the word from getting back that some things aren't working.[4]

Bertrand Russell once wrote, "Education as a rule is the strongest force on the side of what exists and against fundamental change." [5] Worse yet, such a situation tends to create virtually armed camps of students, parents, community leaders, and educators pitted against one another, some ready to destroy the system rather than be ignored any longer, others just hoping to survive the onslaught. It should be of deep concern to all that this alienation will escalate as our nation surges toward a $2 trillion economy by 1980 and leaves in its wake educational problems undreamed of by man.

Pinpointing the Malfunctions

The most glaring deficiency in American education can be stated quite simply: its content for the most part is empty, dull, and meaningless to

---

[4] Living Up To Professed Values," *The Christian Science Monitor* (September 30, 1969), p. 9. © 1969 The Christian Science Publishing society. All Rights Reserved. Quoted by permission from The Christian Science Monitor.

[5] R. Egner and L. Denonn, *The Basic Writings of Bertrand Russell* (New York: Simon and Schuster, 1961).

students; too often, it has no immediate relationship to the adult world they will face; and in too many cases it lacks humanness.

These are generalizations, of course, and there are a number of outstanding exceptions: A. S. Neill's Summerhill; the First Street School described by George Dennison in *The Lives of Children;* [6] the Children's Community Workshop in New York; Fayerwether School in Cambridge, Massachusetts; the Fifteenth Street School directed by Orson Bean; the Francis Parker School in Chicago; the Parkway School in Philadelphia; and the John Adams High School in Portland, Oregon. Except for the latter two, however, these are private institutions. Where public schools operate exciting innovations, such as the model subsystem in Boston, they exist as separate enclaves of excellence which are never allowed to permeate the overall system.

Unfortunately, the rest of American education is much as I described it. Schooling in many places, according to Paul Goodman, has degenerated into custodial operations to keep young people out of their elders' paths, out of trouble with the police, and out of circulation until they can be absorbed by more education, the army, or work. If education has become a mere holding pattern between childhood and legal maturity, the implications are alarming.

The humanistic concept of education, based on warm, supportive interaction between people, is rapidly slipping away. As Harold C. Lyon, Jr., has written: "We have conditioned teachers to deny feelings and, hence, have cut them and their students off from the rich vistas of learning which feeling can open." [7] In view of a growing hostility developed among young people and carried into adulthood, we can ask if the emergence of intellect over instinct has made man the most destructive of all living creatures.

Americans are faced with the growing reality that public education may well be dying. Various bids have already been made for the corpse. Ivan Illich would abolish all schools.[8] Christopher Jencks would give vouchers to parents and make schools lure customers or die. Both are intriguing ideas which bear study and experimentation, but these paths cannot be allowed to replace universal public education. Clearly, a great many aspects of the present situation are untenable, and alternatives

---

[6] George Dennison, *The Lives of Children* (New York: Simon and Schuster, 1961).

[7] Harold C. Lyon, Jr., "Learning to Feel—Humanistic Education and Tomorrow's Schools," *Needs of Elementary and Secondary Education for the Seventies: A Compendium of Policy Papers,* General Subcommittee on Education, Committee on Education and Labor, U.S. House of Representatives, ed. Sharlene Pearlman Hirsch (Washington, D.C.: U.S. Government Printing Office, 1970), pp. 553-62.

[8] See Ivan Illich, "Why We Must Abolish Schooling," *The New York Review* (July 2, 1970), pp. 9-15.

must be offered. Yet, neither obliteration nor resurrection of the existing concept is sufficient. Nothing short of a new renaissance for learning is now in order, and it cannot come about unless we have the courage to change.

The crucial question for the seventies is two-pronged: it asks whether most educators are ready to change and, even more fundamentally, whether the nation has sufficient perseverance, patience, and commitment to support one of its key institutions in the throes of transformation.

THE CASE FOR CAREER EDUCATION

The Twilight Hour

The schools have one final opportunity to prove their worth to the nation, in perhaps the most challenging undertaking of their history, by dedicating themselves to preparation of students for the world of work. "Themselves" does not refer to one lonely curriculum area or specialized group of teachers but to the *total school program*. Issues like opportunities and constraints of the working world, role expectations for men and women in jobs, coeducation in vocational and technical schools, institution building, and man and woman in a technological era, cut across the parameters of individual academic subjects and must bring together the professionals from every field of academic concern.

Our total educational resources must be directed toward a recognition that sooner or later each student must work for survival, maintenance, or mobility. Preparation for the world of work must become an integral part of our basic educational structure if we are to recapture the rewarding promise of the entire learning process. We must once and for all dismiss the notion that some young people should be prepared for higher education while others, less capable, are oriented toward jobs. Our national commitment to education must require that every child leave school with a marketable skill—whether he intends at the time to use it or not. Even those young people aspiring to professions and advanced higher education will work part-time during the school year and summers, and it is important that they have jobs which are productive, rewarding, and lucrative. Today, we are *all* part of the world of work.

To be sure, every board of education has paid lip service to the thesis of educating students for adulthood and employment, but translations into action have been sketchy and weak. Typically, they have tried to discharge this obligation through separate tracks or schools for vocational study.

This has proved adequate for some students. However, many parents, understandably, do not want their children steered toward job training and home economics while their counterparts have a chance for college and better-paying, higher-status positions.

Most students, male and female, will eventually join the labor force. With today's skyrocketing higher education costs, even the college student must be able to help work his way through with gainful part-time employment. However, universal public education to the fourteenth grade and beyond is already a reality in many areas of the country, and young people should be enabled to take advantage of such worthwhile opportunities. Most urgently needed is a system that encourages and educates students to *do both:* one that trains all of them for the working world *and* concurrently prepares them for college entrance, with *every* student a product of both processes.

Freedom is a dual concept: it should offer the right to choose and the chance for equal access to the widest possible range of options. In a democracy public education has a major responsibility to provide such avenues for everyone.

In most basic terms, adulthood could be construed as *work* (including motherhood and housewifery); *citizenship* (the power to evaluate public policy and decision-makers); and the *private domain* (the use of leisure time, appreciation of culture, pursuit of avocations, etc.).

Because limited resources preclude public education's equal involvement in all three areas, priorities must be established, based on the skills required to function in adult society. Work and citizenship must have equal emphasis in the school program, with the private domain in a more marginal position.

Priority for Career Education

A number of factors make career education an imperative for the seventies and, indeed, for the rest of the twentieth century.

For one, the United States has reached a trillion dollar economy. According to the U.S. Bureau of Labor Statistics, eight out of ten jobs to be filled during the seventies will be open to workers without a college degree provided, of course, they have the requisite skills.[9] By 1980 the nation will have close to 100.7 million Americans in the labor force. The fastest-growing occupations will be in professional and technical areas. Service jobs will increase by about 40 percent. Managers, officials, and proprietors, as a group, will rise more than 20 percent; clerical workers, 33 percent; sales workers, almost 30 percent; craftsmen, 10 percent.

---

[9] M. A. Farber, "U.S. Predicts 80% of Jobs Won't Require Degree," *New York Times* (June 28, 1970). © 1970 by The New York Times Company. Reprinted by permission.

Young men and women between 16 and 34 will account for about two-thirds of the net increases in the labor force. "With so much competition from young people who have higher levels of education, the boy or girl who does not get good preparation for work will find the going more difficult in the years ahead," according to a 1970 Labor Statistics Bureau report. Current estimates indicate that less than 5 percent of the total jobs in America by 1975 will be available to unskilled help. Unless we find ways to prepare young people effectively for the world of work, the "unemployables" will bankrupt our public assistance programs.

However, studies conducted by Ivar Berg and others have cast doubts on the ability of education in its present form to lead to better job performance, greater promotions, or more salary increments.[10] Berg's work has shown, for example, that job competence is about the same for high school graduates as for dropouts.[11] Moreover, a study of persons holding civil service jobs showed an equally spurious correlation between education and those other factors. Although educational achievements were strongly related to grades at which government workers entered public service, age and length of service were found to be far more powerful determinants of promotion in GS-1 to -14 categories.[12]

A study by the U.S. Department of Labor related income in various occupations to educational attainment. The study, published in 1965, ranked 300 occupations by earnings and median school years completed and showed that amount of education is not necessarily a primary determinant of income.[13]

Still another reason for schools to concentrate on career preparation is what historian Richard Hofstadter called "a decided crisis in the sense of vocation among young people," [14] which he defined as "a very strong desire to do something in particular and do it well . . . a desire to perform well, the feeling of craftsmanship. . . ." [15] He has also said:

> Young people don't have anything that they want to do. Our culture hasn't been able to perpetuate from one generation to the next, as it used to, the desire to do this or that or the other thing, and I think this is one of the roots of the dissatisfaction. . . .[16]

---

[10] Ivar Berg, *Education and Jobs: The Great Training Robbery* (New York: Praeger Publishers, 1970).
[11] See Berg, "Unemployment and the 'Overeducated' Workers," *New Generation* (Winter 1968), pp. 517-27.
[12] Berg, *Education and Jobs,* pp. 164-65.
[13] David F. Johnston, "The Educational Attainment of Workers," *Monthly Labor Review* (May 1965).
[14] Richard Hofstadter, "The Age of Rubbish," *Newsweek* (July 6, 1970), pp. 20-23. Copyright Newsweek, Inc.
[15] *Ibid.*, p. 21.
[16] *Ibid.*

Youth unemployment statistics also speak to this "crisis of vocation." In 1969, according to the U.S. Bureau of Labor Statistics, overall unemployment for the nation was 3.5 percent, but for 16- to 19-year-olds, the figure was 12.2 percent. Among black teenagers alone, 24 percent were unemployed.

At present, preparing students for work rates only peripheral attention in school curricula. As used here, "work" means readiness for existing and anticipated jobs, based on state and national manpower projections. It also includes training young people to make career decisions, to define new roles for themselves in the economy and social order, and to redesign existing institutions and develop new ones.

Toward a Changing World

The world of work is not a place which everyone enters to find his appointed place and later leaves, unaltered. The Carnegies, Rockefellers, Morgans, Harrimans, Fords, Hills, and Armours of the past left the economy, and consequently society, vastly changed. It is reasonable to expect that today's young people will place their own innovative brand on the future. Therefore, young people in a free society should be motivated to evaluate the working world critically, and to contribute creatively through new organizations and systems which can accomplish major goals for the nation and help them find personal fulfillment.

At the same time, we must remember that the world of work is not perfect. Author Judson Gooding, in a *Fortune* article, blames industry managers who have done little to make jobs more rewarding.[17] Jules Henry describes the dilemma of the working world this way:

> Most people do the job they have to do regardless of what they want to do; . . . With a backward glance at the job-dreams of his pre-"labor force" days the young worker enters the occupational system not where he would but where he can; and his job-dream, so often an expression of his dearest self, is pushed down with all his other unmet needs to churn among them for the rest of his life.[18]

Thomas Jefferson warned that a nation should never bind future generations; in this regard, he was defending the power of the people to amend the Constitution. Likewise, the schools must prepare today's students to make their own unique contribution to tomorrow's world. They must liberate rather than contain human potential, fortifying the young with hard skills and intellectual powers for their adult roles in society.

---
[17] Judson Gooding, "Blue-Collar Blues on the Assembly Line," *Fortune* (July 1970), pp. 69-71.
[18] Jules Henry, *Culture Against Man* (New York: Random House, © 1965), p. 25.

Career education must be viewed as a global commodity. It should combine specific teachings in occupational skills necessary for employment in a technological world with orientation to the broad issues confronting people in the world of work; thorough grounding in the basic learning skills of reading, composition, and computation; and self-knowledge and insights necessary for people to make well-reasoned decisions about career.

THE FEDERAL RESPONSE

Initial Legislation

At the turn of the century, a rapidly expanding economy and growing population created expanding needs for skilled manpower both in factories and on farms. The pace of apprenticeship programs proved inadequate, and the schools showed little interest in providing opportunities in vocational education. Congress responded by passing the Vocational Education Act of 1917, known as the Smith-Hughes Act. Its $7.2 million in annual authorizations offered categorical aid for establishing school programs in three fields—agriculture, trade and industrial education, and home economics. Approximately $1 million a year was earmarked for training vocational teachers.

In the thirties, three additional laws—the George-Read, George-Ellzay, and George-Deene Acts—provided additional short-term support for vocational education.

By the end of World War II, the federal treasury was contributing approximately $20 million annually in support of vocational education in the same three categories. Provision was also made for distributive education beginning in 1936.

Following the war, Congress passed the Vocational Education Act of 1946 (also called the George-Barden Act) which extended the 1917 legislation. Its $29 million in allotments brought to $36 million the annual federal expenditures authorized for vocational education. A 1956 amendment added practical nursing and fishery occupations to the list of approved courses.

Passage of the National Defense Education Act of 1958 brought $15 million in annual authorizations for four years to support "area vocational programs" to train highly skilled technicians necessary to the national defense. Occupations covered included electronics, data processing, computer programming, and mechanical, chemical, electrical, and aeronautical engineering.

The Early Sixties

In his message to Congress in February 1961, President John F. Kennedy requested the Secretary of Health, Education, and Welfare to appoint a panel of consultants to review, evaluate, and recommend improvements in vocational education programs. A panel of distinguished Americans was appointed and a report was submitted in 1962, calling for a new vocational education act and substantial increases in federal appropriations for vocational and technical education.

The Vocational Education Act of 1963, signed by President Lyndon B. Johnson, broadened instruction in agriculture, home economics, and distributive education. Provision was made for establishment of area vocational schools and work-study programs and development of vocational education for those with special educational and other handicaps.

During the sixties the Congress also enacted other legislation dealing with occupational training. The Manpower Development and Training Act authorized federal funds to train persons who are unemployed or underemployed, with payment of allowances to eligible trainees. Amendments authorized teaching of basic education in connection with occupational training. Other programs such as Job Corps, Neighborhood Youth Corps, and Youth Conservation Corps, were authorized under the Economic Opportunity Act of 1964. The National Vocational Student Loan Insurance Act of 1965 established a system of loan insurance and a supplementary system of direct loans to assist students to attend postsecondary business, trade, technical, and other vocational schools. The Area Redevelopment Act of 1962 provided funds for supporting training programs of 16 weeks' duration for target populations in redevelopment areas.

Vocational Education Amendments of 1968

The need to consolidate vocational education legislation and help schools move occupational preparation courses of study into the technological era of the twentieth century prompted the Congress to pass the Vocational Education Amendments of 1968, authorizing $2.8 billion over a five-year period. Extensive hearings on the legislation were conducted by the General Subcommittee on Education. Following are some of the major highlights of these amendments:

State grants. The Amendments authorize federal grants to states to help them develop new vocational education programs and maintain, extend, and improve those already in existence. These programs, planned in light of actual or anticipated employment opportunities, are open to all who can benefit from training or retraining, whether enrolled in school or not. For example, state grants may be used for:

(1) programs for high school students, including advanced or highly skilled post-secondary vocational and technical education;
(2) programs for those who have completed or left high school and are available for full-time study in preparation for entering the labor market;
(3) programs for those already in the labor market who need training or retraining;
(4) programs for those who have academic, physical, socioeconomic, or other handicaps which prevent them from succeeding in the regular vocational education program;
(5) construction of area vocational education school facilities;
(6) vocational guidance counseling;
(7) ancillary services and activities such as teacher training, supervision, demonstration and experimental programs, and periodic evaluations of programs in view of current and projected manpower needs and job opportunities.

Exemplary programs and projects. To reduce the continuing high levels of youth unemployment, exemplary programs and projects may be initiated which promote cooperation between public education and manpower agencies and bridge the gap between school and work.

Such programs may be designed to:

(1) familiarize elementary and secondary school students with the world of work;
(2) provide for work experiences during the school year or summer;
(3) provide for intensive occupational counseling during the last years of school or initial job placement;
(4) broaden vocational education curricula;
(5) arrange for exchange of personnel between schools, manpower agencies, and industry;
(6) release young workers from jobs on a part-time basis to increase their educational level;
(7) offer preprofessional preparation for potential teachers of vocational education.

Cooperative education. Cooperative education programs are designed to provide on-the-job experience which is coordinated with classroom learning and planned jointly by schools and employers. Financial assistance is provided for personnel to coordinate such programs, instruction related to the work experience, reimbursement of employers for certain costs of on-the-job training, and payment of costs of certain services such as transportation of students.

Work-Study programs. In this category fall programs which enable students to work and earn compensation while pursuing their education. Students are limited to 15 hours' work in any week when classes are in session. Maximum compensation is set at $45 a month or $350 per semester in most instances.

Curriculum development. Funds are provided for developing and disseminating vocational education curriculum materials, for evaluation of such materials, and for training of personnel in curriculum development.

Consumer and homemaking education. Available support is reserved for home economics programs which encourage (a) greater attention to diverse social and cultural conditions, especially in economically depressed areas; (b) preparation for professional leadership; (c) preparation for homemaking or the dual role of homemaker and wage earner; (d) consumer education.

Educationally disadvantaged students. A total of $80 million was authorized over a two-year period to develop programs for disadvantaged students. Beginning with fiscal year 1970, 25 percent of each state's allotment which is in excess of its base allotment must be used for vocational education for persons who have academic, socioeconomic, or other handicaps which prevent them from succeeding in the regular vocational education program. In homemaking and consumer education, over a three-year period, states are required to expend 90 percent of such amounts for economically depressed areas or areas with high rates of unemployment.

Educational personnel training. Opportunities are provided for experienced vocational education personnel to pursue full-time studies, update occupational competencies through personnel exchanges with educational institutions and employers, and participate in inservice programs and short-term institutes.

Research and training. Funds are reserved for: research in vocational education; projects in the development of new careers and occupations; experimental, developmental, and pilot programs designed to test the effectiveness of research findings; and training programs to familiarize persons with research findings and successful pilot and demonstration projects in vocational education.

Residential schools. To demonstrate the feasibility and desirability of residential vocational education schools, the U.S. Commissioner of Education is authorized to make grants for construction, equipping, and operation of residential schools to provide vocational education for youths 15 to 21 years old who need full-time study on a residential basis in order to benefit fully from such an education.

Planning and advising. As a requirement for receiving their allotments, each state must submit a plan presenting a long-range program of three to five years for programs, services, and activities to be carried on in the vocational education field. National and state advisory councils are also established under this legislation. Such councils are to be broadly representative—consisting of persons familiar with vocational needs of labor and management and the needs of the poor and disadvantaged from a wide range of educational institutions and manpower and educational agencies.

Other Pertinent Legislation

Besides vocational education, the Congress has enacted a wide range of legislation dealing with other aspects of instruction which can apply to career preparation. For example, the Elementary and Secondary Education Act makes provision for the education of disadvantaged children, exemplary innovative programs, library services, and laboratories to develop new curriculum.

NEW PATTERNS FOR THE SEVENTIES

The challenge of the seventies lies in utilization of federal, state, and local funds for creative means of preparing youth for the world of work. It means reaching out in new directions, lending vitality to the word "relevance" and energy to the concept of career development.

Schools Without Walls

To accomplish this task, the walls between school and nonschool must come tumbling down. Students should have almost daily access to the world of work so they can immerse themselves in the adult environment, beginning at a young age and progressing to apprenticeships, assistantships, internships, and whatever other arrangements are necessary to place them in positions, paid and unpaid, alongside adults. Students should be able to choose widely and have a variety of experiences as participant-observers in the work force, in addition to regular classroom training in basic skills.

Schools then offer hope not only of educating for work and providing young people with role models, but also of easing intergenerational tensions by making "youthhood" more continuous with adulthood.

This could be a dramatic innovation in itself. Operationally, the course is fairly clear. It entails making schools more contiguous with the business community and other employers in the public and private sectors. Students would be "on location" part of the time in business and industry, educational institutions, government, cultural organizations, and various other public and private agencies in the community, and their mentors could be "deputized" as clinical teachers and counselors in the field.

The concept also involves a new approach to working with young people. It requires placing more genuine trust in them and making more adult demands on them—holding higher expectations for their behavior, offering them increased responsibility for their actions, and believing they can learn to make rational judgments at a much earlier age if given the appropriate training. Margaret Mead has recommended, "We must now move toward the creation of open systems that focus on the future—and so on children, those whose capacities are least known and whose choices must be left open." [19]

Such a program also necessitates more effective tutelage from instructors who are sensitive to the difficulties of growing up, conversant with the demands and limitations of the world of work, and committed to opening up the talents of young people and, indeed, of giving them the courage to think, act, and change for themselves. Marshall McLuhan and George Leonard have predicted:

> Future educators will value, not fear, fresh approaches, new solutions. Among their first tasks, in fact, may be *un*learning the old, unacknowledged taboos on true originality. After that, they may well pick up a new driving style in which they glance into the rearview mirror when guidance from the past is needed but spend far more time looking forward into the unfamiliar, untested country of the present and future.[20]

This new imperative also requires more creative organization of both students' and teachers' time in school. Effective utilization of time could best be achieved through the "three- and two-day week." Such an arrangement would provide basic classroom education for students on three school days. For the remaining two, the learners would embark on their community field experiences in the working world, freeing teachers for inservice training and preparation of lessons and materials.

Finally, preparing young people for work requires strengthening the programs of job-skill training offered in occupational education programs. Particularly in the area of technical skills, such programs must keep abreast of the economic changes of the seventies and tune into the manpower needs which have been forecast for this decade. The best of vocational education—e.g., cooperative work-study and apprenticeship

---

[19] Margaret Mead, *Culture and Commitment* (Garden City, N.Y.: Natural History Press/Doubleday, 1970), p. 72.
[20] Marshall McLuhan and George Leonard, "Learning in the Global Village," *Radical School Reform,* Ronald and Beatrice Gross, eds. (New York: Simon and Schuster, 1970), pp. 106-15.

training—must be made the core of preparation for employment in our nation's educational institutions.

Most discussions of the so-called youth revolution have tended to dramatize the negative and overlook the sincere concern of young people about contemporary problems such as war, drugs, pollution, materialism, and life and death. A nationwide survey of 2,000 high school students by the Purdue University Measurement and Research Center found that 91 percent were interested in deferring their personal goals for a year or more to work on one of the nation's problems, such as poverty, pollution, education, and race. Now that the voting age is being lowered to eighteen, our schools should capitalize on this serious interest of young people in vital issues of today and make certain that their voices can be heard through regular channels.

At the same time, education should be reconstructed as a lifetime pursuit, with students of many generations able to return continuously to formal learning. Students should be encouraged as part of their education to shuttle between classroom work and outreach activities that will help them test job and social roles under supervision of school and community. High school graduates should be able to spend a year or two in employment before college, without stigma or threat to status, as a maturing and goal-directing experience.

The point is clear: no longer can learning be forced into a single mode. The essence of education is pluralism, with a sufficient variety of foci, loci, and time lines to satisfy the needs of all.

Leadership can be the vital link to educational change. Reform requires restoring the balance of leadership to reflect the interests of a tripartite constituency, involving parents and students as one legitimate interest, the community as another, and educators as the significant third force.

School people should retain their roles as managers of the system and continue their executive leadership in American education. However, educational planning must grow into an ecumenical process combining the resources and knowledge of business and industry, of space technology, of manpower economists and trainers, of private as well as public vocational school programs, and of the community at large with those of professional pedagogues.

Education in a democracy must respond to aspirations of all. Children and youth in central cities should have as fine an education as students in the suburbs. Nonwhite minorities and females should be as well prepared for work as white majorities and men. Nor can the needs of the general public as a whole be denied, although they are sometimes overlooked in earmarked legislation and special educational programs.

Ultimately, the system must be accountable to its total clientele—

parents, students, employers—for preparing young people to enter the working world. Assessment must be based on the system's ability to place students in permanent employment, to satisfy employer performance criteria, and to meet the needs of students themselves for skills and understandings that can help them cope with major issues in the world of employment. Hopefully, as well, the schools will be able to create a performance-based society, one that asks not what diplomas a person holds but what he can do, what abilities and experiences he can bring to the work situation.

THE IMPOSSIBLE DREAM

This is our vision of education for the seventies. It will mean reconstructing the existing educational environment at the elementary, secondary, and community college levels and creating some new institutions, as well. It will require new teacher training to meet altered demands of instructional roles. At the top—in state departments of education, federal agencies, and the halls of state legislatures and the Congress—new alternatives must also be identified, both in administrative organization patterns and depth and breadth of financial commitment to such an effort.

In short, as contributors to this book will discuss at greater length in their chapters, preparing young people for adulthood involves turning around the system, recognizing the rightful role of all citizens in shaping that system, and exercising leadership with extraordinary vision at all levels of educational input.

II

POWER
TO
THE
PEOPLE

INTRODUCTION

Since the advent of the popularly elected school board, American public education has been officially responsible to the taxpayers of the more than 18,000 school districts and to the states for the schooling it provides. Ultimate power to make policies, establish priorities, and set fiscal boundaries for public education thus resides with the people, through their chosen representatives. This is the cornerstone of universal, free public education.

Complementary to and supportive of this principle, educational visionaries such as Thomas Jefferson, Andrew Jackson, Horace Mann, and John Dewey have infused American education with a legacy of democratic creeds which remain a vital part of the philosophical underpinnings of public schools to this day. Education should treat all students equally, they counseled, providing opportunities for every individual to develop his talents, skills, interests, and knowledge to their fullest capacity and enabling him to realize his highest ambitions in life.

Today, American education continues to face new tests. Whether public schooling can, in fact, fulfill its promises and remain sensitive to the needs of all citizens may well determine its future survival. The authors of chapters in this section have reexamined the issues of democracy, equality, and responsiveness as they apply to the particular problem of career education for the 1970s.

Hugh Calkins challenges the use of diplomas, degrees, and many types of tests as entry-level screening devices for employment when they bear only a limited, if any, relationship to employability factors and tend to deny equality of opportunity to persons who might otherwise qualify. Many diploma-less individuals, and particularly those from minority groups, he asserts, have been the victims of inferior schools—often racially segregated—and thus have not had a fair chance to compete for credentials.

Grant Venn traces the rise of mounting pressures on school officials to become more accountable for the outcomes of American education in terms of student performance. He recommends making the schools responsible to students, parents, and employers for educating students for the world of work, including both basic learning and specific job skills.

Three authors focus on the needs of special school populations which require greater public and professional attention if they are to share in the promise of equal educational opportunity. Paul W. Briggs discusses the unique problems of educating urban students for jobs in an environment filled with physical, social, psychological, and other tensions. He suggests that the cities become "urban laboratories" for various types of internships, assistantships, and on-the-job training programs that will qualify students for specific employment offerings in the city.

Cleveland L. Dennard focusses on the education of Black Americans within the context of national employment and manpower priorities established by the President and the Congress. As long as a policy of 95 percent employment and 5 percent unemployment is maintained, he writes, vocational education and job-training programs for the hard-core unemployed cannot deliver results to the black community. He calls for a massive "Marshall Plan" for Black Americans in the inner cities.

Elizabeth J. Simpson is concerned with the education of women for the world of work. She points to job stereotypes, conflicts in roles and expectations for women, differentials in salary and occupational status between men and women, and inadequate educational opportunities as some contributing factors to problems of preparing women for employment. Her recommendations deal with changes in educational programs, leadership at state and federal policy-making levels in education, and educational research focus—all in recognition of the new "woman power" which has emerged.

School systems, like other social institutions, do not change easily. Adjusting them to accommodate growing demands from all segments of the society for quality education will require unparalleled courage to change in the 1970s.
—S. H. P.

PAPER PASSPORTS TO EMPLOYMENT:
A Challenge to Credentialism

HUGH CALKINS

Quest for Credentials

The most coveted and avidly pursued symbol of achievement in America is the college degree. The quality of the education a person actually receives and what he in fact learns from collegiate life are secondary to the life earning power, career advancement, and purported life style which are assumed to be assured by possession of the degree.

Approximately 80 percent of all jobs in the seventies will require less than the baccalaureate, according to a U.S. Labor Department study. Nonetheless, most parents will continue to prod their children on to higher education. A study conducted by the Survey Research Center of the University of Michigan indicated that 70 percent of American parents of young children expect their sons, and 62 percent expect their daughters, to go to college. In an American Council on Education survey of a cross section of the American population, more than half of the young people of college age who were in college reported that their fathers had wanted them to further their education beyond high school. Parental pressure for college attendance was also reported by 81 percent of students enrolled in two-year colleges and 86 percent of those in four-year schools.

Preoccupation with college attendance is by no means restricted to the

---

HUGH CALKINS is Chairman of the National Advisory Council on Vocational Education and a Fellow of Harvard University. He was formerly a member of the Board of Education of Cleveland, Ohio.

affluent. Inner-city parents are alarmed by the below-average test scores in their schools, because the scores threaten the college education for which they aspire for their children. Nor is preoccupation with college limited to parents. In my experience, only in a few ethnic neighborhoods does a value system survive under which a majority of young people are expected to go to work at age 18.

Reconsideration of the Diploma

The national enthusiasm for a college degree is in part the product of genuine respect for education. In part, it is the product of widespread awareness that employers use high school diplomas and college degrees as selecting and sorting mechanisms which substitute for discriminating personnel policies.

Many—probably most—diplomas and degrees in the United States are "paper" standards which convey almost no information about the potential employee's skills and capabilities for specific positions in the working environment. Almost never do job performance criteria enter into the awarding of certificates by schools and colleges, and in most instances only a spurious correlation exists between those paper credentials and excellence produced in work situations.

The well-known series of studies conducted by Ivar Berg supports these conclusions.[1] Berg's work showed that graduates and nongraduates doing the same jobs performed about equally well; no significant differences in productivity could be attributed to education. Jaffe and Froomkin, in "Education and Jobs," reported that "there is little, if any, relationship between changes in educational level and changes in output per worker."[2] Berg, on the other hand, learned that most employers did not even bother to make such comparisons. Those who concentrated extensive energy and finance on personnel programs had no apparent interest in ascertaining whether their educational requirements could be justified in terms of employee productivity. In six large manufacturing companies, for example, scientists with master's degrees who were designated by management as among the most valuable 20 percent in terms of actual performance and potential were paid $1,000 less in average annual salary than Ph.D.'s considered less valuable.[3]

A study of the 1960 census made by Folger and Nam, "Education of the American Population," showed that in the decade of the fifties, a

---

[1] Ivar Berg, *Education and Jobs: The Great Training Robbery* (New York: Praeger Publishers, 1970).

[2] In David Hapgood, ed., *Diplomaism: Zoning People By Degrees,* to be published in 1971.

[3] *Ibid.*

time of escalating diploma requirements, only 15 percent of the increased educational requirements could be attributed to changes in the nature of work. The other 85 percent were due to added diploma requirements for exactly the same jobs.

Despite their apparent irrelevance in predicting job performance, diplomas and degrees have become a convenient device for eliminating prospective candidates for jobs and making the selection process more manageable for those faced with hiring. The nationwide dependence on credentials has thus arisen from a search for more convenient, objective means of comparing job applicants. Theoretically, it can be justified as a democratic process for judging individuals on merit. In practice, however, it serves to exclude those who lack the proper papers—pedigrees, one might almost say—instead of widening the circle of opportunity for all. Progress up the educational ladder correlates closely with family economic background. Those who start with economic handicaps, and do not overcome them, face insurmountable barriers to employment because, lacking the diploma, they are not afforded the opportunity to demonstrate their talents.

Making one's way in an adult world without the credential can be a difficult and discouraging experience. Most company personnel policies are based on the assumption that an individual with a credential, from a high school or college, is better suited to any particular job than one who is "paperless." He has at least the "basic skills," the hiring officials say, and mere possession of the certificate demonstrates perseverance and fortitude. What they fail to realize is that students regularly graduate from high school and even college without basic skills in reading, composition, and computation, much less the ability to reason carefully, weigh alternatives, and make decisions. A study by David Harman [4] estimates that as much as half the American adult population may be functionally illiterate, unable to master such commonplace reading matter as driving manuals, newspapers, and job applications. The proportion of illiterates among the current generation of 18-year-olds is much lower, but, as any Urban League worker will testify, it includes a significant number of high school graduates. Moreover, in some colleges and many schools, the arts of reason, judgment, and logic—surely of substantial if not paramount importance for practically all jobs today—are never taught at all.

To rely on a diploma as a measure of personal determination is to depend on a slippery wicket indeed. Individuals whom the education system was specifically designed to serve—the white, middle-class young

---

[4] David Harman, "Illiteracy: An Overview," *Harvard Educational Review, 40* (May 1970), p. 230.

people encouraged by their parents to stay in school, who suffer relatively minor financial pressures, whose previous education prepared them to succeed in the system, and who are for the most part products of stable home and neighborhood environments—may reflect flaccid conformity rather than ambition in pursuing a diploma. Individuals who are not academically inclined, who finish a school system not designed for their needs, deserve special citations for valor; but their fellows who give up on a system that has shown little regard for them cannot automatically be labelled unemployable and unfit for the rest of their lives. The truth is that American education, not its victims, must accept responsibility for these rejection factors.

Forcing everyone to stomach college preparatory or settle for "general" material when many do not go on to further education can scarcely be said to serve everyone's needs, nor do schools have a right to brand those they fail as uneducable. The experience of Project 100,000, an undertaking of the U.S. military, demonstrated that individuals with below-average intelligence scores, many of whom were high school dropout, could be taught basic skills successfully as well as be trained for various jobs. Upward Bound and similar programs, as well as the experience of many school systems with some of their students, have shown that able young people from low-income families can move on to college, at least when their regular education is supplemented with remedial and enrichment experiences. Graduates of vocational education, manpower development and training, and Job Corps programs have likewise taught us that appropriate educational opportunities can develop the talents of those previously excluded by schools and employers.

Reconsideration of the Tests

A test is a more rational predictor of job performance than a diploma, but it has limitations, too. A few years ago the Federated Department Stores decided to hire a score of "unqualified" persons, all of whom had failed the routine entrance test. The group received brief orientation and was placed in jobs for a year and followed up. At the end of the year, some had left the company—they had failed, been drafted, or were married. Some were working below the skill level for which they had been hired. Others were performing creditably in their assignments—so well, that they had been promoted. One was the best salesman in the store. Tests were again administered at the end of the year, but as at the beginning, the entire group—including the star salesman—flunked.

A test is a probability predictor. There is usually a positive correlation between performance on the test and performance on the job. Because a test is supposed to be unbiased, it is considered fair to rely on it for screening purposes. The trouble is that tests, even the better ones, measure only a few of the skills and qualities that a job situation demands. They say nothing about dependability, or loyalty, or initiative, or the ability to cooperate. They say little about the ability to absorb oral instruction or to learn by doing.

They measure two particular skills—responsiveness to written instructions and the ability to recall in a test situation; and, if the results are adjusted to take these skills of the person taking the test into account, they give some indication of his knowledge of the material tested. The two skills tested are not distributed uniformly in our society, and their distribution probably correlates quite closely to family economic background. Much of the reliance on testing in our society is as unfair to the economically disadvantaged, who are denied the opportunity to prove their worth on the job, as is our reliance on a diploma.

What Are Some Alternatives?

Job opportunities controlled by employers are national resources which have as much claim to fair administration as radio frequencies, natural resources, waterways, or the air we breathe. Judgments based on group characteristics, decisions unduly influenced by tests which are known to be inadequate, cost savings achieved by denying individuals the opportunity to prove themselves—all are as contrary to the national interest as pollution of the air or destruction of the timberlands.

If we accepted this fact as a basis for policy-making, what alternatives to our present disregard of this national resource would we consider?

1. *Performance standards should, to the extent practicable, replace formal credentials as criteria for selecting, promoting, and retaining employees.* Employers who wish to act in the national interest, and with decent regard for the ethical principle that those with power must use it fairly, will analyze existing job categories to determine precisely what knowledge and skills they require. Then more exacting means of measuring these variables must be devised.

Tests will serve as one instrument for assessing aptitudes. As another, employers will insist that school systems, as well as higher education institutions, issue certificates in addition to their diplomas, specifying the skills an individual can demonstrate. For example, a high school or even junior high school diploma could indicate the individual's proficiency in reading, computation, and specific occupational skills—e.g., the speed at which he can type and take dictation. Revamping the reporting system in this way would mean, in effect, that an individual could be judged on the basis of specified performance criteria which could be understood clearly by students, teachers, parents, and prospective employers, and that such standards would replace the nebulous and arbitrary letter or number grades currently in use.

As a third option, employers will follow the suggestion of S. M. Miller that every set of requirements have an "escape clause which permits the unusual person to be admitted to the realm of the elect." [5] By this he means that at least 5 percent of those hired by a particular company or agency each year be persons who qualify in what are to them unconventional ways in terms of education or test results, but whose background, experience, and ability indicate they would otherwise be suitable. The objective, in Miller's words, is to make "pluralism possible in a complex society" through "a variety of social inventions to provide the structure and the reality of pluralism."

2. *Education should be redesigned to focus on preparing all young people for the world of work.* Students who anticipate a career in one of the professions are all aware that one of the purposes of their education is to prepare them for their life work. A few generations ago, most students in high school contemplated a professional career, and irrelevance was not a problem in high school education.

As the proportion of the population enrolled in high school rose, the vision of the faculty remained fixed on academic careers. Irrelevance became a problem for the many students who did not contemplate spending their lives in a profession. Of what use was the academic curriculum to them?

Vocational education was in theory designed for these students, but until very recently it reached only an insignificant proportion of those who needed it. School districts limited enrollment to those students who could be supported on the inadequate state and federal subsidies. Often, the vocational courses were not very good. They were outdated in content, methods, and equipment and taught by persons who had not participated in the working world in years. Moreover, even when funds were adequate and quality was high, enrollments were limited by the stigma that surrounded voc-ed. As Peter Schrag has written:

> The blue collar is still stigmatized; in the school the vocational students are fender-benders, and occasionally a particularly nasty remark is answered with sudden explosive violence: 'He called us grease monkeys, so we pushed him right through the glass door. We stick up for our rights.' [6]

---

[5] S. M. Miller, "Breaking the Credentials Barrier" (New York: The Ford Foundation, 1967), p. 7. See also Miller and Marsha Kroll, "Strategies for Reducing Credentialism," unpublished paper (New York: The Ford Foundation, 1970).

[6] Peter Schrag, "Growing Up on Mechanic Street," *Saturday Review* (March 21, 1970). Copyright © 1970 by Peter Schrag. Reprinted from *Out of Place in America*, by Peter Schrag, by permission of Random House, Inc.

The first annual report of the National Advisory Council on Vocational Education also addressed itself to this sensitive problem.

> At the very heart of our problem is a national attitude that says vocational education is designed for somebody else's children. This attitude is shared by businessmen, labor leaders, administrators, teachers, parents, students. We are all guilty. We have promoted the idea that the only good education is an education capped by four years of college. This idea, transmitted by our values, our aspirations, and our silent support, is snobbish, undemocratic, and a revelation of why schools fail so many students. . . . It infects students, who make inappropriate choices because they are victims of the national yearning for educational prestige.[7]

These conditions are changing and must be eliminated. Federal and state subsidies can be increased, and local districts can allocate local funds for career-related education. The quality of many vocational programs is improving, and every vocational educator can point to a facility which has recently been opened or newly equipped with highly competent staff and relevant curriculum. Most important, schools must acknowledge to themselves and their students that preparing for a job is a primary mission of the school, and such an attitude must infuse the entire curriculum from early elementary grades onward.

3. *Occupations should be redesigned to eliminate dead-end jobs and create career ladders by which employees can advance on the basis of growth and development.* If employment were treated as a national resource, employers would regroup existing jobs into hierarchically arranged families of occupations and provide routes leading from one to another with procedures for promotion. In addition, employers would reconstitute present jobs into a spectrum of high- and low-level skills. Creating job segments which can be handled by less-trained individuals and developing new combinations which enable a person to upgrade his position would provide a road to occupational opportunity.

In any such arrangement, training and experience should be the keys to mobility. With access to some form of government assistance, often through a local college, the employer would assume responsibility for providing training appropriate to the next job level at various stages in the employee's career development. In this way, as Miller indicates, the usual cycle of education-then-job could be turned around. An individual would find a beginning place for himself on the occupational ladder with full knowledge that appropriate training would be available throughout employment and that he would be rewarded appropriately

---

[7] National Advisory Council on Vocational Education, *Vocational Education Amendments of 1968, P.L. 90-576*, Annual Report (Washington, D.C.: Department of Health, Education, and Welfare, July 15, 1969).

for his efforts. This approach thus provides a highly promising means of revising the credentialing syndrome.

The federally supported New Careers program, fashioned after a model designed by Frank Riessman and Arthur Pearl, provides an example of both the promise and the difficulties of carrying out this suggestion. This program utilizes indigenous community people as paraprofessional personnel in such fields as education, health, and the social services. At the heart of the program lies the career ladder; it consists of a series of promotional steps by which, with appropriate inservice training, a person can eventually attain full professional status in a given field. Such an arrangement opens doors to persons who lack the usual credentials, providing them with experience and on-the-job training and rewarding successful performance with increased levels of professional responsibility and status.

Thus far, however, credentialing standards themselves have in most instances failed to give way; they have provided an almost insurmountable barrier to full realization of the mobility goal. Nurses aides cannot become nurses without taking the regular courses and receiving degrees. Teaching assistants are not certifiable as classroom teachers without the customary preparation in terms of course credits.

Consequently, many New Careers program participants have grown discouraged. They have found themselves locked into their roles, unable to move out into more responsible positions, and many have dropped out. While the professions have refused to bend in the process, however, something not originally predicted has happened. A few educational institutions have begun to adjust their expectations to the needs of paraprofessionals for diplomas. The University of Massachusetts, for example, established a special center in New York to provide on-the-job and after-working hours instruction to 200 paraprofessionals in the Brooklyn schools, along with trips to the university's main campus in Amherst, Massachusetts, on weekends. Working within an appointed schedule and offering a large number of credits for actual experience in their school roles, these paraprofessionals can earn a degree in four years.

The Women's Talent Corps of New York actually established its own institution, the College of Human Services, which is accredited by the New York Board of Regents to offer a two-year degree. Members of the Corps work in their jobs three days a week and attend classes two days. Their classroom work is directly related to their jobs and emphasizes a great deal of field work.[8]

---

[8] See Joseph Featherstone, "Career Ladders for Bottom Dogs," *The New Republic* (September 13, 1969), pp. 17-23.

4. *Education must reform itself.* There are few industries in the United States so hobbled by credentialism as education. If educators are to make what an individual actually knows and can do determine his employment opportunity, they must begin the reform with themselves.

Employment and promotion in public schools in this country depend almost entirely on accumulating course credits; practice teaching constitutes only a minor proportion of the training, and standards vary so much from one institution to the next that performance criteria have never been properly validated. Teaching experience is not considered an acceptable substitute for the university-supervised apprenticeship or internship. Consequently, applicants such as ex-Peace Corpsmen who have taught for two years or more are denied licenses because they are unable to produce the appropriate college credits. James D. Koerner, a long-time critic of teacher-training programs and licensing requirements, has written:

> Educationists ought to abandon the manifestly absurd claim that people can become competent teachers only when they have been through orthodox training programs. . . . Educationists need to recognize that the ideas and claims upon which professional work in Education is now based are extremely tenuous; they should recognize that, despite the fact that almost all teachers now in the public schools have been through the standard preparatory programs, the level of public school teaching lends no particular support to the efficacy of these programs.[9]

The same constraints prevail at the administrative level in education. David Hapgood has described the following case:

> The high school principal [of Princeton, New Jersey] had resigned, unable to cope with a school beset by racial conflict and troubled, in a less measurable sense, by the nameless malaise of white suburban youth, children of the bourgeois intelligentsia. In a rare reach of the imagination, the board decided to go outside the industry for a new principal.
>
> They chose a local notable, Raymond F. Male. Male was a remarkable choice. He is a former mayor of Princeton who had sided with the young in generational conflicts. He is also the state commissioner of labor and industry and an expert in public administration. In the selection of Male, the school board seemed to be saying that the troubles of high school students had mostly to do with the students' relations with the world outside the walls.
>
> But Male is not certified to be a high school principal. When his case went to the Board of Examiners, a sort of supreme court within the state's public education bureaucracy, the examiners voted, 7 to 2, that Male was not qualified to be principal of Princeton High School.

---

[9] James D. Koerner, *The Miseducation of American Teachers* (Boston: Houghton Mifflin Co.; Baltimore: Penguin Books, 1963), p. 17.

Their grounds were that he lacked a teaching certificate and 24 credit hours in school administration, the last although Male has taught public administration and holds a master's degree in the subject from Princeton University.[10]

5. *A national discrimination against blue-collar workers must be eliminated.* Finally, to eliminate credentialism in the United States we must recognize it for what it is—a device by which those with privileges preserve them. It is not surprising that students scorn blue-collar occupations; so does society as a whole. The hourly worker still bears the first brunt of recession. It is he who is laid off when it is time to change models or when a strike shuts down the customer. Last winter it was the blue-collar worker whose pay stopped when a cold wave exhausted the gas supply. True, the blue-collar worker is paid for his risks. True, unemployment compensation cushions the shocks. Nonetheless, an equitable system of equal treatment for all occupational groups is a necessity if the national preoccupation with credentials is to be overcome.

Outlook for the Seventies

Peter Drucker calls our paper passports to employment a "diploma curtain," separating the 15 to 20 percent who never finish school from those who have a high school education, who in turn are separated from those who go to college.[11] As Drucker writes:

> This is stupid in the extreme. There is no correlation between academic accomplishment and capacity to perform (except perhaps in academic pursuits). There is, in other words, little reason to believe that the 50 percent with 'higher education' represent a significantly greater reservoir of ability, maturity, and integrity than the other 50 percent.[12]

The main domestic crisis facing this country today concerns extension of equal opportunity to all to demonstrate their worth and share in the benefits of a productive and wealthy nation. Drucker recommends that:

> Every institution, whether business, university, hospital, government agency, or armed service, owes it to itself as well as to American society to organize for the systematic identification of people without the proper degrees who provide their ability through performance. Every institution owes it to them, to itself, and to American society to provide opportunities for those people, including the opportunity, if necessary, to acquire the lacking

---

[10] Hapgood, *Diplomaism*.
[11] Peter Drucker, "Worker and Work in the Metropolis," *Daedalus*, 97 (Fall 1968), 1243-62.
[12] *Ibid.*, 1251.

sheepskin easily and fast. And it would be very intelligent if educational institutions set up soon an 'earned' degree to be awarded for performance rather than for sitting the required time on school benches.[13]

These must become goals for American education in this decade and for the remainder of the twentieth century.

---

[13] *Ibid.*, 1252.

ACCOUNTABLE FOR WHAT?
Measuring Up to The World of Work

GRANT VENN

It reads like a basic principle of democracy: any public institution must be accountable for its actions to the taxpayers who support it and citizens who depend on its services. Elected officials are subject to public scrutiny through the ballot box. Federal judges may be removed through impeachment. Public accounts are audited at regular intervals.

But what about public educational institutions? Education spends approximately $58 billion a year, second only to the military in the national budget. More than 60 million Americans are engaged full time in the field, 57 million as students and 3 million as teachers and administrators.

What of the education profession, those public servants who are traditionally protected by tenure laws and more informally insulated from public oversight by a bureaucratic wall labelled "for professionals only"? The past five years have witnessed an extraordinary surfacing of citizens' demands for increased excellence in schools. Angry parents and members of the general public have acted on the belief that school personnel have a public trust to maintain and that educators must be held responsible for achievement of learning. For the first time, the public has begun to confront school officials, demanding information on quality of output, such as standardized test results in reading and math, and such data have clearly illustrated the widespread failure of some schools

---

GRANT VENN formerly served as Associate Commissioner for Adult, Vocational and Library Programs in the U.S. Office of Education. He is presently Director of the National Academy of School Executives of the American Association of School Administrators, Washington, D.C.

to impart even basic skills. In the past, teachers might have attributed these deficiencies to home influences or to inadequate tax finance. However, parents of today refuse to accept such explanations. They want results and believe their taxes are high enough to warrant something in return.

To a casual observer of the education scene, the public seems perfectly reasonable in its insistence upon a day's worth of learning for every day of schooling it supports. Placed in proper historical context, however, these events are revolutionary. Until about 1965, school personnel were generally considered accountable only to themselves for the learning that occurred in their classrooms. Accountability was fiduciary—school systems were responsible for balancing their books and for spending money as the taxpayers and school boards intended—but qualitative bookkeeping was strictly an in-house affair. Such evaluation was prefixed with "self," indicating that only the profession was considered sufficiently competent to pass judgment on its own actions or to make decisions about change. Consequently, parents were discouraged from raising questions about the substance of their children's education.

Prior to the mid-1960's, evaluation of school programs was carried out by two types of agencies, state departments of education and regional accrediting associations. However, neither considered it necessary to look at pupils in order to determine whether any education was going on in the schools. Their indices were far more mechanical—number of hours of instruction, number of textbooks being used, number of credit hours in education courses for teachers, etc. From time to time more specialized evaluations were conducted, such as the Eight-Year Study of progressive schools or Paul Mort's studies, but results were always held strictly within the profession. As long as the public did not raise questions about pupil achievement, the educators were perfectly willing not to anticipate them.

What has happened within the last half-decade to generate widespread public pressure for qualitative accountability? At least seven classes of phenomena have given significant impetus to this trend.

1. *Since 1965, federal appropriations for education, while still a minor part of the total budget, have multiplied at a tremendous rate, bringing with them new regulations requiring evaluation of program effectiveness.* Almost all federal laws dealing with education provide for the establishment of various commissions and councils—examples are the National Advisory Council on the Education of Disadvantaged Children, National Advisory Council on Vocational Education, National Advisory Council on Education Professions Development—to assess the impact of federal education legislation and point out new areas of need. The individual federal acts also earmark funds for evaluative purposes. For

the fiscal year 1971, for example, $10 million was appropriated by the Congress for such undertakings. In the context of a total $4 billion federal investment in education, the effort seems miniscule. Its importance, however, lies in having set the legislative precedent that recipients of public funds must be held accountable for their effective usage and in having more generally made the case that program impact should be measured not by teacher academic qualifications or physical plant improvements—which may or may not be related to learning—but in terms of student achievement.

One specific product of federal evaluation has been the Coleman Report, whose purpose was to ascertain whether compensatory education had any impact on the learning of educationally disadvantaged children and, more broadly, to examine the relationship of a whole range of school characteristics to pupil achievement. While the report did not evaluate the makeup of specific programs, its findings—that school facilities, libraries, etc., have less influence on pupil learning than socioeconomic composition of the student body and teacher verbal ability—have had the general effect of focusing on product rather than process, on results rather than resources, and of making such data gathering a standard, acceptable method for assessing school effectiveness.

Yet other consequences of increased federal interest in evaluation have been the growth of a fleet of new educational consultant firms ready to take on assessment contracts and the emergence of a new breed of education specialist in the design of evaluation instruments and processes. For example, the U.S. Office of Education funded more than 80 projects in 1969 and 1970 to develop a new technique called program auditing, based very generally on the model of a fiscal auditor. The educational program auditor was to operate as an independent agent outside the local school system to provide an external, objective review. Part of his task would be to generate feedback to those in the school system charged with planning, operations, and evaluation and to help them learn evaluation techniques that could be used at the local level. By their very existence and their constant search for new clients to buy such services, these consultants and specialists thus have perpetuated concern about evaluation and validated assessment as a necessary and even integral part of any education program budget.

2. *Amid heated controversy, the National Assessment of Education was initiated and has begun to provide valuable new information about the status of American education.* The planning committee first met in 1964 and was responsible for designing an instrument to sample approximately 2,500 nine-, thirteen-, and seventeen-year-olds, as well as young adults, to ascertain level of knowledge and intellectual skills in various academic disciplines which is possessed by Americans in various

age groups. This information will no doubt serve as a guide to making some important judgments about the effectiveness of American education.

At first, the proposed assessment engendered considerable suspicion from the education profession, which feared that it would invite a national curriculum and lead to invidious comparisons among school systems. Ultimately, however, cautious endorsement was given by various professional associations, and the assessment has gone ahead, administered by the Education Commission of the States with support from the U.S. Office of Education and private foundations. As the first comprehensive nationwide educational evaluation ever to be conducted in the United States and reported to the people, as well as the profession, it adds important strength to the notion that education belongs to the public and must provide a regular accounting of itself to its clients.

3. *Parent and grass roots organizations, particularly those in minority neighborhoods of various cities, have demanded a much larger voice in the decision-making apparatus for education, especially the power to hold teachers and administrators accountable for youngsters' academic performance.* The issue of community control of education first gained widespread attention in the controversy over decentralization of the New York City school system—focused most heatedly in the Ocean Hill-Brownsville district—and the concept rapidly spread to other large and medium-sized cities, as well. Parents and other indigenous community people insisted that teachers' professional abilities be judged by pupil growth and development and also that, as clients of the school system, they be recognized as having the right to remove incompetent staff. Despite initial opposition from teachers' and supervisors' unions in New York, their organized voices won support of the mayor and ultimately brought sufficient pressure on the system to decentralize the schools of New York into smaller districts. The voice of the community can be expected to soar during the seventies and beyond, as various groups gain greater political awareness and grow more impatient for tangible improvement in the schools.

4. *American youths in public schools have become more self-conscious and sophisticated and have begun to pose serious questions about the quality of their education.* Confrontations and protests at the college level have served to make high school and even junior high school students more sensitive to their educational environment and have prompted them to raise issues regarding the quality of course content, its value for their present and future lives, and even their rights as students to wear what they please, organize politically, etc. A task force of educators and students organized by the National Education Association in 1970 foresaw a growing level of student power in the making of school regulations which relate to due process as well as substantive educational

policies within the school. For example, the NEA report recommended: "Any admissions requirements an advanced or graduate program may have should be established by representatives selected by and from the student body, faculty, administration and the community."

The New York City Board of Education has produced a policy statement affirming the right of students to peaceful dissent and giving them a legitimate voice in school matters of concern to them. How close the schools will move toward actual participatory democracy is still a remote question. Having to deal with this issue will no doubt prove a challenge to educators; it also raises basic philosophical questions regarding rights and responsibilities of all participants in the schooling process. Whatever the outcome, such new developments have placed the educational system on notice: it must take cognizance of this newly emerging constituency, the students, which can be expected to grow increasingly vocal and facile in dealing with educational issues in the seventies.

5. *Computers have come into widespread use in education, making data on student achievement readily retrievable and facilitating broad-scale evaluation of the schools' efforts.* Being able to develop profiles of data on individual children means that their progress can be traced through their school years and this information can be retrieved at a moment's notice for parents and others to assess. It also means that the effectiveness of individual teachers as well as the entire staffs of various schools can be compared in a single printout which, again, is accessible to all interested parties.

One example of the impact of computer data on educational quality occurred in a project in Southern Mississippi funded under the Elementary and Secondary Education Act. The federal funds provided for computerized record-keeping, and with this assistance the teachers in the McComb, Mississippi, public schools were able to compare their effectiveness with white and black students, in preparation for integration of their schools. The data showed they were failing twice as many black as white students, which led the superintendent to call for reexamination of the entire school curriculum and a search for more useful teaching materials and methods to use with minority youngsters.

Thus, modern technology offers potential for facilitating the call to accountability. The tools and equipment are available for data storage and retrieval. However, two problems still remain. One is that not enough school systems have yet purchased the machinery, which is expensive, or as an alternative have contracted to share data processing services with other schools and institutions.

Another difficulty concerns the nature of the data itself. Considerable thought must be given to the qualitative substance of data about education which is fed to computers. The objective must be to measure output, and if only information about input is considered, this will wash out the potential for in-depth public scrutiny of the crux of educational activity.

6. *The new concept of performance contracting has enabled school systems to contract with private companies to teach subjects such as reading and arithmetic and to pay on the basis of learning that is actually achieved.* An initial project in performance contracting was supported by the U.S. Office of Education in the Texarkana, Texas, public schools, and in 1970 the Office of Economic Opportunity began investing between $3.5 million and $5.5 million to continue testing the value of this approach. OEO has commissioned approximately six private companies to undertake similar ventures in about 24 school districts throughout the nation. Moreover, in at least one urban school district, Gary, Indiana, the board of education has hired a private corporation to assume responsibility for an entire school's program, again with a guarantee that reading and other achievement will be raised to specified levels.

These new developments have helped to reinforce the contention that teaching effectiveness must be judged by pupil performance, measured in objective terms, and that educators are responsible for producing increased knowledge and skills for all their pupils.

If private companies can teach children to read and guarantee results, why can't our schools? Parents have already begun to ask this question, although the full results of performance contracting experiments are still to be analyzed and evaluated, and the burden of proof of their worth clearly lies with their ability to produce results. However, their mere existence reinforces the message that achievement scores must be openly available to the public and that educators must stand ready to assume responsibility for the quality of these outcomes.

7. *At a deeper level still, the quest for accountability in education is related to the widespread distrust of social institutions which has swept our nation.* As James Reston has observed: "The authority of the Government, of the church, of the university, and even of the family is under challenge all over the Republic, and men of all ages, stations and persuasions agree that this crisis of confidence is one of the most important and dangerous problems of the age." [1] Thus, the central issue of our age for education involves the question of whether institutions will merit respect from the people or simply will have to be changed. If they refuse to conform to demands for greater credibility, then the society will have to deal with the issue of change—by legal and peaceful means or illegal coercion and violence.

---

[1] James Reston, "The Hypocrisy of Power," *New York Times* (April 8, 1970), p. 42. © 1970 by The New York Times Company. Reprinted by permission.

In retrospect, therefore, a number of new events and developments over the past five years or so have given momentum to the soaring pressures for accountability. The schools belong to the people, they have cried, and few can dispute the validity of this contention. In response, the education community has reacted with mixed emotions, not always positive. Several years ago, for example, the superintendent of schools in Philadelphia wanted to make principals in his system more accountable for learning in their schools. They were asked to list their goals, in terms of pupil performance, and then agree to have their professional competence judged by their ability to meet those stated objectives. The principals balked, and the plan had to be withdrawn. In a similar vein, psychologist Kenneth B. Clark proposed to the District of Columbia Board of Education that teachers' salaries and promotions depend on their ability to teach reading with successful results. The president of the teachers' union protested, and the idea was scrapped.

Recommendations

Assuming that the principle of accountability is a clearly-established right of the American public, and that it will eventually find acceptance within the profession, then the more fundamental question concerns what goals the schools should be held accountable for achieving. In one sense, the schools have already accepted responsibility for their students, at least those going on to college, and interestingly enough, they have not resisted being judged by the percentage of any senior class which pursues further education. The real shame lies in their treatment of the rest—those who leave school permanently, before or after graduation. The Ford Foundation's Educational Facilities Laboratory reports that of every 100 high school graduates, 46 do not go on to further education. Only about nine of these are trained for a craft or white collar job; 37 are lost and forgotten. In 1970, approximately 18 percent of all young Americans and 30 percent of all black young Americans were unemployed, and about half of unemployed youth were functionally illiterate. Moreover, about 50 percent of those students who do start college never finish.

At some point, therefore, almost every product of the public schools goes out to face the world of work, and most are in total bewilderment. They have little information about their own skills and abilities, much less about the range and varieties of occupations open to them. Their understanding of the nature of work is superficial. *The schools should be held accountable for their ability to prepare young people for the world of work.* James A. Rhodes, as governor of Ohio, has written: "What this nation needs is an educational system with a purpose focussed on youth as workers in our productive society."[2] This should be the stated policy of every local school board in every local district in the nation. It should become the major priority of the U.S. Office of Education, the Congress, state legislatures, and state departments of education. It should constitute a goal supported by every PTA, professional education association, and concerned citizens group.

This raises the immediate question of how school districts should be expected to meet such a goal. What criteria are most valid for judging their effectiveness? The schools should be held responsible for three types of efforts. Most immediately, they must be responsible for imparting to all students the basic skills of reading, exposition, and mathematics, which are fundamental to all types of roles in the working world. This should be regarded as a serious priority. School systems which continue to fail sizable numbers of students in this regard should be penalized in their allotment of state and federal funds.

Second, the schools should assume responsibility for placing students in jobs. A U.S. Office of Education official once remarked, "Every secondary school in the country can prepare a youngster for college, but not one can find a job." This situation can no longer be tolerated. Schools should establish their own extensive placement services which can help all students identify and locate suitable employment and which can also continue to offer them counseling on the job and follow them throughout their careers.

Finally, the schools must vastly improve their ability and commitment to teach various job skills. They must take responsibility for the employability of all students and be answerable to parents and pupils as well as employers. Viewing education from this perspective requires wholesale reconsideration of the content presently comprising the school curriculum. It also necessitates that factors constituting employability be isolated and analyzed and that the most effective means of teaching them be developed. Evaluation of a district's effectiveness should entail specification of quantifiable or otherwise assessable performance criteria and constant reappraisal of the progress of the school district in meeting them. Statements of objectives produced by school systems usually include something like education of "useful citizens" and "responsible adults," but these words are so vague and general that the schools have felt free to pursue practically any direction they wished. The new accountability demands that all such goals be translated into terms of pupil performance which can be objectively determined.

In insisting that education prepare pupils for the world of work, the

---

2 James A. Rhodes, *Alternative to a Decadent Society* (Indianapolis: Howard W. Sams and Co., Inc., 1969), p. 48.

public would be saying, for probably the first time, that schools must be held responsible for what their students do after leaving. They would be judged by student performance on the job, as determined by employers, and by the student's own appraisals of the quality of preparation relative to demands of the working world. The schools would also be subject to a third layer of scrutiny, from outside appraisers or program evaluators. The schools would be required to publish the results of these findings for all citizens to discern and would be required to demonstrate ways in which the findings would be used to modify school programs.

Accountability implies that penalties exist for those who fail to measure up. Thus far, the American public has been infinitely patient with the faltering efforts of schools to do their job, but their level of satisfaction or dissatisfaction is ultimately reflected in the level of public support provided for education, and this is always in jeopardy and subject to change. The time has come for school systems to measure up, to welcome opportunities to demonstrate their competence to their clients, and to begin making a major commitment to preparation of students for the working worlds of today and tomorrow.

SCENE OF HOSTILITY AND HOPE:
The City as Educator for Work

PAUL W. BRIGGS

In July 1969 two Americans walked on the moon and gathered samples of lunar soil. An Ohio farm boy and a fellow astronaut spent more than two hours exploring the moon's surface, and through the miracle of live television people throughout the world witnessed this magnificent scientific achievement.

America's educational enterprise can take pride in its contribution to development of the technological and scientific expertise which enabled man to accomplish this daring mission. Likewise, it can share in the credit for having helped make this nation the best fed and housed and most healthy, affluent, and highly trained ever known to the world. With 7 percent of the world's land area and 6 percent of the globe's 3 billion inhabitants, the nation's output accounts for about one-third of the world's total industrial production. Viewed in this perspective, our know-how seems almost infinite; the production of goods and services, limitless. However, the benefits of such material advancement have not accrued equally to all Americans; opportunities to savor the fruits of man's labors have been denied to millions; and nowhere is this disparity more starkly evident than in our nation's cities.

Disparities at the Core

Every city is but a microcosm of all the hopes, dreams, and human misery experienced by Americans everywhere. This is the best fed nation

---

PAUL W. BRIGGS is Superintendent of Schools in Cleveland, Ohio. He has also headed school systems in Bay City, Michigan, and Parma, Ohio.

in the world, but some of its poor citizens in inner cities eat starch because they cannot afford to buy food. Modern housing can be designed for comfort and easy living, but millions of city families are packed into small, unheated, crumbling surroundings because adequate apartments and houses in the city are expensive and scarce, and many buildings have been abandoned by their owners. In some cities mass transportation is crowded, slow, dirty, and at times unsafe; and public utilities are in a state of deterioration and disrepair. While living in a nation with the most advanced hospitals and best-trained doctors anywhere, many city children and adults have never seen a physician or dentist.

Poverty, the need for social services, the demand for expanded municipal services—all are highest in the city. Cities are rapidly losing population in terms of numbers; middle-class blacks and whites have fled to the suburbs, and cities are gaining migrants from poor and underprivileged sections of the U.S. Between 1950 and 1960, according to the U.S. Census Bureau, the white exodus from all of America's central cities averaged 450,000 a year; it is now running 800,000 annually. Meanwhile, in the 1950's, 1.5 million Black Americans left the rural South, and this rate continued in the sixties, attracting those with least education and poorest preparation for employment in greatest need of social welfare and rehabilitation. Today, 30 percent of all blacks in the central city live in poverty. Thus, it costs the city more per citizen to operate than ever before.

At the same time, the flight of middle-class Americans and increasingly of large corporations to the suburbs means that the tax base is eroding, leaving cities worse off than ever, and jobs are disappearing, as well. A Census Bureau study found that while the number of jobs in St. Louis dropped by 50,000 between 1952 and 1966, they rose in nearby suburbs by 193,500. Philadelphia lost 14,600 jobs in this period, while its suburbs gained almost 250,000. From 1945 to 1965, about 53 percent of all industrial building took place outside the core city. In 1969, between 75 and 80 percent of new jobs in trades and industry were situated on the metropolitan fringe.

Crime is growing more dangerous and frightening, and drug addiction and alcoholism have increased dramatically. In cities over half a million in population, total robberies reported to the police, including armed holdups of individuals and business, as well as forcible purse snatchings and muggings, jumped fivefold between 1960 and 1968. Even that understates the problem, however, because a third of all robberies are not reported by their victims. In municipalities of 100,000 to 299,000 people, it costs $14.60 per person per year for police protection; in cities of 500,000 to 1 million, the cost is $21.88.

Cities are vulnerable places, as well. They can be crippled by strikes, riots, layoffs. Operations as diverse as garbage disposal, post offices, and schools can be and have been paralyzed by mass walkouts of employees.

In the relatively short span of less than 50 years, America moved from an agrarian nation to one dominated by industry. During that period, no models and few guidelines existed to guide the metamorphosis. There were no patterns to follow, previous experiences to tap, or experts in urbanology to hire as consultants. Thus, urban America is now forced to pay the premium for its random experimentation and frenetic expansion. With an anticipated seven-tenths of the nation's population expected to be concentrated in metropolitan areas by 1975, a study by the National Planning Association estimates the cost of transforming metropolitan centers into viable communities at some $2.1 trillion, representing both public and private expenditures, spread over 20 years.

At the same time, however, those families who fled to the suburbs for relief have not fared as well as they expected. They have learned instead that social and economic crises of the urban environment follow them. Total metropolitan areas, whether cities or suburbs, have become similarly infected with problems of drugs, crime, rising taxes, deterioration of goods and services, rising welfare rolls, costly housing, breakdowns in transportation and communications, and even polluted air and water.

Education in the City

All of America's urban ills have converged on one central point, the nation's schools, and these institutions have found themselves almost totally unequipped to handle them. Suddenly, it seems, the country has awakened to its urban predicaments, but the schools have been struggling with them for decades, largely unassisted. Increasing numbers of teachers trained to work with middle-income, well-fed, confident youngsters ready for the most part to follow prescribed school routines now discover themselves confronted with classrooms full of poor, neglected, hungry children, unprepared to cope with the traditional school environment, victims of broken homes, unable to concentrate because of the environmental distress pressing in on their lives, and often finding school unrelated to their lives and their skills too poor to deal with the tasks at hand. The schools themselves have withered with old age, and capital expansion has lagged far behind the rate of increase in school population, causing overcrowding and double sessions. In Cleveland, for example, between 1960 and 1965 the city's total population dropped by 130,000 while the school enrollment rose by 50,000. The same eroding tax base which has crippled the extension of municipal services is also encumbering the efforts of the public schools in their hour of greatest need.

Meanwhile, vandalism and riots plague the schools. In Washington, D.C., a principal has been shot and killed trying to protect his school in an attempted holdup. A principal in New York was beaten by seven youths while working in his office on a Saturday morning. Terrified teachers in East St. Louis, Illinois, have carried guns to class for protection. In the past five years assaults have risen by 500 percent in the Philadelphia school system alone.

Vandalism and violence have imposed a tremendous financial burden on every urban school system. The nation's 36 largest cities reported that school vandalism, including arson, caused damage totalling more than $6.5 million in 1968. An Associated Press survey of vandalism in school systems between 1967 and 1968 showed an increase of 25 to 30 percent. The New York schools reportedly suffered a gross loss of $5 million to vandals; Philadelphia, $1 million, the District of Columbia, $400,000; Milwaukee, $335,000; New Orleans, $100,000; Miami, $269,000; Cleveland, $479,000. Many big-city systems have felt compelled to install such costly items as special lighting, burglar alarms, and hidden microphones to meet this problem.

At the same time, schools in some cities have become bastions of broad-scale drug operations. Outside school buildings, pushers hawk their wares while inside plainclothes or uniformed police have had to be posted to keep order.

Veteran educators and even fresh newcomers to the profession face this dramatic influx of social problems with a sense of shock and bewilderment. Most had anticipated careers in tranquil school environments similar to those from which they emerged as youngsters. They were never trained for today's city schools, nor did they expect to be teaching in such volatile circumstances. Most are dedicated, committed professionals, determined to remain in the system and do their best; but how can they hope to succeed, when they are equipped with essentially the same texts, tools, and assumptions about learning which guided their predecessors in totally different situations?

The Cleveland Scene

With a school enrollment of approximately 150,000 pupils, the Cleveland public schools serve about 7 percent of the state's public school population but enroll more than 30 percent of Ohio children who receive public assistance, and this proportion is increasing. In 1969, school districts throughout Ohio received, on the average, 67 percent of the total local real estate tax dollar. In Cleveland suburbs, the share was 66 percent for schools; but Cleveland itself had only 52 percent available for this purpose.

Cleveland is a city with 50,000 adults who cannot read and write, a city whose daily newspapers list column after column of well-paying jobs waiting to be filled, while unemployment rates in the inner city are among the highest in the nation. The city faced devastating riots in 1966 and in the spring of 1970, 200 policemen were necessary to open one of the large high schools. During the summer of 1964, schools were built under armed guard. The preceding school year had been marked by heated controversy with violent street fights and rock throwing as well as demonstrations and sit-ins in the board of education building.

Encapsulation in Hough. Cleveland's Hough area in the inner city was the scene of riots in 1966. It covers approximately two square miles, bordered on the east by University Circle, a rich complex of cultural institutions, and on the west by Cleveland's industrial heart. To the north and south run two main thoroughfares, traveled most heavily at the beginning and end of the business day as commuters from the other sections of Cleveland and from the eastern suburbs move in and out of Cleveland's central business district.

Once a favored residential area of wealthy Cleveland families, Hough today is covered with blight. Forty years ago, more than 90 percent of its homes were owner occupied. Today, fewer than 10 percent of the residents are homeowners. Hough's population of about 60,000 represents virtually a complete turnover since 1940. Rare, indeed, is the recent graduate of a high school in Hough whose father or mother also attended the same school.

The exodus from Hough was rapid. As former residents were replaced by families with large numbers of children, the schools became totally inadequate to serve the area. During the 1960's, Hough's school enrollment more than doubled, and it was not uncommon for a Hough school to experience 100 percent turnover in enrollment. Today, ten elementary schools—seven of them built since 1954—serve an area for which three were adequate prior to World War II.

Hough's new immigrants came from small towns in Appalachia and from the rural South to escape poverty and the burdens of discrimination. However, they were unprepared for the perplexing demands of urban living, and Cleveland was not equipped to help them become assimilated into the mainstream of city life. Jobs were not readily available for those with poor skills. Adequate housing at reasonable prices was scarce.

The change in Hough since 1940 has been dramatic. Delinquency has risen 300 percent and population density is almost 300 percent greater for Hough than in the city as a whole. School enrollment has doubled since 1950, and public welfare is up 700 percent in both number of cases handled and proportion of total funds expended in Cleveland. Since 1960, the income level for residents of Cleveland as a whole is up 16 percent, but for Hough income level is down 12 percent. The proportion of out-of-school youth is 200 percent greater than the city average.

A junior high school student in the ghetto today has a better than 50-50 chance of becoming a high school dropout, unemployed, and unemployable without salable skills. All around him he sees the devastating effects of social decay and economic decline—junkies on the street, hustlers, alcoholics, numbers runners, the ever-present pawnshop, litter, dingy stores with poor quality and overpriced wares owned by nonresidents, and worst of all, despair. His immediate goal is survival and his aspiration is to break out of the inner city, to gain a measure of economic security, and perhaps also to help his people. But the prospects, given his situation, are grim, indeed.

Preparation for Work

The urban schools have an obligation to provide excellence in education for all in the city. Public education must be the portal of opportunity for the denied, the underprivileged, underchallenged, undereducated, and undermotivated, identifying and responding to the varied needs of all children and youth. It must create an appropriate environment and marshal the necessary resources that will uncover, develop, refine, and encourage the abilities and talents of every youngster to the fullest possible extent.

In these perilous times for cities, the schools cannot afford to act as bulwarks of isolation or impervious retreats which fail to communicate with or understand the urban environment in which they dwell. This means that city schools cannot be like any others. They must respond to the vibrations of their own special setting and build upon the raw materials at their own front door. This is particularly necessary if the schools are to fulfill their commitment to prepare students for the world of work.

For the child of urban education, that working world is the city, and the schools must create a unique combination of experiences which help him "make it" in the working world. Teaching the literature, history, and culture of yesterday or the mathematics, science, and economics of today and tomorrow is not sufficient. The city must become the central learning laboratory for education, and city pupils must be approached not as naive children but as relatively sophisticated young people who themselves can serve as special resources in any study of city life. Many young people know far more about crime, police activities, political confrontations, and other urban issues than most of their teachers. It is ludicrous to pretend such knowledge does not exist in favor of repeating many of the irrelevant generalizations about cities found in most textbooks. Far more valuable, educationally, is a program which encourages students to utilize and build upon the knowledge they already possess about their changing city.

Ethnic studies. Working, living, and surviving both economically and psychologically in the city of today and tomorrow will require ability to relate to and interact with all of the multicultural and multiracial elements in its midst. Through the years, assimilationist efforts of the schools and society have helped to stifle many of the non-Anglo cultures which thread through the rich cultural fabric of the city. Consequently, many young people have grown up knowing almost nothing about their own cultural heritage, much less about the backgrounds of other groups around them. The movement for black studies first brought this deficiency to national attention. It made Americans cognizant of the fact that black people have been denied the opportunity to learn about their own history, music, heroes, and achievements, and that as a result most white people have been equally uninformed. This lesson, in turn, has led to recognition of an even more pervasive "culture gap" in our education programs, one which prevents students from gaining respect for and appreciation of the city as a polyglot enclave, a mosaic of America's history and growth. Today, the mounting tensions between diverse groups in the city make the need for such education even more imperative. If America is to make democracy work, with all people achieving a level of mutual understanding and willingness to share the benefits of living in a free society, then its educational system must begin by enabling every student to gain a fix on his own identity and enhance his sense of self-respect at what his people have been able to achieve. At the same time, he should develop a deeper understanding of the multiethnic nature of his environment and the forces which bind the various national and racial entities within a common framework called the city.

Part of this knowledge can be gleaned from books, but the most powerful learning will come from personal contact with students and adults from all neighborhoods in the city. Young people live and study in starkly isolated ethnic barrios, a poor beginning to prepare for a pluralistic working world. On the nation's 100 largest school districts, for example, only 12.9 percent of black students attended predominantly white schools in 1968,[1] and neighborhood patterns also tend to reinforce the inbred cultural orientation of children and young people from other groups, as

---

[1] "Desegregation Report," *Congressional Quarterly,* 28 (January 9, 1970), 124. See pp. 6-7 B.S.

well. This live interaction must be frequent and penetrating, and the school is in an advantageous position to help unite dissident or disparate segments of the urban population in deeply meaningful ways.

Urban studies. A second part of preparing students for work in the city involves strengthening their knowledge and sharpening their perceptions about their own urban surroundings. The social and neighborhood patterns which comprise a city, architecture as a reflection of its history, the economic pursuits of its people and their impact on the character of the city, the general ecology of urban living, city government, the phenomenon of metropolitanism—these are just a few of the topics which could be part of a curriculum in the urban schools. Every academic field, whether science, math, social studies, or English, can contribute to a penetrating study of the city. They should involve the students in almost daily encounters with resource persons from and on-the-spot participant observation of their city.

Basic skills. Students must have the opportunity to develop basic skills necessary for learning—whether they go on to further education or join the world of work immediately upon leaving school. City schools have made a very poor showing in this area and must commit themselves to giving Number One priority here. They should be able to insure that every city youngster will be able to read, perform basic computational tasks, and gain proficiency in the skills of studying and learning before they leave school.

Job training. Finally, the schools must be prepared to offer effective programs of education and training for specific jobs in the city. This means close cooperation between the schools and facets of the world of work in both the private and public sectors. As early in school as possible, students should be encouraged to "follow" and explore those careers in which they are interested. Some of these should be urban service careers which would develop their commitment to improve life in urban America. Students should be enabled to participate in the life of their city as junior assistants in various types of urban endeavors—city planning, housing, welfare and social service programs—and as teaching assistants and hospital aides, etc.

Students must also be able to receive specific skill training for jobs in the business and industries found in the city, and toward this undertaking the private sector must be willing to assume a sizable share of the financial burden.

The Cleveland school system has been extremely fortunate in developing a close working relationship with General Electric Company in what is popularly known as the "factory school." In 1968, GE's Lamp Division gave the school system an air-conditioned building valued at approximately $5 million with 4.5 acres of usable space. The facility, located in a high unemployment area, serves actual and potential dropouts in their upper teens, as well as some young men and women in their twenties. Establishment of the school was prompted by the fact that approximately 58 percent of young people between 17 and 25 years old in Cleveland's inner city were unemployed in 1968 and 4 million students were dropping out of school in the city every year.

On this one site the students can obtain both basic education and job training with pay. The public schools provide basic courses in reading, writing, and mathematics; classes in citizenship and work habits; and intensive counseling in money management and personal hygiene. The companies offer on-the-job training with immediate compensation. GE and other businesses and industries have leased and equipped office and light manufacturing space in the building. A large cafeteria provides training in food preparation and service. Classes are scheduled flexibly, learning is geared to individual rates of progress, and the school's head is called "manager" rather than "principal."

Prognosis

Can men of variegated backgrounds with plural ambitions and life styles coalesce in the social invention called the city? Forging common themes from disparate and sometimes dissonant harmonies must be a primary theme of public educational institutions. The schools must educate for work in the city, for grappling with the problems and challenges of life in the urban milieu, and for the hopes and dreams of the city of the seventies and beyond.

BLACK MAN, WHITE WORLD
Necessary National Manpower Priorities

CLEVELAND L. DENNARD

> . . .
> the child of years from me
> the eyes of a grandfather days from me
> will know this strange word
> freedom.
> —Gaston Neal (1967) [1]

Need for change is a constant in human affairs. Laws and institutions must keep pace with the progress of the human mind. As Thomas Jefferson recognized, truths continually discovered must fan out to transform opinions and structures that regulate and inspire human conduct.

School board members and professionals who spend valuable time at workshops, conferences, and seminars reviewing new trends have a sincere desire to uplift public education. Unfortunately, however, intentions do not automatically translate into results. Inhibitions to action loom up like mountains out of mists, and neither ESP nor radar is needed to spot them.

Facing these issues and moving beyond them to creation of comprehensive programs for career preparation demands high courage. It also

---

CLEVELAND L. DENNARD is President of Washington Technical Institute, Washington, D.C., and Chairman of the Board of Trustees of the Washington Center for Metropolitan Studies.

---

[1] Gaston Neal, "Today," in *The Black Power Revolt,* Floyd B. Barbour, ed. (New York: Collier Books, 1969; and Boston: Porter Sargent Publisher, 1968).

requires determination that so-called vocational training of the past will take on broader dimensions and greater diversity than ever before.

This issue impinges on one of the most vital concerns of the Black American community now and in the remaining third of the twentieth century—the need to develop economic viability through career opportunities and options in all levels and segments of the American work force. U.S. Labor Department statistics showed as of June 1970 that 79.3 million persons were employed and 4.7 million were unemployed, with a seasonally unadjusted rate of 5.6 percent unemployment for the nation as a whole. For Black Americans the unemployment rate, unadjusted, was 10.6 percent—nearly twice as great as the national average. Critical examination of selected Standard Metropolitan Statistical Areas, in which center city population is concentrated, indicates that the unemployment rate for Blacks in the 15-29 age group approached 20 percent. Hence, the job problem is a real one for Blacks, grounded in experiences of the past and cold, hard statistics of the present. As was obvious to every American educator and interested layman at the close of the sixties, the quality of public vocational education was totally out of phase with the employment picture in today's economy. Philosophical commitment to the principle that public educational opportunity for all includes a chance to acquire occupational skills stands unchallenged. Implementation of that precept, however, remains an issue of unremitting debate.

Parents, White or Black, tend to believe that vocational education is a fine academic alternative—for someone else's child. The stratification of white- and blue-collar jobs in America is a manifestation of social elitism further expressed and reinforced by mass preoccupation with college. Despite the high rejection rate, however, educators and public policy-makers continue to assume that vocational training offers the best hope of preparing Black people for employment.

Black Americans tend to view vocational education as a hoax, as perpetrating a fraud on the Black male, whether he is a 15-year-old student or 47-year-old head of household. Payoff is measured in terms of job delivery, on the assumption that gainful employment can lead to "good" housing in "respectable" neighborhoods where there are usually "better" schools that prepare youngsters for "good" jobs and so on in the merry-go-round. When jobs are not forthcoming, then Black people lose faith in the entire process, which becomes for them a "misery-go-round."

Furthermore, serious doubts exist even within the White community about the capacity of public education to achieve its goals, even under optimum conditions. Assuming that Blacks and other minority groups did not pose a special challenge for full-time employment in the labor force, it is entirely possible that the system still could not produce jobs.

Blacks have been raising substantive questions about the areas of development and implementation of public policy and legislation as they affect career education and training.

National Employment Policy

With passage of the Employment Act of 1946, the Congress established basic direction for the issue of full employment. Since the early sixties, interpretation of this policy by the President's Council of Economic Advisers has meant that a full-employment economy represents 96 percent of the employment age population at any point during the year and assumes that the nation's economy can absorb a 4 percent unemployment rate (3.2 to 3.6 million persons) annually through social policy and manpower- or welfare-oriented legislation.

In the abstract, such a concept may appear quite reasonable, but when viewed in perspective of Black population densities in blighted urban centers, the net effect of Black unemployment in any given central city area is national travesty. Unemployment did not drop below 8 percent for Black American males in the 24 years following World War II. The productive question then becomes: Is it truly feasible to design a job-training system that meets the nation's manpower requirements at the subprofessional, technical, and skill levels in an economy geared to a 96 percent full-employment concept?

Framed in this way, the question must be answered with an emphatic "no." Manpower excesses at a 4 percent level totaling more than 3.2 million able-bodied Americans, of which more than 68 percent are minorities, cannot be absorbed into the mainstream of industry and business unless public policy is changed to reflect a full-employment concept at the 98.5 to 99.5 percent level. A 2.5 to 3.5 percent increase in full-employment level would require a long-range commitment of Marshall Plan-type grants to cities and states to assure job opportunities. Such responsible political behavior would then enable state education agencies to plan vocational education that would assure matching with the economic thrust of the states and territories.

Analogous to the impact of public policy formulation on vocational education programming, as it affects the Black community, is the present plight of manpower development programs in the United States. As President, Dwight D. Eisenhower established a commission in 1960 to formulate goals and priorities for the decade of the sixties. The goals, translated into 15 major recommendations, included the following: increased concern for status of the individual; lowering barriers to equality; perfecting the democratic process; strengthening the educational system; diffusing and balancing the centers of economic power; promoting economic growth; and remedying slum conditions and reversing the process of decay in cities.

Following two years of discussion and review, the National Planning Association established its Center for Priority Analysis in 1962 to study the goals of the commission. By 1966, the National Planning Association had quantified those goals into dollar requirements and published their findings in *The Dollar Cost of Our National Goals* [2] by Leonard Lecht.

Not until 1969—nine years later—were national goals for the decade of the sixties translated into manpower requirements. The second Lecht publication, *Manpower Needs for National Goals in the 1970's*,[3] although a worthwhile document, had zero relevance to problems of the previous decade, because a ten-year period had elapsed before it was possible to determine types of manpower programs to be continued or initiated and competencies needed to conceptualize, design, develop, maintain, evaluate, and finance public and private sector efforts. This delay also foreclosed any opportunity for such data to be useful in determining appropriate input for entry-level and inservice occupational training.

Trying to meet manpower development requirements without examining the nature of vocational education programs approaches folly. In the absence of such effort, the Black community knows that its needs cannot and will not be met through regular educational channels.

As an alternative, Blacks have chosen to endorse and promote short-term, crisis-oriented manpower programs which are accepted as band-aids in the absence of a national manpower policy. They take the form of high visibility subsidies for the unemployed, under the aegis of training, with no realistic expectation that jobs will be forthcoming. The Area Redevelopment Act of 1960, Manpower Development Training Act of 1962, Office of Economic Opportunity Act of 1965, and Civil Rights Act of the same year represent badly needed manpower development action from the federal level with direct impact on the Black community. At their best, however, they are simply brush-fire alternatives like the nation's response to the Great Depression of the 1930's, but not nearly so extensive.

Manpower programs implemented through the National Youth Administration, Works Progress Administration, Civilian Conservation Corps, and other administrative mechanisms have their modern parallels

---

[2] Leonard A. Lecht, *The Dollar Cost of Our National Goals* (Washington, D.C.: National Planning Association, Center for Priority Analysis, May 1965).
[3] Lecht, *Manpower Needs for National Goals in the 1970's* (New York: Frederick A. Praeger, 1969).

in the Neighborhood Youth Corps, Job Corps, and Bureau of Work Training Programs. One important difference is that present emphasis on minority business enables Black-owned and related consultant firms to contract with both the private and public sectors to carry on recruitment, counseling-testing, basic education, skill training, job development, initial job placement, and program evaluation.

Persistently high unemployment rates for Blacks suggest that short-term, high-visibility manpower alternatives do not lead to permanent jobs. Rather, they reinforce the subsidy concept—soil banks, farm price parity, and oil depletion, to cite only a few—so often used legislatively.

It is no secret that, irrespective of geographic and regional biases, Black Americans are not usually given priority in normal consideration of national manpower needs. A new dimension for the seventies, however, is the perception of Black people that synthesizes the violence, marching, looting, burning, and fatalities of the fifties and sixties into a special sense of personal involvement and commitment in the struggle for equality of opportunity, justice, housing, jobs, and education.

Perennial attacks on public education from the Black community reflect a fantastic height of frustration with educators over their limited ability to link education and training to demands of the employment sector for highly literate, well-trained job applicants. Blacks tend to attribute racist sentiments to White Americans who refuse to be aggressive in securing organized labor's cooperation for placing their sons and daughters in cooperative work-study programs. Accusations intensify when school personnel are reticent about permanent job placement of Black students upon graduation. Subtleties and nuances of dealing as individuals with a personnel office in a private company can be dealt with as part of the Black people problem; however, Blacks automatically question what the White coordinator, supervisor, or teacher is doing on a public payroll, if not to assist Black students in a curriculum which by statute is dedicated to training them for gainful employment. Black Americans want vocational education to be effective in helping them open personnel office doors. They also want to be able to participate in adult vocational extension courses as a part of industry efforts to upgrade personnel. Processes for achieving mobility are often included in negotiated union agreements. However, general lack of responsiveness from White educators at federal, state, and local levels to the call for new training avenues leaves them open to charges from the Black community of repression, racism, and consorting with the "system."

Couriers of Change

Change agents on whom a just and substantive policy for career education and employment policy will largely depend are as follows:

1. *The President of the United States*—who provides leadership for public policy at the national level, direction for the economy, and guidance through appointments to various federal commissions in regulating the economy and behavior of the private and government sectors in employment. The President is directly responsible for both employment and manpower policies and, most important, for establishing broad national priorities in the critical areas of concern to Black people—job training, employment, housing, justice, education, and equal opportunity. The faith of Black Americans in their country is influenced to a large extent by their understanding of where the President stands on these issues.

2. *The Congress*—with responsibility for enacting laws to establish and support occupational training and related programs. Significantly, the Congress can append clauses to such legislation requiring accountability for results. The imperative to improve quality of life for Black Americans, and especially the Black American male, rests in large measure with such statutory action. The Congress must command results from its job training investment in the form of full employment for Black people. In return for every federal dollar spent in occupational education, there must be a recognizable return as measured by gainful employment.

3. *The private sector*—whose participation in regular channels of the governmentally energized and regulated economy represents a major opportunity for change with tangible results. Along with labor unions, they still present a major obstacle to realization of economic fulfillment for the Black community. Only the federal government, through strengthening agencies such as the Equal Employment Opportunity Commission, can trigger the mechanism for assuring that the real challenge to the American dream can become a "right-now" reality in the life of the Black American.

4. *State and local boards of education*—which can most effectively evaluate programs and press for more adequate output. As cities become more densely Black and Brown in population, educators must in exchange for tax support produce a student product that can read the language, articulate thought, compute as consumer and artisan, spell accurately, analyze and synthesize, and perform specific marketable tasks in the American economy. Boards of education have the most favorable vantage point from which to insure that these results do in fact occur.

5. *Higher educational institutions*—which train the leadership for public education, government, and business. Their graduates must now become students of the human condition rather than exclusively craftsmen for particular work environments. In particular, colleges and universities can provide more sophisticated capability for educating leaders in career

education, including the training and credentialing of increased numbers of Black educators.

Prospects for Fulfillment

Thus, the challenge of full employment in America, which is so dependent on a responsive public educational system, can be met through human courage, a sense of history, and the need for immediate changes in attitude, program emphasis, resource allocations, and accountability.

The need for change and the courage to change both operationally and attitudinally pose a great challenge to America in the seventies. Within the hearts and minds of Black men and women, the haunting question remains one of whether change is really possible. They are told to have patience, but meanwhile parents and children are born and die, and still the doubt lingers on.

Yet, it has been America's ability to recognize challenges, respond to them, and move on to higher plateaus that has made this nation the best hope for realization of man's dreams ever witnessed in the history of the world. The latter third of this century must show America equal to the challenge. It must be remembered as the period in which national leaders and the common man undertook to erase both overt and more subtle traces of racism; when equal educational opportunity meant access to a quality vocational and academic education; when Black Americans could at last feel justified in believing that the Constitution includes them, as does the message of the Statue of Liberty, "Give me your tired and your poor, your huddled masses . . ."; and when national resources of Marshall Plan magnitude were allocated to move Black America into the economic, political, and social mainstream of American society.

THE NEW WOMANHOOD:
Education for Viable Alternatives

ELIZABETH J. SIMPSON

> Oh, oh, you will be sorry for that word!
> Give back my book and take my kiss instead.
> Was it my enemy or my friend I heard,
> "What a big book for such a little head!"
> Come, I will show you now my newest hat,
> And you may watch me purse my mouth and prink!
> Oh, I shall love you still, and all of that,
> I never again shall t ll you what I think.
> I shall be sweet and crafty, soft and sly;
> You will not catch me reading any more:
> I shall be called a wife to pattern by;
> And some day when you knock and push the door,
> Some sane day, not too bright and not too stormy,
> I shall be gone, and you may whistle for me.
> —Edna St. Vincent Millay [1]

Edna St. Vincent Millay's sonnet may not be in the fiery spirit of the more militant members of the Women's Liberation Movement. But it expresses, albeit rather gently, the kind of frustration felt by many

---

ELIZABETH J. SIMPSON is a Research Associate in the U.S. Office of Education. She was formerly a professor of vocational-technical education at the University of Illinois and is a Past President of the American Vocational Association.

The author bears sole responsibility for opinions expressed. They do not necessarily reflect official positions of the U.S. Office of Education.

[1] From *Collected Poems,* Harper & Row. Copyright 1923, 1951 by Edna St. Vincent Millay and Norma Millay Ellis.

women today when their abilities are downgraded because they are women; they repeatedly are figuratively or literally patted on the head and told, "Men are the *logical* thinkers, women *intuitive*"; they are asked to contribute cookies rather than ideas to a professional committee meeting; they are passed over in favor of males for promotion to administrative or executive positions; they labor at supporting roles while males "star."

The poet, Judith Viorst, expressed it in her own special style.

> Where is it written that husbands get twenty-five dollar lunches and invitations to South America for think conferences while wives get Campbell's black bean soup and a trip to the fire house with the first grade? . . . And if a wife should finally decide to let him take the shoes to the shoemaker and the children to the pediatrician and the dog to the vet while she takes up something like brain surgery or transcendental meditation, where is it written that she always has to feel guilty? [2]

This is not a chapter on the movement for female equality—but this revolution of the seventies is significant for the field of education and highlights special challenges for vocational education. At the upper echelons, the latter is male dominated (heavens, the upper echelons are exclusively male), and perhaps this is one reason why little attention is being given vocational education for women in national seminars and conferences of the field. Another may be lack of militancy among the largest groups of female vocational educators, the home economists and those in business education and health occupations. A national committee to study problems and challenges of vocational education for women and implications of the "women's revolution" should have been formed by the U.S. Office of Education or the American Vocational Association months—or even years—ago.

MAGNITUDE OF THE PROBLEM

Role Conflict Situations

- Thirty million American women are gainfully employed, accounting for two out of every five workers. This is 42 percent of all women of working age 16 years old and over.
- It is estimated that there will be an annual net increase of one-half million women entering the labor force during the 1970s.
- Nine out of ten women will be gainfully employed at some time during their lives.

---

[2] Reprinted by permission of The World Publishing Company from *It's Hard To Be Hip Over Thirty . . . Other Tragedies of Married Life* by Judith Viorst. An NAL book. Copyright © 1968 by Judith Viorst.

- The nation's rapidly expanding technology is opening broad vistas of employment possibilities, both at the technical and professional levels.

Hence, increased emphasis on vocational and technical education for women and preparation for their dual role of homemaker and wage earner may be seen as an imperative of the seventies. Herein lie both challenge and opportunity for the field of vocational education—and implications for the total field of education. But the challenge carries with it some concomitant problems.

There are no basic differences in intelligence between the sexes, and women can succeed at almost any job a man can do. *These are well-established facts.* However, stereotypes are operative which limit the vocational opportunities open to women. Certain occupational roles, such as nurse, teacher, or secretary, are generally considered acceptable; others, such as business executive or airplane pilot, are frowned upon not only by men but also many women.

Of the "acceptable" roles for women, that of wife-mother is still the *most* acceptable. Opting for the career role as first in importance, as a reasoned choice, raises questions about the woman's femininity among "Freud-and-Spock-thinking" males. And ambivalence with respect to her role almost certainly comes to the female sooner or later. This is probably true whether she has chosen a career or full-time homemaking in the traditional sense. In this ambivalence are inherent problems needing intensive examination by the field of vocational education.

Such ambivalence is not unknown to the male, but tradition is on his side when he makes a job or career central in his life. Particularly for the male, self-identity is found in the occupational role, and he can concentrate his energies on it with little feeling of guilt or conflict.

On the other hand, many females find their identity through association with husband, lover, or boss. It is rare to find a couple which chooses its geographic location in terms of the female's occupational situation. If the woman's employment is a primary consideration, she connives to make the man somehow feel that he gains by the choice. She assiduously sets about mending the purple toga of male ego which she feels has been rent by her dominance. Thus, she seeks to reassure him and assuage her own guilt feelings.

Whether the roots are in tradition and training or in female anatomy, most women respond with considerable submissiveness in their personal relationships with the men they love. Certainly, loving men are also giving, gentle, and considerate in intimacy. But, for the most part, it is the woman who is the more accommodative and adaptable, who accedes rather than proposes—although, admittedly, she may have stage-set the proposing. It is she who experiences most conflict in shifting from the softness of the one role to the greater toughness and aggressiveness that may be required by her occupation.

Most men do not experience the dramatic role conflicts of women. Or, if role conflicts exist, they are different in nature. Those who are concerned with women's educational and work lives need, at a minimum, an awareness of the existence and nature of feminine role conflict. And they need an awareness that this conflict may be lessening as women achieve greater equality and, in a very real sense, liberate their men from some of the unfair overprotective demands that society has made on them.

Child Rearing, Marriage, and Career

In considering women in the world of work and their occupational education, a basic fact to be recognized is that women still have to bear the children. There is a play in which a 16-year-old boy becomes pregnant, but there seems little likelihood that such a situation would ever prevail outside the world of fantasy. Because of motherhood, the woman's work and educational lives are likely to be discontinuous in nature. Just as a majority of men desire fatherhood, so do most women desire, and achieve, motherhood.

But the problems of population explosion are forcing us to take another look at parenthood. Stringent limitations on family size would appear inevitable, for they are essential from a social standpoint and possible from a medical perspective. This will result in greater availability of many women for the work force for more years of their lives. Hence, the concept of "the discontinuous nature of women's work and education" will be a somewhat *less* important factor in considering woman power in the economy as well as in education.

In addition, modern methods of contraception, changing abortion laws, and the social necessity for family size limitation, along with changes in sexual mores and other social changes that impinge on family life, are bringing about alterations in family forms and functions. Forms which are used increasingly include those based on various short- or long-term contractual marriage arrangements, depending on personal and family-life objectives, and communal family life styles with their youthful, and more recently middle-aged, experimenters.

A current de-emphasis on materialistic values among the young *may* have its impact on vocational aspirations and certainly on life styles. Hence, this must be a consideration in planning vocational education, including vocational guidance programs for both girls and boys.

It would not be surprising if a somewhat larger proportion of men and women decide against marriage in the foreseeable future. This thought is suggested by considerations previously stated and also by the career commitment for more women that will emerge from the female revolution in the seventies.

However, it would seem realistic to expect that a majority of women will combine marriage and homemaking. Hence, their education for the world of work must include induction into the role of homemaker, in addition to occupational training.

Of course, someone always raises questions regarding social desirability and effects on the child of mothers working outside the home, particularly when children are young. A number of studies lead to the conclusion that it is the *quality* of the parent-child relationship rather than the *frequency* that is significant in determining such effects, although it seems reasonable to assume some relationship betwen quality and quantity.

Lee G. Burchinal and Jack E. Rossman, using a sampling of 1,172 children, found in their study, "Relations Among Maternal Employment Indices and Development Characteristics of Children," that:

> Within the limitations of the methodology used in the study, apparently maternal employment *per se* cannot be considered as an index of maternal deprivation with consequent detrimental effects on the development of children. If maternal employment during pre-school years of children had negative effects upon the children's development, these effects were not observed by techniques used in the study. This conclusion holds for both sexes.[3]

Eleanor E. Maccoby, in *Work in the Lives of Married Women,* points out:

> Some mothers should work while others should not, and the outcome for the children depends upon many factors other than the employment itself. Some of these factors are: the age of the children, the nature of the mother's motivation to work, the mother's skill in child care and that of her substitute, the composition of the family . . . , the stability of the husband, and the presence or absence of tension between the husband and wife.[4]

The increasing availability of day-care facilities for children, their improving standards, and increasing emphasis on the training of child care workers open the way for more mothers to work away from home with peace of mind concerning their children's welfare. One of the immediate challenges to vocational education is training girls and women as child care workers and simultaneously preparing them for their own "mother roles." Since 1963, home economics education has made great strides toward meeting this challenge.

---

[3] Lee G. Burchinal and Jack E. Rossman, "Relations Among Maternal Employment . . . ," *Marriage and Family Living,* 23 (November 1961), 339.

[4] Eleanor E. Maccoby, "Effects Upon Children of Their Mothers' Outside Employment," in National Manpower Council, *Work in the Lives of Married Women* (New York: Columbia University Press, 1957), pp. 150-72.

Another challenge to vocational education lies in the life expectancy of women. For a woman born in 1940, total life expectancy was 66 years and work-life expectancy 12 years. But women born in 1960 could expect to live an average of 73 years and work 20 years.

The most startling increase in the labor force in the 1970s is expected among older women workers. There will be a million fewer females in the 40-to-54 age group and 8 million more above age 55. The greatest population increase will be among women 45 and over—triple the rise among their male counterparts.

Summary. Because life styles, roles, and expectations of women are changing, largely in response to technological advances and social changes, and these new developments appear to expand the possibilities and probabilities of women working outside the home for a longer period and in a greater variety of occupations, the need for increased attention to the problems, opportunities, and challenges of vocational education for women is underlined.

Women at Work

In a nation that has already achieved a trillion dollar economy, the contributions of women to the work force are absolutely essential. Full use of their talents and training should be made for the benefit of society, as well as for fulfillment of the individual. But it is a sad fact that most women hold jobs that are not commensurate with their abilities and educational achievements. A significant proportion of women college graduates labor in nonprofessional roles as clerks, sales or service workers, or factory operatives.

The failure to make effective use of woman power resources in the economic life of the nation, the failure to develop its woman power fully through education and training, and the failure in many instances to reward the female worker appropriately—these are matters of national disgrace.

Significant statistics. That the work of women is significant *to the economic well-being of the country* may be inferred from the following statistics. In 1940 women comprised a quarter of the civilian work force. Today they account for nearly 38 percent of the 80.4 million persons in it. By the mid-1970s it is expected to climb to 91.4 million. About 60 percent of that increase will be women, meaning there will be 22 percent more women workers and only 9 percent more men workers. Whereas 37 percent of women of employment age now work, experts expect nearly 47 percent will be doing so by the middle of the next decade.

The work of women is essential for family well-being. In 1968, according to the U.S. Women's Bureau, about 2.7 million women workers were heads of their families. According to the U.S. Department of Labor, of the 34 million women who worked at some time during 1965, 18 percent were widowed, divorced, or separated from their husbands; another 24 percent were single. A number were "parents without partners" with all the attendant responsibilities and problems. Married women whose husbands' incomes are inadequate or barely adequate to support families often are compelled to seek gainful employment. For example: 11 percent of all women who worked in 1965 had husbands with incomes below $3,000 a year; 13 percent of all women who worked in 1965 had husbands with incomes between $3,000 and $5,000; and 33 percent of all working women had husbands with annual incomes of $5,000 or more.

About three in five working women, old and young, are married. In fact, 34 percent of all married women work. The number of wives in jobs exceeded that of single women in 1950, and the gap has been widening ever since. The National Industrial Conference Board expects 22 million wives will be working by 1980.

Working wives have not abandoned the home. They simply do both—pursuing an outside-the-home occupation and keeping house (and sometimes caring for children). A recent study in France shows that the typical working wife with two children spends 37 hours a week on her job, 36 hours a week on housework, and another eight hours taking care of her children, for a total work week of 84 hours. American studies show a similar range of 50 to 80 hours in the total work week of employed wives.

A large proportion of mothers are employed outside the home. In March, 1967, 10,582,000 or 38.2 percent of all mothers with children under 18 were in the labor force; 6,443,000 or 48.6 percent of all mothers with children 6 to 17, and no children under 6, were in the labor force; and 4,139,000 or 28.7 percent of all mothers with children under 6 years (mothers who also may have had other children) were in the labor force.

The Women's Bureau indicates that 46 percent of the children of employed women are cared for at home in whole or in part by someone other than the mother; 28 percent are cared for entirely by the mother; 16 percent are cared for away from home; and 2 percent are in group care facilities. Eight percent are reported as having *no care*. The low percentage of children cared for away from home indicates that child care facilities either are not available or are not utilized widely.

At what kinds of jobs are women employed? Table 1 sheds light on this issue and raises questions for the vocational educator.

A large proportion of women (42 percent of all female employees) work at clerical and sales jobs. These, together with the service occupations, provide 58 percent of all jobs held by women in the United States. Fifteen percent of women are employed at semiskilled (operator) work.

Table 1 OCCUPATIONAL STANDINGS OF MEN AND WOMEN

People Employed As	Percent of All Women Workers	Percent of All Male Workers
Proprietors, managers	4%	14%
Professional, technical workers	15	14
Craftsmen	1	20
Factory workers	15	20
Clerks, sales workers	42	13
Service workers	16	7
Household workers	6	less than 1

Source: U.S. Department of Labor, as presented in *U.S. NEWS AND WORLD REPORT* (April 13, 1970), 37.

Broadening the range of possibilities for women in deciding on an occupation should be a goal for vocational education, rather than merely accepting and accommodating to the *status quo.*

Black women. In particular, black women suffer from "appropriate job" stereotyping. More than 50 percent of employed black women are domestic servants, chambermaids, cleaners, or cooks. The nation's highest rate of unemployment, found among 16- and 17-year-old nonwhite girls, is 33.7 percent.

If the black woman, as well as the black man, is to have wider occupational possibilities open, a reduction in discrimination is clearly imperative. Another is increased occupational and training possibilities, including preparation of females for the dual role of homemaker-wage earner.

According to the U.S. Bureau of Labor Statistics, the proportion of black women in the labor force may be expected to decline from the 1968 level of 49 percent to 47 percent in 1980. This change, though slight, will reflect the improving economic situation of black men and the decreasing pressure on the female to contribute toward support of the family.

Salary gaps. Table 2 shows salary differentials with respect to sex. Here, too, are challenges to those concerned with the preparation of women for occupational roles.

On the average, men earn considerably more than women. Unfortunately, this gap between men's and women's wages has been widening rather than narrowing in recent years. In 1955, the average American woman who worked full time earned $63.90 for each $100 earned by the

Table 2 MEDIAN WAGE OR SALARY INCOME OF FULL-TIME WORKERS IN 1968 BY SELECTED MAJOR OCCUPATION GROUP AND SEX (1968)

Occupation	Women	Men
Scientists	$10,000	$13,200
Professional, technical workers	6,691	10,151
Proprietors, managers	5,635	10,340
Clerical workers	4,789	7,351
Sales workers	3,461	8,549
Craftsmen	4,625	7,978
Factory workers	3,991	6,738
Service workers	3,332	6,058

Source: U.S. Dept. of Labor, National Science Foundation, as presented in *U.S. NEWS AND WORLD REPORT* (April 13, 1970), 37.

average American man. By 1960, she was earning $60.80 to his $100, and, by 1968, her average was only $58.20.

Bernice Sandler, of the Women's Equity Action League, testified before the U.S. Senate Judiciary Subcommittee on Constitutional Amendments:

> Sex prejudice is so ingrained in our society that many who practice it are simply unaware that they are hurting women. It is the last socially acceptable prejudice. The Chairman of a [university] department sees nothing wrong in paying a woman less because 'she is married and therefore doesn't need as much,' or paying her less because 'she is not married and therefore doesn't need as much.' [5]

Partial explanation for the disparity in earnings between men and women lies in the fact that women tend to be employed in lower paying jobs—in clerical work, sales, and service occupations. Sixty-four percent are so clustered, as opposed to about 70 percent of men employed as professional and technical workers, managers, proprietors, craftsmen, foremen, or factory workers—jobs which pay better. However, even when comparing men's and women's earnings *within occupational categories,* it is a disturbing fact that women still earn less than men, as shown in Table 2. Correcting these inequalities is one of the purposes of the several new groups working for equal occupational opportunity for women.

Career education. In *The Role of the Secondary Schools in the Prepa-*

---

[5] Bernice Sandler, "Statement Before Senate Judiciary Committee, Subcommittee on Constitutional Amendments. Re: S.J. Res. #61 (Equal Rights Amendment)," (Washington, D.C.: May 6, 1970).

ration of Youth for Employment, Jacob J. Kaufman and associates state the truism that "females are in many ways being ignored by vocational education." [6] They continue:

> In effect, society, through its schools, tells young girls who do not plan to go on to college that they are not capable of obtaining and holding jobs other than as clerks and secretaries. Although this condition would seem to stifle aspirations and to induce frustration, young women do not seem to respond in these ways, apparently because their vocational self-concepts are so limited by the cultural conditioning to which they are exposed that they see very few occupations as appropriate to them.[7]

They found that "females regarded post-high school employment as an interlude before they assumed their real roles as wives and mothers." [8] The authors conclude that:

> [Girls] have learned their cultural lessons well: there are few occupations appropriate for girls; girls should only plan on working until they get married; girls should not prepare themselves for important jobs because they will get married and waste their training. All of these cultured stereotypes restrict the schools in the programs they offer to girls, and, even more, they restrict the vocational self-concepts of young girls so that they are satisfied with these limited offerings.
> . . . the schools should take the lead in expanding the vocational self-concepts of young girls. Through expanded offerings and skillful guidance, young girls can be led to prepare themselves for the variety of occupations where their skills are needed.[9]

However, it must be recognized that combatting the stereotypes will require modifications in educational materials and methods from nursery school upward. It may be noted, without tongue in cheek, that an elementary school textbook writer recently reported in a press interview that his new first grade reader will include—along with the intact family and Tan, the dog—a swinging aunt who enjoys a full single life and an engrossing, rewarding job.

Family life education will have to come to grips with the problems of feminine stereotypes in new ways. But the real challenge is to vocational education to assume leadership in improving the occupational and professional lot of women.

Forecast. Expansion of vocational opportunities for women is in-

---

[6] Jacob J. Kaufman, Carl J. Schaefer, *et al., The Role of the Secondary Schools in the Preparation of Youth for Employment* (University Park, Pa.: Institute for Research on Human Resources, The Pennsylvania State University, 1967).
[7] *Ibid.*
[8] *Ibid.*
[9] *Ibid.,* 11-12.

evitable because of increasing pressures from women and recognition of resulting social and economic losses when their abilities are not fully utilized. Today's executive secretary, who plays a key role in the functioning of her organization but earns a fraction of her male boss's salary, will be tomorrow's top executive with pay commensurate with her improved status. Increasingly, women may be expected to enter the medical and legal professions and to advance to positions of prestige and influence. Such developing areas as environmental management, transportation, and allied health, family, and community services have exciting potential for the employment of women at all occupational levels.

Realization of this potential will result as vocational education, vocational counseling, job placement services, business, and the professions share increasing responsibility and cooperate in meeting the challenges of enlarging vocational opportunities for the nation's women.

Job, Career, Home, and Family?

That many—perhaps most—females today experience some confusion about their roles, life styles, and goals is not surprising. For many, two of the most pressing problems are: What shall be the place of a job or career in my life? What relation does the job or career have to my personal life as a woman? And, of course, whether to opt for a less demanding "job" or more ambitious "career" is a matter of concern.

The concept of "career" carries with it a sense of commitment. Marilyn J. Horn, in discussing professional commitment, stated:

> Commitment usually implies a devotion, a dedication, a loyalty to a cause. In more specific terms, committed individuals are serious in their intent to continue in their profession, in contrast to the noncommitted person who does not intend to remain in the profession for very long. Studies show that in general most men have a relatively high degree of commitment to their occupation or profession. Women, on the other hand, have a tendency to regard work as an intermediate step between schooling and motherhood, and even if they continue to work after marriage, their major orientation is toward the economic gains involved rather than toward the intrinsic satisfactions inherent in a career.[10]

Philip E. Slater, in a provocative discussion of the lives of modern women, expresses the opinion that "career" is a masculine concept.

> Career has connoted a demanding, rigorous, preordained life pattern, to whose goals everything else is ruthlessly subordinated—everything pleasurable, human, emotional, bodily, frivolous. . . . When a man asks a woman if she

---

[10] Marilyn J. Horn, "The Rewards of Commitment," *Journal of Home Economics*, *61* (February 1969), 87.

wants a career, it is intimidating. He is saying, are you willing to suppress half of your being as I am, neglect your family as I do, exploit personal relationships as I do, renounce all personal spontaneity as I do? [11]

He suggests that women work toward a *new* definition of career which recognizes the importance of meaningful, stimulating, "contributing" occupational activity, challenge, and social satisfactions without a sacrifice of the human values implicit in the finest definitions of marriage, family, motherhood—and friendships. He foresees the possibility of a woman adopting a revolutionary stance with respect to work. She need not fall into the masculine trap of finding her major definition of self in and through her work. She can make her commitment to work *and* to human values and find these goals compatible.

One example of such compatibility might include many of the service occupations—such as child care aide, food service worker, clothing service worker, interior decorator's aide, and group care worker—which require knowledge and skills in common with those needed by homemakers. Thus, preparing for one of these fields has a carry-over value for homemaking.

Legislation for Women

Federal laws relating to women and work include the following:
  1. Equal Pay Act—requires equal wages and salaries for men and women in equal work.
  2. Executive Order 11246, as amended by 11375—prohibits discrimination based on race, color, religion, sex, and national origin by federal government contractors and sub-contractors.
  3. National Labor Relations Act, as amended—is primarily concerned with union representation elections, but also deals with complaints of discrimination based on sex by employers and unions.
  4. Title VII of the Civil Rights Act—prohibits discrimination based on race, color, religion, sex, and national origin. It covers discrimination by employers of 25 or more employees, employment agencies, and unions with 25 or more members which operate hiring halls.
  5. Age Discrimination in Employment Act of 1967—prohibits discrimination based on age affecting workers 40 to 65 years old. Although it does not specifically mention sex discrimination, it is considered of assistance to women over 40 who wish to return to the job market.
  6. Civil Service Act of 1883—permits women to compete in civil service examinations on the same basis as men.

---

[11] Philip E. Slater, *The Pursuit of Loneliness* (Boston: Beacon Press, © 1970 by Philip E. Slater), p. 72. Reprinted by permission of Beacon Press.

7. Classification Act of 1923—establishes the present pay system for federal employees, whereby the salary rate for each position is determined solely on the basis of the job's duties and responsibilities.

Organizations such as Women's Equity Action League (WEAL), the National Organization of Women (NOW), and Federally Employed Women (FEW) keep a close watch on the progress of proposed legislation related to the rights of women and on enforcement of existing laws. These groups have initiated complaints when laws prohibiting sex discrimination have not been enforced and have actively campaigned for a constitutional amendment to guarantee equal rights for women.

Most states have laws "protecting" women workers; some of these, originally well-intended to protect women against discrimination, now appear needlessly discriminatory. They involve such matters as weight-lifting, long hours, bartending, and mining. As Elinor Lander Horwitz comments, however, "It is significant that no one has wished to legislate against women cleaning office buildings at midnight." [12]

However, certain equalizers are being demanded by women's rights groups—and here and there are being effected. These include time off from jobs for pregnancy and childbirth, adjustments in working hours to accommodate child rearing, and improved day care facilities for children.

Conclusions

1. An increasing proportion of women is working outside the home. The proportion of employed women may be expected to increase in the foreseeable future. They may be expected to enter new fields, including those stereotyped as men's occupations.

2. Practically all employed women are homemakers in a very real sense, whether married or single. Most are married and a very high proportion are mothers with children still at home.

3. Most women (nine out of ten) may expect to be gainfully employed at some time during their lifetimes.

4. The most startling increase in the labor force in the seventies is expected among women workers aged 45 and over.

5. The work of women is essential to the economic well-being of the nation. Society is the loser when women are confined to certain approved occupational roles and life styles and when their vocational self-concepts are as restricted as at the present time.

6. Many women work because of dire economic necessity, to support a household, or to supplement a husband's inadequate income. Others

---

[12] Elinor Lander Horwitz, "Are You a Sexist?" *Washington Star* (April 5, 1970), p. 12.

work to improve a family's standard of living, for personal fulfillment, or to satisfy a desire for communication with husband and children.

7. Many women have not achieved a personally satisfying combination of occupation and homemaking for their own lives. They feel ambivalent with respect to occupational aspirations and limit themselves both professionally and personally by viewing work as a stop-gap to marriage or to the husband's improved economic status. And our culture offers meager support for a genuine career commitment on the part of women.

8. There is no question that women suffer discrimination in employment. They tend to be employed in female-stereotyped jobs, at lower pay, and with less opportunity for advancement than is afforded men in the same occupational category. Rarely do they ascend to important policy-making positions.

9. The black woman suffers two kinds of job discrimination and is the least advantaged of any group with respect to her employment—except at certain professional levels. In the higher education setting, the black professional, both male and female, is much sought after in the current job market.

10. Job stereotyping occurs in the elementary school (but may begin earlier) through readers and other teaching materials that almost always present an intact family with the mother as full-time homemaker and the father as the only parent employed away from home. Men are frequently used as resource persons to tell about their jobs; women, rarely.

11. There are a variety of women's groups, such as the National Organization of Women (NOW), Federally Employed Women (FEW), Women's Equity Action League (WEAL), and the more radical Female Liberation Movement, all of which have the primary objective of improving vocational opportunities for women, including wider occupational choices, with salary and promotion based on ability. It is regrettable that this laudable objective has, in some groups and some instances, been confused with irrelevancies which have not served to advance the status of women either in a professional or personal sense.

12. Very few women hold key administrative roles in vocational education, either in state education departments or on college and university faculties. There is no woman in a top administrative position in vocational education in the U.S. Office of Education. As Director of the Women's Bureau of the U.S. Department of Labor beginning in 1969, Elizabeth Koontz has come closest to meeting this requirement, but her concerns are far broader than vocational education.

13. Vigilance with respect to enactment and enforcement of legislation for women is an essential concomitant to an effective program of vocational education for women. The women's rights groups have assumed the watchdog role that seems called for at this time.

A PROGRAM OF ACTION

Federal Guidelines

A harbinger of things to come in the improvement of the vocational lot of women is found in guidelines issued by the U.S. Secretary of Labor in 1970. They require that federal contractors maintain written personnel policies stating that there shall be no discrimination against employees because of sex. Union contracts must be consistent with these guidelines.

The guidelines apply to companies with contracts of $50,000 or more or those that employ more than 50 people and are supervised by the Labor Department's Office of Federal Contract Compliance. Under the guidelines, employers are prohibited from:

(1) Making any distinction based upon sex in employment opportunities, wages, hours, or other conditions of employment;
(2) Advertising for workers in newspaper columns headed "Male" or "Female" unless sex is a bona fide occupational qualification;
(3) Denying employment to women with young children unless the same exclusionary policy exists for men;
(4) Making any distinction between married and unmarried persons of one sex unless the same distinctions are made between married and unmarried persons of the opposite sex;
(5) Penalizing women in their conditions of employment because they require time away from work for childbearing. Whether or not the employer has a leave policy, childbearing must be considered a justification for leave of absence for a reasonable length of time;
(6) Maintaining seniority lines or lists based solely on sex;
(7) Discriminatorily restricting one sex to certain job classifications and departments;
(8) Specifying any differences on the basis of sex in either mandatory or optional retirement age;
(9) Denying a female employee the right to any job that she is qualified to perform in reliance upon a state "protective" law.

The guidelines also require contractors to recruit women for jobs from which they have been previously excluded.

Task Force Report

The report of the President's Task Force on Women's Rights and Responsibilities issued in 1970 [13] recommended such guidelines. Their other recommendations included:

---

[13] *A Matter of Simple Justice*. The Report of the President's Task Force on Women's Rights and Responsibilities (Washington, D.C.: U.S. Government Printing Office, April 1970).

(1) Establishment of an Office of Women's Rights and Responsibilities headed by a woman as a special assistant to the President;
(2) Convening of a 1970 White House Conference on Women's Rights and Responsibilities to study ways to improve the status of the American woman;
(3) Enactment of an amendment to the Constitution to assure men and women equal protection under laws relating to marriage, guardianship, dependents, property ownership, business ownership, dower rights, and domicile;
(4) Passage by the Congress of legislation to equalize educational opportunities, access to public accommodations, benefits under Social Security, and professional salaries (women professionals, executives, and administrators having been excluded from the equal provisions of the Fair Labor Standards Act);
(5) Establishment of a national goal of a system of well-run child care centers available to all pre-school children and after-school activities for school-age children, with priority given to the needs of low-income working mothers;
(6) Establishment of a special Women's Unit in the U.S. Office of Education to end discrimination against women in higher education and to improve the counseling of girls and women.

Recommendations

The current and predicted status of career education for women indicates the need for a number of significant changes, in addition to those recommendations already made in the report of the President's Task Force on Women's Rights and Responsibilities.

Research. Research on roles of women in the work force and on women's vocational education should be brought together. It is recognized that some such efforts have been made or are currently underway. Analysis and synthesis of research in such areas as the following are needed to provide direction for a major effort to improve vocational opportunity for girls and women:

- roles of women and role behaviors and expectations;
- men's expectations and attitudes concerning women's roles;
- the influence of guidance counselors on girls' vocational and educational aspirations and decisions;
- problems and practices associated with the "dual role" of homemaker and employee;
- employment of mothers and its effects on children;
- motivations for working or for full-time homemaking among women;
- women's performance in various occupational roles;
- women's opportunities for salary increases and advancement in various occupational roles;
- effects of involvement in women's rights groups on personal and work lives and on employers' attitudes and practices;

- problems and satisfactions associated with a woman's employment at different stages in the family life cycle;
- influences on girls' developing concepts of work, appropriate jobs for women, and leisure;
- the impact of an increasing female work force on social institutions;
- factors associated with women's employment, part time or full time;
- problems faced by women in job re-entry and retraining in later years.

Each of the women's rights groups appears to be conducting its own studies. Where feasible, coordination would seem desirable. As a minimum, an attempt should be made to determine what studies are in progress.

Hopefully, such research can be undertaken with the support of federal and state funds and participation of higher educational institutions.

Advisory mechanism. Immediate steps should be taken by the U.S. Office of Education to establish a separate Advisory Council on Vocational Education for Women or, as an alternative, to make it a subcommittee of the National Advisory Council on Vocational Education. It should be unnecessary to insist that this council include vocational educators, among them recognized leaders in vocational education for women. Concerned leaders from business and industry should also play a major role in the deliberations of the council. The council should be convened at regular intervals, perhaps every three or four months, to review and advise on policies and programs of the U.S. Office of Education related to vocational education of women.

Organizations. Women's rights groups should be encouraged to continue and expand their efforts on behalf of legislation to prohibit sex discrimination in employment. The establishment of a clearing house for their activities would be a great aid in effecting their objectives. Professional staff members of OE working with the Advisory Council of Vocational Education for Women should remain cognizant of the goals of such women's rights groups as WEAL, FEW, and NOW as they affect education. These groups fill a need and will continue to function, grow, and develop.

Thus, we should develop a strong base in research, cooperative activity among federal agencies, and legislation for the development of courageous innovation needed in meeting the challenges of improved vocational opportunity, including vocational education, for women.

Education for women. The following recommendations would be the base for improved vocational education for women.

• Kindergarten and elementary school educators should help open new vistas of occupational opportunity to girls through promoting an awareness of women as employed persons and helping girls enlarge their

vocational self-concept by developing understanding of the great variety of occupational roles they might fill.
- From grammar school on, females should be encouraged to pursue their own intellectual interests and concerns.
- Employed married and single women from a variety of occupational fields, both traditionally feminine fields of endeavor and otherwise, should serve as resource persons along with men in promoting awareness of occupational possibilities.
- New student text materials which present a variety of socially constructive life styles and roles, including a range of occupational roles for women, should be developed and tested.
- Nursery school, kindergarten, and elementary school teachers should be educated to assume greater responsibility for helping girls expand their vocational self-concept.
- Guidance counselors should be made aware of the very significant role that they can play in helping girls develop their potential for employment in a wide variety of occupational fields.
- Teachers of such subjects as English and social studies should be oriented to the whole area of vocational preparation for women. The unique contributions that these fields can make are needed in the total effort to improve the vocational lot of women—but making the contributions could enhance the relevance of the content for each field, itself.

For example, the communications problems of the woman at work, particularly as she tries to "make it" in traditionally male bastions of employment, would be provocative and meaningful for the job-oriented girl—and young man. The fascinating literature on women, from that of Simone de Beauvoir to the writings of Oriana Fallaci, Judith Viorst, and Robert Graves, to name only a few, could be reviewed and discussed in literature classes. A social studies class might consider the impact of an increasing number of women in the work force on the institution of the family, volunteer social services, the personal service industry, males, etc.
- Women's history might be included in social studies textbooks for the role identification of young girls and for the role models of concerned and responsible women in the political, social welfare, and economic life of the nation.
- Opportunity should be provided for girls and women to prepare for occupations in any field of endeavor that interests them. This is the challenge to vocational education. Females should be recruited for some programs of study that were virtually closed to them in the past. Emerging occupations not already stereotyped as "men's jobs" might offer special opportunities to women. For example, positions in environmental management and transportation could offer special opportunity and challenge in widening occupational choices for females.

- Recruitment programs and literature should be used as means of attracting girls into new areas of study in the post-secondary technical education programs.
- Surely such organizations as the American Association of Junior Colleges and the American Technical Education Association, along with the American Vocational Association, will respond to the challenge of opening new occupational and training opportunities to women. Perhaps the fact that one woman, Ruth E. Midjaas, has already been elected the first female President of ATEA is a harbinger of things to come in that organization's developing concern for women in the world of work.
- Each substantive area of vocational education should consider its potential for serving the occupational preparation needs of girls and women.

Home Economics. The field of Home Economics is in a particularly strategic position to respond to the challenges of improving the vocational opportunity of women. A number of service occupations are related to content of the field, among them child care and guidance services; food management; clothing management, production, and services; and home furnishings, equipment, and services.

- Preparation for occupations in these areas may begin in the secondary school and extend into the community college and/or four-year institution. To some extent, hierarchies of occupations in the aforementioned service areas have been identified. Curriculum materials completed or in process take cognizance of these and provide for a number of job exits as a student progresses in her studies in one of the service areas.
- There is need for more specialists in the occupational programs of Home Economics. There is need for cooperation with other related fields of vocational education. There is need for more tested curriculum materials. Nevertheless, there is an increasing sense of commitment to the goals of the occupationally oriented aspect of Home Economics education and considerable progress has been made. Many fine efforts have not been given the visibility that they deserve.
- A young woman preparing for a Home Economics-related occupation receives the bonus of preparation for certain of her homemaking responsibilities. Many of the knowledges and skills needed for the occupational role are the same ones needed for the homemaking role. Thus, in entering the occupational training programs of the field, she is training for her dual role of homemaker-wage earner.
- Part F, "Consumer and Homemaking Education," of the Vocational Education Amendments of 1968 authorized federal reimbursement for a program to, among other purposes, "prepare youths and adults for the

role of homemaker, or to contribute to the employability of such youths and adults in the dual role of homemaker and wage earner." Such a program would be geared to the realities of homemaking today and emphasize such areas as personal development; understanding the roles of women (and men); management of resources and decision making in terms of goals and values; family financial management, including consumer buying and consumer ethics; personal relationships at home and on the job; child care and guidance; nutrition; and continued education for home and family living.

- Such a curriculum would enhance the employability of young women—and men, too. Such programs are already in evidence around the country, supplanting the garment-making and cooking-centered programs of the past.
- Researchers at Cornell University, Ohio State University, and Purdue University are cooperating in a study entitled "The Efficacy of Home Economics Courses Designed to Prepare Disadvantaged Pupils for their Homemaker–Family Member Role and the Dual Roles of Homemaker and Wage Earner." The study, near completion, has resulted in tested curriculum materials for preparing high school students for their dual role.
- There is abundant evidence that Home Economics education should do the following:

(1) Give more attention to its theoretical and philosophical base. Like the whole field of vocational education, Home Economics can be a victim of its success with the practical in failing to give sufficient cognizance to the theoretical.
(2) Establish priorities, because it cannot do *all* of the things that cry for attention from its specialists. Home Economics has tended to add areas of content but eliminate little or nothing. This is unrealistic and results in a watering down of content, continued attention to outmoded content, and "cream on the pie" methods in relation to new and vital areas of content.
(3) Provide for much greater access to occupationally oriented Home Economics courses and courses that realistically prepare for the dual role of homemaker-wage earner. Such courses should be available to all young people in both secondary and post-secondary educational programs.
(4) Provide for prevocational education in its programs in the junior high and middle schools. Curriculum materials for this purpose have been prepared and tried in practice at the University of Illinois.
(5) Provide for continuing development and testing of curriculum and evaluation materials for occupationally oriented Home Economics and homemaking programs aimed at improving employability and preparing for the dual role.
(6) Provide for continuing development of supporting teacher education and research programs.

Special programs. Particular efforts should be made to motivate and train the economically and educationally deprived woman for occupational and homemaking roles. Special counseling and guidance services are needed for girls and women of all ages and circumstances.

Higher education. Kate H. Mueller has made a recommendation which is worthy of consideration by all institutions of higher education:

> . . . the naming of an expert on educational needs of women for each 1,000 women students on a campus. The major assignment of this specialist would be to induct teachers and administrators into the study of woman as an individual—her intellectual, physical, glandular, motivational, and sexual makeup.[14]

New programs. Both women and men should be educated concerning "women in the world of work," whether in home economics, social studies, vocational education, or elsewhere. As a graduate student at the University of Minnesota, Richard J. Thoni, working under faculty members Mary Klaurens, Wes Tennyson, and Lorraine Hansen, has developed a curriculum guide on the subject as part of a larger Career Development Project. The objectives of Thoni's unit of study are found in Table 3.

As an administrator in the U.S. Department of Labor's Manpower Program, Charles Phillips described the following training program which is on the "front burner" in meeting needs of adults, particularly women, in preparing for entry or reentry into the world of work.

> Mrs. Donna Seay, of Montgomery, Alabama, has directed the development of a system of individualized programed instruction (IPI) which should be a tremendous aid to basic and vocational education for many whose educational opportunities have either been lacking or undeveloped, and who, as a result, have been left behind in a competitive economic development.
>
> A vocational educator, Mrs. Seay directed the development of this system during six years of work in a Department of Labor Manpower Program. Programed instruction—self-paced lessons that permit many different individuals in a class to work at different speeds and levels—was not new. Results were promising, not the least in that slow learners eventually achieved the same proficiencies as faster ones. Yet many problems appeared in administration and the methods were not easily translatable to teachers in general. Problems ranged from knowing the right materials to select and prescribe for particular deficiencies to a general management of the learning sequences, to a linking of basic education to vocational goals and training. Much experimentation, field-testing, measurement, and manualizing of the results has [sic] led to a system for diagnosis, prescription, and management which can be communicated to any competent teaching staff in a minimal training time.

---

[14] Kate H. Mueller, "Education: The Realistic Approach," in *The Challenge to Women,* Seymour Farber and Roger H. L. Wilson, eds. (New York: Basic Books, 1966).

Table 3 WOMEN IN THE WORLD OF WORK: CURRICULUM OBJECTIVES

Terminal Performance Goals

The student will demonstrate an attitude toward women that is consistent with present social trends by displaying that he:

1) considers the work contribution of woman to be socially significant as that of man;
2) acknowledges that many women will need the stimulation and rewards of a work role in addition to a family role.

Enabling Objectives

1) Discovers elements within our culture which have contributed to the traditional view of women;
2) investigates the opinions that contemporary women hold of themselves and their place in the world of work;
3) reads and discusses significant literature dealing with women, their traditional roles, and their place in the world of work;
4) participates in and observes situations in which women are found in roles other than traditional ones;
5) cites examples of change within the modern work society which have affected the traditional division of labor by sex;
6) identifies several life patterns which might be followed by women and discusses the significance of these in connection with the personal development and family life of a woman;
7) gathers information concerning vocational opportunities for women in various areas of work.

Source: Richard J. Thoni, "Women and the World of Work," unpublished curriculum guide (St. Paul: Division of Vocational and Technical Education, University of Minnesota, 1970).

The expansion of the system to include vocational skill linkages is under development. It can be of enormous value in training many women in a variety of fields—women for whom an educational catch-up is necessary to make them economically self-sufficient.[15]

This is an exciting program with potential for application far beyond its setting or original success.

The needs, the challenges, and the possibilities in improving the vocational opportunity and the lives of employed women seem endless. In achieving this goal, the field of vocational education *can* and *should* take the lead.

Women can help by being more respectful of other women. Women who put down women, who aspire to be the only woman on a staff of men, and who downgrade the woman boss or supervisor, who trade on

---

[15] Letter to Elizabeth J. Simpson from Charles Phillips, Manpower Administration, U.S. Department of Labor, Washington, D.C., March 10, 1970.

their sexuality in lieu of competence—such women limit by just so much the occupational opportunity for all women.

Out of the efforts to improve the vocational lot of women may come a new concept of what it means to be a mature, fully functioning woman. Such a woman will be a partner to men, neither subservient nor threatening and "emasculating"; feminine in the sense of womanly rather than helpless and childlike; more interesting to her husband and children; and fully responsible in her roles as homemaker, employed person, and citizen. In a satisfying, contributing, wholly "human" synthesis of her various roles she will find her identity.

III

TURNING AROUND THE SYSTEM

INTRODUCTION

Strengthening the capability of American public education to prepare youth for technologically oriented careers will necessitate dramatic changes in schooling as presently conceived. New and inventive efforts will be needed in such familiar areas as curriculum development, teacher training, and pupil personnel services. On a broader level, the input into education must be greatly expanded and lifelong educational experiences systematically organized through redesigned or newly established institutional vehicles. The doors must be opened to participation from the private and public sectors of American enterprise, in addition to the education profession, to maximize the learning potential of career education experiences.

Contributors to this section have centered their attention on these needs for the seventies. Garth L. Mangum discusses manpower requirements for the decade. He suggests that career education will have to broaden its horizons to include more comprehensive orientation to the work environment and at the same time become more specifically focussed on emerging occupations in a technical economy, if manpower needs are to be met.

Marvin J. Feldman perceives the community college as the focal point for career education efforts. He suggests that career preparation from kindergarten through adult education be conceptualized by community colleges, which in his view are best qualified to bridge the theoretical and practical worlds of academia and employment.

Making rational career decisions is the subject of David V. Tiedeman's essay. He presents a theory of decision making which can be taught to students with use of a computerized "guidance machine," freeing counselors to attend to individual psychological problems which prevent students from making choices.

Teachers must increase their understanding of technology and the world of work, according to Carl J. Schaefer. He would have both preservice and inservice teachers spend more time in actual work experiences as part of their training and would design special facilities to familiarize teachers with new technological concepts and design curriculum materials to utilize this knowledge in the classroom.

Samuel M. Burt and Lowell A. Burkett hope to open up the system to fresh inputs from the nonacademic world. Burt calls for greater efforts by school people to involve the business community in formulating educational goals and designing programs to prepare young people for work. He presents several successful examples of industry-education cooperation. Burkett suggests that manpower trainers and vocational educators strive for greater cooperation, both at policy development and program implementation levels, because both groups are concerned with many of the same goals and problems. He stresses, however, that the public school system, which has a mandate to provide for all learners, should act as the central institutional mechanism for career education.

Finally, Sherwood Dees recommends that state education bureaucracies dealing with vocational training be revitalized through reorganization with greater emphasis on the Vocational Education Amendments of 1968, and through removal of staff from civil service tenure, better salaries, and greater opportunities for mobility to attract competent professionals.—S. H. P.

WORKPOWER FOR THE SEVENTIES:
Requirements for Talent, Knowledge, and Skills

GARTH L. MANGUM

Since World War II, the United States has graduated from an industrial stage of economic history, with capital resources the critical element, to a postindustrial phase in which human resources have soared in importance. Consequently the nation finds itself facing (1) a hunger for manpower with specialized skills and talents; (2) a need for greater investment in occupational training at both entry and inservice levels; (3) severe difficulties finding jobs for the unskilled; and (4) direct competition between men and machines, with a worker's survival hinging on his ability to perform new functions or to underbid the cost of machine labor. There is no sign of work becoming obsolete, but the nature and definition of work are changing rapidly.

This chapter will compare ways in which people earned their living in the 1960s with the occupational outlook for the 1970s, and then explore the implications of those trends for the determination of education and training policies and procedures in contrast with the present structure of education.

The transition from agrarian to industrial to postindustrial economy is most dramatically illustrated by tracing shifts in the structure of employment. In 1850, over half the labor force was employed in agriculture. By 1940 one out of eight workers was employed on a farm; in 1969,

---

GARTH L. MANGUM is McGraw Professor of Economics and Director of the Human Resources Institute at the University of Utah, and Research Professor of Economics and Associate of the Center for Manpower Policy Studies at The George Washington University.

one in 22. The production of physical goods in agriculture, mining, manufacturing, and construction absorbed about the same number of workers in 1950 as 1960 and only slightly more in 1969, while the total labor force increased dramatically from 64 to 72 to 84 million.

Thus, nongoods-producing industries accounted for all employment growth between 1950 and 1960 in all but 2 million [1] of the 12 million new jobs created between 1960 and 1969, despite the nation's involvement in the latter year in a conventional war demanding high production of military goods and creating an inflationary boom in the consumption of consumer goods.

However, these totals by industry can be misleading. Within the goods-producing industries, an increasing proportion of jobs consists of "paper shuffling," management, and other activities separate from the actual production of goods.

Employment Projections

An average 77 million people were working or seeking employment during 1965 and that number will average 92 million by 1975. The most rapidly growing portion of the labor force in the 1950s was a middle-aged group (45 to 64 years old); during the 1960s it was a youthful under-30 population. The growth of the 1970s is shifting to young careerists, 25 to 34 years old. Thus, the labor market will long feel the effects of a system which educated youth during the 1950s to enter the labor market in the 1960s and become its mainstay in the seventies. Continuing education will be required to improve the skills and knowledge of this group, which will represent a progressively greater bulge in the labor force anatomy until they retire around the year 2020. Therefore, community colleges, business and industry, or institutions yet to be created will have to expand their efforts considerably to meet this new need.

Youth and minority groups encountered enormous difficulties finding jobs in the 1960s. The 1970s will offer less resistance to young people (as Table 4 suggests), but for minorities the future will be even more desperate (see Table 5). Between 1960 and 1970 the number of nonwhites in the labor force expanded by 22 percent and constituted 17 percent of the total labor force. In the remainder of the seventies, the pace of white growth will remain constant; at the same time, the nonwhite labor force will increase another 27 percent. The number of 16- to 19-year-old nonwhite youths in the labor force in 1975 will have

---

[1] Figures have been rounded.

Table 4 CHANGES IN THE TOTAL LABOR FORCE, BY SEX AND AGE, 1950 TO 1980 (Numbers in thousands)

	ACTUAL		PROJECTED		NUMBER CHANGE			PERCENT CHANGE		
	1950	1960	1970	1980	1950-60	1960-70	1970-80	1950-60	1960-70	1970-80
Both Sexes										
16 years and over	63,858	72,104	84,617	99,942	8,246	12,513	15,325	12.9	17.4	18.1
16 to 24 years	12,440	12,720	18,921	22,554	273	6,208	3,633	2.2	48.8	19.2
25 to 44 years	29,263	31,878	33,442	43,407	2,615	1,564	9,965	8.9	4.9	29.8
25 to 34 years	15,145	15,099	16,957	24,937	-46	1,858	7,980	-.3	12.3	47.1
35 to 44 years	14,118	16,779	16,485	18,470	2,661	-294	1,985	18.3	-1.8	12.0
45 years and over	22,156	27,506	32,254	33,981	5,350	4,748	1,727	24.1	17.3	5.4
45 to 64 years	19,119	24,127	29,055	30,545	5,008	4,928	1,490	26.2	24.4	5.1
65 years and over	3,037	3,379	3,199	3,436	342	-180	237	11.3	-5.3	7.4
Male										
16 years and over	45,446	48,933	54,960	64,061	3,487	6,027	9,101	7.7	12.3	16.6
16 to 24 years	8,045	8,101	11,746	13,888	49	3,652	2,142	.6	45.1	18.2
25 to 44 years	20,996	22,394	22,993	29,674	1,398	599	6,681	6.7	2.7	29.1
25 to 34 years	11,044	10,940	12,063	17,590	-104	1,123	5,527	-.9	10.3	45.8
35 to 44 years	9,952	11,454	10,930	12,084	1,502	-524	1,154	15.1	-4.6	10.6
45 years and over	16,405	18,438	20,221	20,499	2,033	1,783	278	12.4	9.7	1.4
45 to 64 years	13,952	16,013	18,113	18,403	2,061	2,100	290	14.8	13.1	1.6
65 years and over	2,453	2,425	2,108	2,096	-28	-317	-12	-1.1	-13.1	-.6
Female										
16 years and over	18,412	23,171	29,657	35,881	4,759	6,486	6,224	25.8	28.0	21.0
16 to 24 years	4,395	4,619	7,175	8,666	224	2,556	1,491	5.1	55.3	20.8
25 to 44 years	8,267	9,484	10,449	13,733	1,217	965	3,284	14.7	10.2	31.4
25 to 34 years	4,101	4,159	4,894	7,347	58	735	2,453	1.4	17.7	50.1
35 to 44 years	4,166	5,325	5,555	6,386	1,159	230	831	27.8	4.3	15.0
45 years and over	5,751	9,068	12,033	13,482	3,317	2,965	1,449	57.7	32.7	12.0
45 to 64 years	5,167	8,114	10,942	12,142	2,947	2,828	1,200	57.0	34.9	11.0
65 years and over	584	954	1,091	1,340	370	137	249	63.4	14.4	22.8

Source: *MANPOWER REPORT OF THE PRESIDENT*, January 1969.

Table 5 CHANGES IN THE TOTAL LABOR FORCE, BY COLOR, SEX, AND AGE, 1960 TO 1980 (Numbers in thousands)

COLOR, SEX, AND AGE	ACTUAL 1960	ACTUAL 1965	1970	PROJECTED 1975	PROJECTED 1980	NUMBER CHANGE 1960-65	NUMBER CHANGE 1965-70	NUMBER CHANGE 1970-75	NUMBER CHANGE 1975-80	PERCENT CHANGE 1960-65	PERCENT CHANGE 1965-70	PERCENT CHANGE 1970-75	PERCENT CHANGE 1975-80
Total													
16 years and over	72,104	77,177	84,617	92,183	99,942	5,073	7,440	7,566	7,759	7.0	9.6	8.9	8.4
White													
Both Sexes													
16 years and over	64,210	68,627	75,055	81,436	87,872	4,417	6,428	6,381	6,436	6.9	9.4	8.5	7.9
16 to 24 years	11,239	13,814	16,566	18,252	19,394	2,575	2,752	1,686	1,142	22.9	19.9	10.2	6.3
25 to 44 years	28,111	28,337	29,360	32,757	37,902	226	1,023	3,397	5,145	.8	3.6	11.6	15.7
45 years and over	24,860	26,475	29,129	30,427	30,576	1,615	2,654	1,298	149	6.5	10.0	4.5	.5
45 to 64 years	21,747	23,638	26,198	27,408	27,422	1,891	2,560	1,210	14	8.7	10.8	4.6	.1
65 years and over	3,113	2,837	2,931	3,019	3,154	-276	94	88	135	-8.9	3.3	3.0	4.5
Male													
16 years and over	44,119	45,862	49,263	52,946	56,822	1,743	3,401	3,683	3,876	4.0	7.4	7.5	7.3
16 to 24 years	7,171	8,621	10,320	11,311	11,998	1,450	1,699	991	687	20.2	19.7	9.6	6.1
25 to 44 years	20,123	19,882	20,532	22,830	26,237	-241	650	2,298	3,407	-1.2	3.3	11.2	14.9
45 years and over	16,825	17,359	18,411	18,805	18,587	534	1,052	394	-218	3.2	6.1	2.1	-1.2
45 to 64 years	14,582	15,401	16,474	16,888	16,660	819	1,073	414	-228	5.6	7.0	2.5	-1.4
65 years and over	2,243	1,958	1,937	1,917	1,927	-285	-21	-20	10	-12.7	-1.1	-1.0	.5
Female													
16 years and over	20,091	22,765	25,792	28,490	31,050	2,674	3,027	2,698	2,560	13.3	13.3	10.5	9.0
16 to 24 years	4,068	5,193	6,246	6,941	7,396	1,125	1,053	695	455	27.7	20.3	11.1	6.6
25 to 44 years	7,988	8,455	8,828	9,927	11,665	467	373	1,099	1,738	5.8	4.4	12.4	17.5
45 years and over	8,035	9,116	10,718	11,622	11,989	1,081	1,602	904	367	13.5	17.6	8.4	3.2
45 to 64 years	7,165	8,237	9,724	10,520	10,762	1,072	1,487	796	242	15.0	18.1	8.2	2.3
65 years and over	870	879	994	1,102	1,227	9	115	108	125	1.0	13.1	10.9	11.3

Table 5 (Continued)

Nonwhite												
Both Sexes												
16 years and over	7,894	8,551	9,560	10,746	12,072	657	1,009	1,186	1,326	8.3	11.8	12.4	12.3
16 to 24 years	1,481	1,839	2,335	2,809	3,161	358	516	454	352	24.2	28.1	19.3	12.5
25 to 44 years	3,767	3,882	4,081	4,618	5,505	115	199	537	887	3.1	5.1	13.2	19.2
45 years and over	2,646	2,830	3,124	3,319	3,406	184	294	195	87	7.0	10.4	6.2	2.6
45 to 64 years	2,380	2,561	2,856	3,046	3,124	181	295	190	78	7.6	11.5	6.7	2.6
65 years and over	266	269	268	273	282	3	−1	5	9	1.1	−.4	1.9	3.3
Male												
16 years and over	4,814	5,084	5,695	6,409	7,241	270	611	714	832	5.6	12.0	12.5	13.0
16 to 24 years	930	1,137	1,426	1,684	1,891	207	289	258	207	22.3	25.4	18.1	12.3
25 to 44 years	2,271	2,276	2,460	2,839	3,437	5	184	379	598	.2	8.1	15.4	21.1
45 years and over	1,613	1,671	1,809	1,886	1,913	58	138	77	27	3.6	8.3	4.3	1.4
45 to 64 years	1,431	1,498	1,638	1,716	1,744	67	140	78	28	4.7	9.3	4.8	1.6
65 years and over	182	173	171	170	169	−9	−2	−1	−1	−4.9	−1.2	−.6	−.6
Female												
16 years and over	3,080	3,467	3,865	4,337	4,831	387	398	472	494	12.6	11.5	12.2	11.4
16 to 24 years	551	702	929	1,125	1,270	151	227	196	145	27.4	32.3	21.1	12.9
25 to 44 years	1,496	1,606	1,621	1,779	2,068	110	15	158	289	7.4	.9	9.7	16.2
45 years and over	1,033	1,159	1,315	1,433	1,493	126	156	118	60	12.2	13.5	9.0	4.2
45 to 64 years	949	1,063	1,218	1,330	1,380	114	155	112	50	12.0	14.6	9.2	3.8
65 years and over	84	96	97	103	113	12	1	6	10	14.3	1.0	6.2	9.7

Source: MANPOWER REPORT OF THE PRESIDENT, January 1969.

doubled since 1955 and increased by more than half since 1965.[2] The training of minorities for employment therefore becomes a special issue of concern for educational institutions in the seventies.

The past twenty years have witnessed a dramatic increase in the number of women in the labor force. The rate of expansion for women has far outdistanced that of men; in the 1950s it was more than three times as high as the growth rate for men; in the 1960s it was more than twice as high. This upward surge will continue in the seventies, although in terms of actual numbers the total males in the labor force will outdistance females by 50 percent. Women can be expected to make increased inroads into the traditional male management and professional jobs at the top of the occupational structure, while men may have to compete with increasing numbers of women in the middle-level nonmanual jobs where females have made their past advances. The education of women for employment will merit special consideration in the planning of policies for manpower training in the seventies.

Occupations of the Decade

America is a white-collar economy; white-collar workers have comprised a majority of the labor force since 1956. By 1975 less than one out of three American workers will be employed in goods-producing industries (mining, contract construction, and manufacturing); and increasing proportions will be placed in service industries (transportation, wholesale and retail trade, public utilities, finance, insurance, real estate, government). While employment in goods-producing industries will rise by one-eighth between 1965 and 1975, employment in service-producing industries will grow a third, with wholesale and retail trade, insurance, and state and local government making widest gains (see Table 6). On the goods-producing side, contract construction, which in 1965 accounted for only a little over 3 million jobs, will add as much to total employment by 1975 as durable goods manufacturing with its base of between 10 and 11 million jobs in 1965, and twice as much as nondurables, with its base of about 8 million.

By broad occupational groupings, one-fourth of the total increase of 16 million jobs in the seventies will be professional and technical (see Table 7), requiring primarily bachelor's degrees or above. Despite the automation of "paper shuffling," another 3 to 4 million clerical workers will be needed in the same period. Clerical and service workers, along

---

[2] *Manpower Report of the President* (Washington, D.C.: U.S. Government Printing Office, 1969), p. 68.

Table 6 ACTUAL AND PROJECTED EMPLOYMENT BY INDUSTRY DIVISION, 1960 TO 1975 (Numbers in thousands)

Industry division	ACTUAL 1960 Number	ACTUAL 1960 Percent distribution	ACTUAL 1965 Number	ACTUAL 1965 Percent distribution	PROJECTED[1] 1975 Number	PROJECTED[1] 1975 Percent distribution	NUMBER CHANGE 1960-65	NUMBER CHANGE 1965-75	PERCENT CHANGE 1960-65	PERCENT CHANGE 1965-75
Agriculture[2]	5,723	—	4,585	—	3,745	—	-1,138	-840	-19.9	-18.3
Total nonagricultural wage and salary workers[3]	54,234	100.0	60,832	100.0	76,040	100.0	6,598	15,208	12.2	25.0
Goods-producing industries	20,393	37.6	21,880	36.0	24,530	32.3	1,487	2,650	7.3	12.1
Mining	712	1.3	632	1.0	620	.8	-80	-12	-11.2	-1.9
Contract construction	2,885	5.3	3,186	5.2	4,190	5.5	301	1,004	10.4	31.5
Manufacturing	16,796	31.0	18,062	29.7	19,720	25.9	1,266	1,658	7.5	9.2
Durable goods	9,459	17.4	10,406	17.1	11,480	15.1	947	1,074	10.0	10.3
Nondurable goods	7,336	13.5	7,656	12.6	8,240	10.8	320	584	4.4	7.6
Service-producing industries	33,840	62.4	38,953	64.0	51,510	67.7	5,113	12,557	15.1	32.2
Transportation and public utilities	4,004	7.4	4,036	6.6	4,580	6.0	32	544	.8	13.5
Transportation	2,549	4.7	2,532	4.2	2,935	3.9	-17	403	-.7	15.9
Communication	840	1.5	881	1.4	1,020	1.3	41	139	4.9	15.8
Electric, gas, and sanitary services	615	1.1	623	1.0	625	.8	8	2	1.3	.3
Wholesale and retail trade	11,391	21.0	12,716	20.9	16,115	21.2	1,325	3,399	11.6	26.7
Wholesale	3,004	5.5	3,312	5.4	4,135	5.4	308	823	10.3	24.8
Retail	8,388	15.5	9,404	15.5	11,980	15.8	1,016	2,576	12.1	27.4
Finance, insurance, and real estate	2,669	4.9	3,023	5.0	3,725	4.9	354	702	13.3	23.2
Service and miscellaneous	7,423	13.7	9,087	14.9	12,945	17.0	1,664	3,858	22.4	42.5
Government[4]	8,353	15.4	10,091	16.6	14,145	18.6	1,738	4,054	20.8	40.2
Federal[4]	2,270	4.2	2,378	3.9	2,745	3.6	108	367	4.8	15.4
State and local	6,083	11.2	7,714	12.7	11,400	15.0	1,631	3,686	26.8	47.8

[1] Revised 1968. See also footnote 1, table E-8.
[2] Represents total employment for persons 14 years and over as covered by the Current Population Survey prior to the change in age limit introduced in 1967; includes wage and salary workers, the self-employed, and unpaid family workers.
[3] Represents wage and salary employment as covered by the monthly establishment survey; excludes the self-employed, unpaid family workers' and domestic workers in households. (These data are not affected by the change in the lower age limit introduced into the Current Population Survey in 1967.)
[4] Data relate to civilian employment only, excluding the Central Intelligence and National Security Agencies.

Table 7 ACTUAL AND PROJECTED EMPLOYMENT FOR PERSONS 16 YEARS AND OVER, BY OCCUPATION GROUP, 1960 TO 1975

	1960 Number (thousands)	1960 Percent distribution	1965 Number (thousands)	1965 Percent distribution	1975 Number (millions) PROJECTED[1]	1975 Percent distribution[2] PROJECTED[1]	NUMBER CHANGE[2] (millions) 1960-65	NUMBER CHANGE[2] (millions) 1965-75	PERCENT CHANGE[2] 1960-65	PERCENT CHANGE[2] 1965-75
Total employment[3]	65,777	100.0	71,088	100.0	87.2	100.0	5.3	16.1	18.1	22.7
Professional, technical workers	7,474	11.4	8,883	12.5	12.9	14.8	1.4	4.0	18.9	45.2
Managers, officials, proprietors	7,067	10.7	7,340	10.3	9.0	10.4	.3	1.7	3.9	23.3
Clerical workers	9,759	14.8	11,129	15.7	14.8	16.9	1.4	3.6	14.0	32.5
Sales workers	4,216	6.4	4,497	6.3	5.6	6.4	.3	1.1	6.7	25.0
Craftsmen and foremen	8,560	13.0	9,222	13.0	11.4	13.0	.7	2.1	7.7	23.1
Operatives	11,950	18.2	13,336	18.8	14.7	16.9	1.4	1.4	11.6	10.5
Service workers	8,031	12.2	8,936	12.6	12.0	13.8	.9	3.1	11.3	34.4
Nonfarm laborers	3,557	5.4	3,688	5.2	3.6	4.1	.1	-.1	3.7	-2.4[4]
Farmers and farm laborers	5,163	7.8	4,057	5.7	3.2	3.6	-1.1	-.9	-21.4	-21.6

[1] These projections of civilian employment assume 3 percent unemployment whereas the projections of total labor force shown in the preceding tables are consistent with 4 percent unemployment. The lower unemployment assumption implies a slightly larger labor force; e.g., the total labor force in 1975 at 3 percent unemployment would be about 92.6 million as compared with 92.2 million at 4 percent unemployment.
[2] Based on data in thousands.
[3] Represents total employment as covered by the Current Population Survey.
[4] Employment is projected at about the level of the past decade; however, because 1965 employment was unusually high, reflecting a sharp increase in manufacturing, the projected percent change from 1965 indicates an apparent decline.
Source: MANPOWER REPORT OF THE PRESIDENT, January 1969.

with professional and technical workers and managers, officials, and proprietors, will account for nearly three-fourths of all new jobs.

The nature of work will continue to change in the seventies. A world where the majority is engaged in manual labor is quite different from one in which most employees manipulate sophisticated tools and equipment and is even more remote from one in which most employees sit in

Table 8 JOB OPENINGS RESULTING FROM CHANGE IN EMPLOYMENT AND DEATHS AND RETIREMENTS, BY MAJOR OCCUPATION GROUP, 1965 TO 1975 (Thousands)

Major occupation group	Total	OPENINGS Due to employment change	Due to deaths and retirements
Total	38,780	16,525	22,255
Professional, technical workers	6,513	4,020	2,493
Managers, officials, proprietors	3,921	1,860	2,061
Clerical workers	7,835	3,430	4,405
Sales workers	2,533	1,085	1,448
Craftsmen and foremen	3,967	2,180	1,787
Operatives	4,563	1,610	2,953
Service workers, including private household	7,892	3,260	4,632
Nonfarm laborers	546	−155	701
Farmers and farm managers, laborers and foremen	1,010	−765	1,775

Note: detail may not add to totals due to rounding.
Source: MANPOWER REPORT OF THE PRESIDENT, January 1969.

offices processing information. Such new developments will require adjustments not only in the psychological orientation of employees but also in the way society organizes its expectations for the world of work. With all of these gains, access to good jobs becomes more difficult for the underprepared; the routine work and restricted mobility of industrial and service workers grow more frustrating; and lower-level white-collar employment loses its relative prestige and attractiveness.

The trillion dollar economy of 1970 represents a doubling of output in real terms since 1951. Overall employment has increased by 30 percent during that time, but employment in goods-producing industries (minus agriculture) has risen only 23 percent. Releasing labor from the production of goods allows the expansion of service activities and particularly of such areas as research, finance, insurance, and government. A shift in the focus of employment from manufacturing, with its susceptibility to fluctuations based on shifts in consumer demand and the inventory and investment judgments of employers, to the more stable areas of utilities, services, finance, and government, should ease familiar fluctuations in employment rates.

Preparing for Employment

The first grader of the seventies is likely to retire from the labor force in the year 2029; the decade's first high school graduate will reach average retirement age in 2017; and the preschool youngster will be a potential worker until 2035. This does not mean that all education must be relevant to those years or that manpower requirements should be projected to those points for training to be useful. It does point to the need for the continuous availability of up-to-date education and training to keep people permanently employable.

To varying degrees, those general attributes which seem to characterize an effective member of the world of work include: good mental and physical health; a commitment to work as the source of income; self-discipline and ability to work within various external constraints; basic skills in communications, computation, and interpersonal relations; familiarity with fundamentals of science and technology; and ability to make sound judgments in the choice of a career. These variables are all at least equal in importance to the possession of specific job skills.

Therefore, *education which is restricted to training in the traditional skilled trades is obsolete by any gauge of the modern economy.* Today's world of work is a totally different scene from home or school. For the farm youth, home and school were a continuous, unitary environment. The child of an industrial worker, though never visiting his parents on the job, probably still absorbs some sense of production processes. Even a typewriter can be recognized by a youngster as an instrument of work. But when the core of a job consists of manipulating abstractions and handling people rather than products, it becomes increasingly difficult for the uninitiated to visualize the multifaceted spectrum of employment existing in the world of work.

Education for Occupations

General orientation to work is critical to a successful career, but employers pay for production. At some point in or out of the school system, in an education or training institution or on the job, skills must be acquired. What are the implications of this occupational outlook for the provision of future employees with the appropriate skills? One way to consider the educational levels required in various occupational categories is by examining the education and training which have been attained by persons already holding such jobs.

As pointed out earlier, over one-quarter of all new job openings expected in the seventies will occur in professional and technical occupations. Approximately two-thirds of the incumbents in such jobs in 1963 reported that they had completed three or more years of college, while another quarter had had formal occupational training short of that level [3] (see Table 9). There was a higher percentage of college-trained employees among younger workers.

The observed trend toward college-level training could be offset to some degree by current advocacy of a higher ratio of two-year trained technicians to each professional in such fields as engineering. At the same time, the small proportion without any formal training in that professional-technical category will decline even further. Therefore, it seems reasonable to assume that about one-fifth, or 800,000 of all new jobs and 500,000 of the replacement jobs in this category, will be filled by persons with two years or less of postsecondary education and will most likely consist of draftsmen, nurses, and technicians in electronics, engineering, medicine, and other fields.

Managers, officials, and proprietors, a category expected to grow by about 2 million and to require another 2 million replacements in the next five years or so, are rarely trained at less than college-level education. However, other training frequently contributes to their achieving managerial status. It seems reasonable to expect that over a million persons without college education in fields such as automobile mechanics, bookkeeping, shoe repairing, and construction trades may end up as managers, officials, and proprietors, but this is an exceedingly difficult area for which to plan. Essentially, the less than three years' college education received by this group consisted of training for other purposes which served incidentally to increase their ability to move up into managerial levels.

Clerical workers, a group in which only a small proportion had three

---

[3] *Current Occupation and Past Training of Adult Workers,* Statistical Evaluation Report No. 7 (A report prepared by Ann R. Miller, Consultant to the Office of Statistical Standards, Bureau of the Budget, Executive Office of the President, March 1968). This study is a further analysis of a supplement to the April 1963 Current Population Survey, originally published as Manpower Automation Research Monograph No. 2, *Formal Occupational Training of Adult Workers* (Washington, D.C.: U.S. Department of Labor, Manpower Administration, December 1964). Included in the formal but less than three years' college training is that received in the military, in apprenticeship, and formal on-the-job training as well as that gained in proprietary and public vocational and technical schools, community colleges, and less than three years of enrollment in four-year colleges. Estimates of those likely to be trained in this category in the future are therefore likely to be overestimated and an outside limit to the role of vocational-technical education during 1965-75.

Table 9. MAJOR OCCUPATION GROUP BY EDUCATION AND TRAINING STATUS: EXPERIENCED CIVILIAN LABOR FORCE AGED 22 TO 64, BY AGE AND SEX (Percent distribution)

Major occupation group and age	MEN				WOMEN		
	Completed 3 or more years of college	Completed less than 3 years of college — With formal occupational training	Completed less than 3 years of college — Without formal occupational training	Completed 3 or more years of college	Completed less than 3 years of college — With formal occupational training	Completed less than 3 years of college — Without formal occupational training
Total, aged 22-64	15.1	37.6	47.4	12.8	41.1	46.1
22-34	18.8	41.5	39.7	16.5	47.6	36.0
35-44	16.5	42.7	40.8	11.5	44.1	44.4
45-64	11.3	31.1	57.6	11.2	35.0	53.9
Professional, technical, and kindred workers, aged 22-64	66.2	23.6	10.2	64.9	23.7	11.4
22-34	70.4	21.5	8.1	71.7	20.4	7.8
35-44	66.5	26.1	7.3	65.9	24.6	9.5
45-64	60.3	23.9	15.9	58.5	26.0	15.4
Managers, officials, and proprietors aged 22-64	22.0	38.9	39.1	13.6	44.5	41.9
22-34	26.5	44.6	28.8	16.7	53.2	30.2
35-44	24.2	42.8	33.0	16.6	49.0	34.4
45-64	18.9	34.4	46.7	11.7	40.4	47.8
Clerical and kindred workers, aged 22-64	15.7	47.6	36.8	7.2	66.3	26.5
23-34	19.5	47.6	33.0	8.0	69.8	22.2
35-44	15.5	55.5	28.9	6.8	66.5	26.7
45-64	12.0	41.4	46.6	6.8	62.4	30.9

Table 9 (Continued)

Sales workers, aged 22-64	22.2	40.8	36.9	4.7	43.1	52.2
22-34	26.2	42.3	31.5	6.2	54.9	39.3
35-44	25.8	42.7	31.5	2.6	48.5	48.9
45-64	15.9	38.1	46.0	5.4	36.4	58.1
Craftsmen, foremen, & kindred workers, aged 22-64	2.0	51.8	45.3	2.6	36.3	61.6
22-34	4.1	57.5	38.4	1.8	46.4	50.0
35-44	3.0	58.6	38.4	3.9	47.1	49.0
45-64	2.1	42.9	55.0	2.4	21.4	75.0
Operatives & kindred workers, aged 22-64	1.3	34.7	64.0	0.9	26.3	72.8
22-34	2.9	41.9	56.2	0.7	32.4	66.9
35-44	1.2	37.4	61.3	1.2	31.3	67.5
45-64	0.7	25.6	73.7	0.7	18.7	80.6
Service workers, aged 22-64	4.3	40.8	54.9	1.8	33.2	65.0
22-34	8.3	46.3	45.4	2.7	44.3	53.0
35-44	3.6	50.6	45.8	1.3	34.6	64.1
45-64	2.5	32.8	64.7	1.7	27.1	71.3
Private household workers, aged 22-64	n.a.	n.a.	n.a.	1.6	21.3	77.2
22-34	n.a.	n.a.	n.a.	2.7	33.0	64.3
35-44	n.a.	n.a.	n.a.	1.1	21.2	77.7
45-64	n.a.	n.a.	n.a.	1.4	16.7	81.9

97

Table 9 (Continued)

Major Occupation group and age	MEN				WOMEN		
	Completed 3 or more years of college	Completed less than 3 years of college		Completed 3 or more years of college	Completed less than 3 years of college		
		With formal occupational training	Without formal occupational training		With formal occupational training	Without formal occupational training	
Service workers, except private household, aged 22-64	n.a.	n.a.	n.a.	1.9	38.9	59.2	
22-34	n.a.	n.a.	n.a.	2.7	48.7	48.7	
35-44	n.a.	n.a.	n.a.	1.3	40.2	58.4	
45-64	n.a.	n.a.	n.a.	1.8	32.7	65.5	
Farmers and farm laborers, aged 22-64	3.2	22.9	73.8	2.5	20.1	77.4	
22-34	4.2	35.8	59.9	—	36.6	63.4	
35-44	4.7	27.0	68.3	4.1	14.9	81.0	
45-64	2.1	15.7	82.3	3.1	14.1	82.8	
Laborers, except farm and mine, aged 22-64	1.2	24.0	74.9	—	21.9	79.5	
22-34	1.1	31.6	67.3	—	(1)	(1)	
35-44	1.5	30.3	68.2	—	(1)	(1)	
45-64	1.0	13.3	85.7	—	(1)	(1)	

(1): percents not shown where base is less than 50,000.
n.a.: not available.
Note: the sums of components may not equal totals because of rounding.
Source: CURRENT OCCUPATION AND PAST TRAINING OF ADULT WORKERS, Statistical Evaluation Report No. 7, Bureau of the Budget, March 1968.

or more years of college but where approximately half reported other shorter training, are promised about three and a half million new jobs and about four and a half million replacement jobs in this decade. The college-trained portion is increasing rapidly for men and moderately for women, but 4 million may well be the proportion of clerical training which secondary schools will handle.

Trends toward increased college education are modest for sales workers, suggesting training needs for 400,000 to meet job growth in addition to 550,000 for the extraordinarily high replacement needs, particularly for women in sales jobs. However, only 40 percent of the trained men in this category had education in any field directly related to business or sales, suggesting the difficulty of foreseeing the exact training needs for this area.

Half of the men and a little over a third of the women in craftsmen, foremen, and kindred jobs in 1963 had formal education consisting of less than three years of college. Because under 5 percent of workers under 30 had three or more years of college, it is reasonable to expect the vocational-technical apprentice and formal on-the-job proportions to grow. Apprenticeship is important for this grouping, with vocational education providing related instruction, but vocational-technical training should play some more dominant role in educating about 3 million persons for this classification during the present decade.

Not all workers in this classification received formal training for the jobs they were doing. Only half of the brick masons reporting training had been formally trained in that particular skill.[4] Four out of seven carpenters who had received formal training had been trained for crafts other than carpentry. Two out of three electricians, about half of the compositors, typesetters, machinists, plumbers, and tinsmiths, and under half of the linemen and electrical servicemen who indicated formal training had been trained for the craft in which they were working. The same was true for six of ten aircraft repairmen, four of nine painters, and two-thirds of TV and radio repairmen. Therefore, half of the craftsman training presently being offered in schools may contribute somewhat to craft employment in a general way but may be wasted as preparation for specific assignments.

More than two of five male operatives and one-third of the female operatives claimed formal skill training, although most of this training was probably acquired on the job and in a wide variety of occupations. Figures are not available for male private household and service workers, but one-fifth of the females in the latter category and two-fifths in the former reported formal training for jobs which normally require no

---

[4] *Ibid.*, pp. 25-30.

such training. Approximately one-fourth of male farmers, farm laborers, and other laborers also had formal training, but these are occupational categories which are declining in absolute numbers.

Based on this information, it can be concluded that unless occupational education shifts its focus, projected trends threaten it with a declining labor market role. No more than one of every four jobs newly emerging or requiring replacements in the seventies is likely to be filled with a person trained in high school vocational education, postsecondary education of two years or less, or formal apprenticeship or on-the-job training. The approximately 22 million job openings expected to result from death and retirement during this period are expected to absorb half of new entrants,[5] and the primary outlet for those with less than college training will have to be in meeting such replacement needs. Preparing replacements and new job entrants, plus those who never work in fields for which they have been trained, will undoubtedly keep enrollment at or above the 1967 total of 7 million.

With the exception of clerical skills, employment trends are shifting away from skills traditionally taught in vocational education. If formal education below the college level is to respond to manpower training needs, it must accomplish the following missions: (1) assume responsibility for orientation to the world of work; (2) expand its technical component; (3) relate to the trend toward subprofessional job categories; (4) provide more meaningful training for sales workers, particularly those requiring technical knowledge; and (5) play a larger role in preparation of craftsmen as preliminary, supplementary, or replacement to apprenticeship and on-the-job training. Given the expectation that sales and craft jobs will expand at only an average rate and also assuming limited training needs of operatives and service workers, and persistent declines in farm categories, the first three recommendations constitute dynamic areas for future opportunity.

Relevance of Current Enrollments

The previous section presented a discussion of projected employment trends in the context of probable future needs for formal career education at the less-than-college level and identified the proportion of expected new jobs likely to be amenable to formal training. But to what degree is federally supported vocational education currently concentrating in those areas of present and foreseen demand?

Table 10 illustrates 1966 employment, average annual openings for 1966-75 (replacement needs as well as new jobs), vocational education

---

[5] *Manpower Report of the President*, p. 67.

enrollments in fiscal 1967, completions in 1967, and training-related placements in the same year. While no information is available as to alternative sources of supply, experience indicates that the jobs will be filled whether or not educational institutions or any other formal training sources provide the skills. Heavy reliance on apprenticeship in training accounts for low enrollments in crafts such as the building trades and die-making. There are no self-evident criteria for establishing educational priorities among other occupations which have completion rates far under average annual openings. The divergence between projected demand and vocational education output appears greatest for associate degree nurses and nursing assistants, medical technologists, law enforcement officers, firemen, barbers, and most occupations for which postsecondary but less than college training is the customary preparation. As broad occupational categories, health and technical occupations appear to be supplying manpower in numbers furthest below demand levels.

Enrollments and completions for food service workers, general merchandise clerks, blacksmiths, auto body and fender repairmen, automobile mechanics, and those trained in the graphic arts appear to be excessive in relation to demand. Most of these are secondary school enrollees, however, who have no long-term commitment to either the particular occupation they are learning or more generally to the labor force. Experience has shown that low proportions tend to enter the occupations for which they are trained; hence, high enrollments do not necessarily lead to oversupply in these fields. Nevertheless, they can result in waste of both training dollars and investment of human resources and time. While enrollments in computer programming and hotel occupations are relatively high compared to openings, their completions are not.

The same is true of familiar occupations of long-standing popularity in vocational education—such as automotive sales, finance and credit, real estate, transportation, secretarial occupations, airplane mechanics, electrical occupations, drafting, machine shop, sheet metal, welding, and shoe repair. All have enrollments which, in relation to average annual openings, would lead to an oversupply were it not for low completion rates. In some instances, moreover, enrollment figures cannot be used as the most accurate base of assessment; for example, commercial art and photography are types of occupational training often pursued for interest rather than employment. Nevertheless, this high dropout rate should be of concern to education. These comparisons of employment opportunities to enrollments reflect a reasonably good fit for familiar occupations, general underenrollment for many emerging and expanding occupations, and possible over-rapid expansion of some of the newer ones, such as computer programming and hotel management.

Table 10 COMPARISON OF EMPLOYMENT, PROJECTED ANNUAL OPENINGS, ENROLLMENTS, COMPLETIONS, AND PLACEMENTS FOR VOCATIONAL EDUCATION OCCUPATIONAL TRAINING PROGRAMS

Instructional Program	Employment 1966	Average[1] Annual Openings, 1966-75	Vocational Education Enrollment 1966-67[2]	Vocational Education Completions 1967[3] Total	Post-Secondary	Vocational Education Placements 1967[4]
Health Occupations	2,020,900 (1,882,000)[5]	203,400	117,073	31,065	23,464	27,900
Dental assisting	93,000	7,700	6,742	2,042	903	
Dental hygiene	15,000	2,000	1,312	452	452	
Dental laboratory technology	25,000	1,700	1,337	257	189	
Medical laboratory assisting	50,000	8,400	4,818	1,044	749	
Nursing	620,000	61,000	9,954	2,280	2,056	
Practical nursing	300,000	39,000	58,721	18,711	16,420	
Nursing assistance	700,000	77,000	22,802	4,588	1,039	
Radiologic technology	72,000	6,300	1,683	475	383	
Optician	7,000	300	257	118	77	
Technical Occupations	2,239,100 (2,134,000)[5]	187,300	249,825	28,224	19,861	14,800
Engineering related technology	885,000	72,000	5,277	691	336	
Scientific data processing	100,000	13,600	26,367	3,989	2,731	
Commercial pilot training	80,000	7,200	4,401	202	202	

Table 10 (Continued)

Police	300,000	16,000	3,391	206	206
Distributive Occupations	11,902,000 (2,602,000)[5]	159,100	481,314	118,584	38,567	32,200
Advertising services	158,000	11,000	4,224	1,096	450
Automotive	218,000	7,500	11,834	5,151	52
Finance and credit	280,000	25,000	23,074	4,010	1,079
Food distribution	255,000	10,000	24,747	11,345	666
Food service	43,000	2,800	33,389	4,871	54
General merchandise	43,000	3,600	62,263	15,096	773
Hotel and lodging	280,000	18,000	14,115	2,505	428
Insurance	400,000	43,000	11,105	1,231	531
Real estate	215,000	16,000	58,036	8,591	8,246
Transportation	200,000	5,000	10,902	1,878	711
Office Occupations	9,953,000 (7,180,000)[5]	555,000	1,580,441	423,243	73,717	137,800
Business data processing	120,000	14,000	85,063	5,442	2,271
Personnel, training, etc.	100,000	6,200	1,806	366	61
Stenographic secretarial	2,400,000	175,000	504,602	154,976	31,574
Typing, etc.	715,000	60,000	222,649	27,988	3,701
Trades and Industrial Occupations	14,283,700 (11,588,200)[5]	577,500	1,483,584	151,275	28,829	71,100
Air conditioning	80,000	3,500	23,176	2,009	568
Appliance repair	195,000	10,000	4,270	865	156
Automotive body and fender	95,000	3,700	16,007	3,748	799

103

Table 10 (Continued)

Instructional Program	Employment 1966	Average[1] Annual Openings	Vocational Education Enrollment 1966-67[2]	Vocational Education Completions 1967[3] Total	Vocational Education Completions 1967[3] Post Secondary	Vocational Education Placements 1967[4]
Automobile mechanics	580,000	20,000	103,200	25,191	4,165	
Aircraft maintenance	130,000	6,500	18,491	1,304	590	
Aircraft operations	7,200	500	5,587	746	39	
Ground operations	14,000	400	2,605	217	212	
Business machine maintenance	80,000	3,700	1,284	317	112	
Commercial art occupations	60,000	2,200	10,828	2,151	600	
Maritime occupations	100,000	2,000	2,653	143	66	
Commercial photography	30,000	1,300	6,576	957	294	
Carpentry	850,000	32,000	46,211	7,177	795	
Electricity	175,000	6,400	32,282	2,206	525	
Operation, heavy equipment	275,000	16,000	2,859	168	124	
Masonry	260,000	10,600	19,965	3,825	323	
Painting and decorating	460,000	19,000	6,547	512	111	
Plastering	80,000	3,300	606	8	—	
Plumbing and pipe-fitting	350,000	16,000	31,988	805	121	
Construction and maintenance trades	300,000	15,000	14,726	2,934	92	
Custodial services	1,000,000	80,000	20,538	569	92	
Diesel mechanic	76,000	4,000	4,955	935	528	

Table 10 (Continued)

Drafting	270,000	16,000	63,167	9,448	2,494
Electrical occupations	240,000	7,500	17,291	2,023	542
Linemen	35,000	1,100	30,907	91	76
Communications	209,000	9,000	6,612	736	147
Graphic arts	310,000	8,000	34,405	7,300	1,272
Instrument maintenance and repair	80,000	4,500	3,448	571	365
Machine shop	900,000	27,000	72,497	11,445	1,378
Sheet metal	55,000	2,100	20,245	1,668	348
Welding and cutting	460,000	23,000	79,330	6,524	2,632
Metalworking	15,000	600	12,355	1,473	—
Barbering	205,000	12,000	4,888	449	333
Cosmetology	450,000	43,000	30,088	8,416	2,011
Fire training	183,000	10,000	128,789	172	170
Waiter/waitress	970,000	64,000	2,313	725	46
Stationary energy sources	305,000	9,000	2,959	46	24
Pumping plants	23,000	1,500	282	2	—
Shoe repair	30,000	1,200	3,760	369	43
Upholstering	40,000	1,000	7,444	650	280

[1] Department of Labor Occupational Outlook projections to 1975 including employment increases and estimated replacement for death and retirement.
[2] Office of Education data from state reports for fiscal 1967. Enrollments by program title do not necessarily add to totals for broad occupational training category because of adjustments to correlate program titles with employment projections.
[3] Office of Education data from state reports of completions during academic year 1966-67.
[4] Placements reported by state as of September 1967 for fiscal 1967 completers.
[5] Number employed in the category who are included in occupations covered by Occupational Outlook projections and therefore more appropriate than the total employment for comparison with projected openings.

105

Table 11 VOCATIONAL EDUCATION ENROLLMENT SUMMARY, BY OCCUPATIONAL CATEGORY AND EDUCATIONAL LEVEL, FISCAL YEARS 1964-1967

FISCAL YEAR 1964

	Total	Secondary	Post-Secondary	Adult	Special Needs
Grand Totals	4,566,390	2,140,756	171,495	2,161,223	—
Agriculture	860,605	501,819	—	265,879	
Distribution	334,126	55,132	2,688	276,306	
Health	59,006	5,478	41,698	11,830	
Home Economics	2,022,138	1,308,453	1,652	712,033	
Technical	221,241	20,755	71,824	128,662	
Trades and Industry	1,069,274	249,119	53,633	766,513	

FISCAL YEAR 1967

	Total	Secondary	Post Secondary	Adult	Special Needs	
Grand Totals	7,047,501	3,532,823	499,906	2,941,109	73,663	(92,925)*
Agriculture (Off-farm)	935,170 (151,781)	508,675	8,093	413,454	4,948	(12,488)
Distribution	481,034	151,378	21,003	303,783	4,870	(9,065)
Health	115,109	16,734	54,135	42,721	1,519	(1,146)
Home Economics (Gainful)	2,186,992 (62,245)	1,475,235	3,506	685,225	23,026	(33,437)
Office	1,572,325	985,398	192,639	389,174	5,104	(18,475)
Technical	266,054	27,614	97,156	140,431	853	(2,927)
Trade and Industry	1,490,807	367,374	123,374	966,301	33,343	(15,387)

*Figures in parentheses indicate persons with special needs enrolled in regular classes.
Source: Data furnished by the Division of Vocational and Technical Education, Office of Education.

Even agriculture enrollments do not exceed the number of openings, including off-farm occupations, and home economics enrollments certainly do not surpass the number of potential housewives. However, the real issue concerning these categories (not included in Table 10) relates to priorities. Health and technical occupations appear to be the primary categories requiring expansion; but within these general classifications there is need for reallocation from practical nurses to registered two-year nurses and health technologists and from electronic to engineering technologists.

Discussion of the fit between vocational education curriculum and occupational trends must not overlook an important category—expanding occupations. Examples are environmental health occupations, various medical technologies, floristry, systems and budget analysis, quality control clerks, and traffic rate clerks. Skill requirements for this area could in general be handled by vocational training, but no courses relating specifically to such occupations were reported in 1967.

Implications for Future Education

Employment and education trends appear to be moving away from those occupations and types of training traditionally encompassed by vocational education. At the same time, the experiences in the family, neighborhood, and school environment are less and less helpful in preparing youths to work and make critical decisions about their own careers in the working world. These facts pose a grave problem for the nation's schools and offer the real challenge to those who are preparing to change them.

Educators have been highly reluctant to commit their total energies to preparation for employment. They have responded instead by defending the importance of more general goals of education for "life"—usually referring to citizenship, culture, social skills, and pursuit of learning for its own intrinsic value. A dichotomy between employment training and academic goals has arisen because of a short-sighted tendency to think of specific job skills as the only necessary ingredients for employment. This constitutes a failure to recognize that participating in world of work experiences necessitates being able to meet broader but equally crucial requirements of employability.

The goals of such career education are difficult to pinpoint, but they can be expected to include knowledge and understanding of one's society and of oneself in relation to its requirements and opportunities; the ability to accumulate and process information and make rational judgments based on it; identification and development of one's talents as a productive member of society; and taking positive steps toward developing one's own life values. These overarching goals are complimentary to skill training, and nothing about preparing oneself for effective labor market participation should preclude the development of this wider vantage point on employment.

What must be recognized is the beginning of a new stage of economic life in which human resources are critical and in which formal education and training are primary determinants of income and employment status. A school system which once offered a modicum of the three R's to the population as citizens of a democracy, then selected out the relatively few persons needed to fill the demands for skilled workers and the even smaller number needed for professional positions, now must place immediate emphasis on employment goals of the individual as they relate to demands of the labor market. Because most members of society find greatest satisfaction in vocational accomplishment (including homemaking), preparation for employment is critical not only to income and living standards but also to self-realization and personal happiness.

OPTING FOR CAREER EDUCATION:
Emergence of the Community College

MARVIN J. FELDMAN

Tensions in American Education

Student alienation from learning has become a fashionable denominator for contemporary discussions about the state of American education. Especially during the last two years, the nation has witnessed serious disruptions in the routine of its high schools and colleges; in fact, close to 50 percent of all recorded civil disorders during that period involved schools. In part, these conflagrations have erupted in reaction to phenomena in the local and national political arenas; in part, their roots are deeply ingrained in the educational system, itself—in its curriculum, authority structure, classroom routine, reward system, and in the absence of a range of viable educational options for young people.

The schools have failed to communicate with learners as distinctive human beings; they have failed to demonstrate to young people that their talents can register an impact on the environment; they have made little genuine effort to connect schooling with the burning issues of existence in the real worlds of adulthood and employment; nor have they bothered to organize a systematic, long-range plan to provide career development for youth.

In short, many students have written off education in part because they no longer have real hope that it can help them find their niches in

---

MARVIN J. FELDMAN is Executive Director of the Planning and Review Committee, U.S. Office of Economic Opportunity. He has served as a consultant on community colleges to the U.S. Commissioner of Education and as a Program Officer of The Ford Foundation.

life—those roles which in good conscience they can fill with some sense of meaning and significance for themselves.

The public disturbances which have occurred in many educational institutions highlight the fact that, as good as our public schools have been—helping our immigrant grandparents and parents assimilate new cultural values and sending their sons and daughters to college and work—they are no longer addressing the issues of the time. They are not equipping young people to overcome adversities and limitations in environment, experience, or background, or to utilize the unique skills, motivations, concerns, and interests arising from these diverse situations.

People learn differently. Some do best with the spoken or written word. Some flourish through handling tools and materials or graphic processes. Still others express themselves most succinctly through making films or participating in or watching drama. Any of these or other approaches might be used to teach a subject, depending on the pupil's style of learning, but the crucial factor is the availability of a wide range of alternatives to meet every educational situation.

A companion notion to the existence of diverse individual learning styles is the assumption that every person has some inherent talent to offer society. The schools are mandated to help each pupil discover his own strengths and to design opportunities for him to develop these abilities. Today this means even more—it guarantees the student a chance to explore his own career potential and acquire job skills in addition to a basic education.

More than 122,000 educational institutions—from elementary schools through universities—operate in the United States, serving nearly 58 *million students* at any one time. Close to 3 million teachers and 210,000 administrators work in these environments. The nation spends over $50 billion per year for operating expenses alone and has a current capital outlay of over $8 billion for educational purposes.

Despite this massive investment of human and dollar power, however, the entire system is constructed within a narrow academic framework geared toward college entrance requirements. Well over 40 million of the 46 million students in school will not graduate from college, but their needs will have rated only fleeting attention from the educators. Proposed alternatives to college preparatory programs or university degrees have continually been misunderstood and rejected by both the managers and consumers of American public education. Consequently, the educational system continues to ignore the preponderant majority of its students, who never get a college diploma.

There has been a steady decrease in availability of jobs for the unskilled and a simultaneous increase in the number of young people looking for work but totally unprepared to meet the demands of skilled employment in this technological age. The roster of causes has become familiar: the advance of automation on all fronts—business, industry, and agriculture—and the disappearance of skills within job classifications. Jobs now require more mental ability, fewer physical skills, higher educational attainment at the entry level, and greater versatility or adaptability in the worker over his productive lifetime.

The problem with this analysis, however, is that it places the blame on the job, the markets, society, everywhere except the schools and colleges. Some other culprits might be denounced—the apprenticeship system because of the high cost to industry, obsolete curriculum content, and restrictive union practices—but primary responsibility for assuring that young people are prepared to function productively in adult life lies with the educational system, from preschool through postsecondary.

What has gone wrong? On one level, the deficiencies are fairly clear: failure to bring outmoded training facilities into line with on-the-job working conditions; failure to make changes in training content itself to meet new needs in the job market; failure to provide effective vocational guidance to a large enough group of students. But there is a broader and more subtle deficiency that pervades the educational system. It can be traced to the time that general and vocational studies were conceived as two different tracks leading to separate life goals, the former a preparation for liberal or professional higher education and the latter for those who lacked either the desire or the intellectual capacity for further schooling. It also goes back to the time when vocational education—manual training they called it then—was used for "schooling" delinquents and acquired a lasting stigma as an inferior form of instruction.

Concern for career education has rarely been focused in the proper places or processes within the educational system, and its misplacement has deprived the educational system of a vast array of alternative techniques and methods with which to meet the needs of all students. The community college has a key role to play in introducing such curriculum options into education in the earlier years.

A necessary first step is to *reconstitute* education as a series of experiences which help a person to discover, define, and refine his talents to use them in working toward a career. Thus, for example, education would embrace but not be confined to development of manual skills; and such skills would serve not only as preparation for vocationally oriented tasks but also as supplements or even alternatives to verbal performance in the entire learning process.

Enter: The Community College

In recent years, a new type of career development institution, the community college, has been created to help fill this vacuum. Under this general rubric fall public and private community two-year colleges, junior colleges, technical institutes, university extension centers, and satellite campuses. Community or junior colleges may be public or private; they may be independent of much external control or integral branches of large universities. They may be part of a unified school system, as City College of San Francisco; a division of higher education, as in New York; part of a university program, as in Pennsylvania; or under a community college board, as is the case in California.

The various publicly supported community-junior colleges seem to have three distinct types of undertakings:

(1) transfer or university-parallel programs designed primarily for students planning to graduate from senior colleges;
(2) terminal programs, which usually include technical, subprofessional, and other vocationally oriented training designed for those who seek immediate employment;
(3) service operations, most of which are community oriented and which may include short courses, adult education programs, and general cultural activities.

Statistics on the rapid growth of the two-year community college have been reported widely. There are about 1,000 such institutions now in existence, almost double the 1960 count. In September 1969 at least 50 new public community colleges were established, and some 200 more were scheduled to open in the succeeding four years. The Carnegie Commission on Higher Education called for 500 additional community colleges by 1976, and that ambitious goal may well be realized.

Enrollments have increased even more sharply. Today, two-year colleges serve about two million students, three times the 1960 enrollment. Significantly, for the first time there are more freshmen entering junior than senior colleges. Estimates are that the total will reach almost three and a half million by September 1973.

At this very moment, virtually every state is planning to create, expand, or reorganize its public two-year college system. California's complex is probably the most comprehensive, with more than 80 percent of all freshmen commencing postsecondary studies in two-year public institutions. In Florida the figure is 60 percent. In New York, nearly one-half of all full-time students in public higher education are enrolled in two-year colleges.

Apart from the Southeast's traditionally black institutions, the big-city public community college is the most important educational resource for black students and probably will continue to be for the rest of the seventies. To illustrate, about one-fourth of all black American collegians are concentrated in public two-year colleges in New York, Chicago, and Los Angeles. In virtually every large American city—

Cleveland, St. Louis, San Francisco, Philadelphia, Miami, Dallas—more blacks are enrolled in public community colleges than in all other nearby institutions combined. The reasons are obvious: public two-year colleges are the most accessible institutions, geographically, financially, and academically.

All evidence indicates that America will continue to move rapidly toward universal education for all Americans through age 20, and that the two-year college is one of the chief means for making this possible. At the beginning of the twentieth century, only 4 or 5 percent of Americans between the ages of 18 and 21 years old were students in higher educational institutions. Today 45 percent of that age group is enrolled for degree credits. If present trends continue, by 1980 at least 60 percent of all Americans between 18 and 21 years old will be enrolled for credit in higher institutions and virtually all young Americans will at least be in formal postsecondary education, to say nothing of adult education.

The Captain Was Called "Junior"

As a relatively new type of educational institution offering instruction in fields not ordinarily associated with higher education, the two-year college has encountered difficulty in establishing an identity and gaining acceptance from the education establishment. Some critics have labeled it a mere extension of high school—or even a finishing school. Others have considered it a substandard college, unworthy of the designation, higher education—a training school rather than an educational institution. Some have even classified it as little more than a custodial agency.

Image is not the only difficulty of the community college, however, Approximately two-thirds of all students in two-year colleges require remedial or compensatory programs. Dropout rates are high; 60 to 70 percent of all enrollees and nine out of ten students from low-income homes do not complete the two-year program.

The conventional curriculum has prolonged the silence between career and college parallel programs. Most career programs are offered in the areas of business and engineering technology and, more recently, in the health occupations. College parallel offerings are in the arts and sciences. What happens when students enter a community college? A large majority, uncertain about their future plans, choose the college parallel route, in the event they later decide to transfer to a four-year institution. In this way, they avoid being trapped in a terminal career training program with no guarantee of acceptance in a college or university.

Understandably, parents are anxious that their children have all the education possible, although such aspirations may at times be unrealistic. At least two-thirds of the students elect college parallel courses, and many find their studies dull and useless. They end up with a skimpy slice of education and little if any vocational orientation or preparation. Only a third of the 75 percent continue on with college; the others drop out or complete their community college programs quite unprepared to start a career. Conversely, those students who do elect the career education curriculum and want to transfer to four-year institutions discover that their chances of acceptance are reduced because they do not have sufficient credits in college parallel subjects.

Yet another serious problem exists in the form of poor administration from the state level. In many states, overlapping authorities make it impossible for any single official to exercise responsibility for community colleges. The state superintendent of public instruction, state director of vocational education, state chancellors of higher education, and now the new comprehensive manpower boards all want the deciding voice in control of career development programs.

Finally, disagreement prevails over the role and function of the community college in such areas as educational research and experimentation; faculty training and recruitment; community service activities, particularly as they relate to minority community groups; and veterans' programs. Some of these problems, particularly those related to curriculum development, modern instructional processes, and better articulation between secondary and higher education, are real and persistent; others are manifestations of institutional growing pains.

Christopher S. Jencks and David Riesman, in *The Academic Revolution*,[1] have discussed some of these problems at length. While community colleges have not been tied to traditional academic definitions of appropriate qualifications for teaching, they write, "neither have they been especially imaginative in utilizing new kinds of instructors. Like their public school cousins, they have often insisted on just enough academic certification to bar the employment of gifted amateurs from other occupations."[2] They also accuse community college faculty members of generally perpetuating what they term "a quite rigid pattern of instruction,"[3] continuing to teach whatever they learned in four-year colleges, "immunized from new ideas by isolation and by the prestige of the models they are emulating."[4] Finally, perhaps their most serious

---

[1] Christopher S. Jencks and David Riesman, *The Academic Revolution* (Garden City, N.Y.: Doubleday, 1968). Copyright © 1968 by Christopher Jencks and David Riesman. Excerpts reprinted by permission of Doubleday & Co., Inc.
[2] *Ibid.*, p. 484.
[3] *Ibid.*
[4] *Ibid.*, p. 488.

indictment concerns career education. "While the community college may in principle exist to serve new sorts of students and offer new sorts of programs," they conclude, "most faculty and administrators are still primarily interested in traditional academic programs and in students who will eventually transfer to a four-year college." [5]

Interlocking the Educational Systems

The basic components of a K–16 system that could change the complexion of American education already exist; but at present they are essentially autonomous, uncoordinated units. By using the community college as the focal point, elementary and secondary schools, higher education, and various government programs could be joined into such a unitary system.

The role of the community college cannot be understood in isolation from the rest of education. Instead, education must be designed as a total system composed of several sequential modules, none of which prevents a student from moving on to a more advanced phase. The job of the elementary school, for example, should be to identify and develop a child's learning style and ability. It should perform both diagnostic and prescriptive services, using whatever devices are necessary to make learning "real" to a child. It is pointless, for example, to have a youngster read, "Billy builds a boat," if he has never built or even seen one. The school has a responsibility to create learning experiences to which the child can react from his own environment. Finally, the school curriculum should begin to develop fundamental concepts about the world of work, including an awareness of the many options existing in various fields of employment.

The middle school years, covering fifth through eighth grades, are a period of early adolescence. A major concern of the middle school should center on helping young people learn to cope with the turmoil of early adolescence when they are undergoing severe emotional and physical changes. This is the place for more extensive exploration of careers, a subject of considerable concern to adolescents. It should build on the pupil's talents by helping him learn what adults with similar abilities do in society—what jobs they have, what objectives and life-styles they pursue, etc.

In high school, earlier learning should begin to fall into place within some broader framework of meaning for the student—an integration of knowledge about subject matter and his own career ambitions. High school learning experiences should also encourage teenagers to try out a

---

[5] *Ibid.*, p. 487.

number of adult roles, free of impediments to further education such as tracking systems.

The community college, rather than being a bush-league university, thus emerges as a transitional instrument for expanded career and educational opportunities. It should provide entry to the working world via specific career training, especially through work-study programs, and should be the gateway as well to professional schools and universities.

Community colleges, working very closely with both vocational and academic educators, should create—beginning with the elementary schools and continuing on to the high school level—a coordinated curriculum where occupational and basic liberal education interface with and reinforce one another. Students should be taught general work skills that are transferable from one occupation to another. In addition, carefully designed programs should prepare youth for advanced career training in such modern fields as medical technology, graphic arts, police and fire science, hotel and restaurant management, all the engineering technologies, and other paraprofessional fields.

Interinstitutional ties are essential if career development is to have any continuity or interrelationship. For this purpose the community college is a natural coordinating force. The community college should build on experiences of at least the last two years of high school. In addition, technical institutes and community colleges should work with senior institutions and state colleges to provide avenues toward still further training and assurance that such education is available at all. The community colleges should also work very closely with the 800 area vocational schools that provide skill training.

Connecting with Four-Year Institutions

Our present stereotypes of education dictate that only the vocational, technical, or trade schools need be concerned with the serious shortage of qualified manpower at the technologist level in all professions. Rapid changes in technology and the overall explosion of knowledge, along with artificial divisions of knowledge caused by the separation of liberal and vocational education, have combined to create a mandate for upgrading courses once considered strictly trade, vocational, or technical.

However, very few institutions offering technical education have concerned themselves with nonvocational skills, such as teaching students how to study independently, an essential skill for successful college-level work. Their curricula have been formulated in stark contrast to the liberal education offered by four-year colleges and universities. The community college must be ready to assert leadership in bringing together liberal arts and occupational education as a strategy for nationwide manpower development in every professional and vocational field.

Pursuing this goal requires that the two approaches be integrated throughout the entire educational experience. The current tendency to give a student general education initially, then specialization, is inappropriate on pedagogical grounds, and is at the root of some of the major problems in education; nor is it consistent with the educational philosophy which holds that culture and vocation cannot be separated.

Higher education has demonstrated narrow perspective on the question of who should be admitted as full-time degree candidates. American colleges are now beginning to recognize that a much larger portion of the population can profit from study on the college level than had been assumed earlier. The problem for them is that this enlarged group includes students of more diverse backgrounds and career interests and, in many instances, more deficient secondary school preparation and achievement than has been considered acceptable. To help meet these pluralistic needs and provide a transitional phase between high school and the traditional academic college curriculum, the four-year institutions must be able to look to the community colleges.

Some take the position that accommodating this large base in a new community college career program will inevitably lower the quality of higher education and narrow the range of individual opportunity. Such an assumption is based upon a narrow definition of higher education and a rigid and simplistic view of its role and process. It ignores the concepts of flexibility, options, and multilevel goals whch should be implicit throughout a model educational system. The real issue is whether further extensions of educational opportunities will multiply and broaden the pathways to higher education and personal achievement. As a key part of this commitment, the community college offers promise of educational renewal, better lives, and ultimately a better society in which excellence of all dimensions and varieties can flourish.

Manpower Training and Community Colleges

Most good engineering designs contain redundant systems; thus, if a component in a missile or weapon breaks down, a backup unit can be engaged to continue the mission. This is how we try to ensure the success of a space vehicle, but in education we allow ourselves to fail students. Education as a system has for some time now required a backup capacity to ensure its success.

Each year over 3 million students leave secondary education—one million enter institutions of higher education, a second million complete high school, and the remaining million drop out before graduation. Of the two-thirds who do not go on, about a half million have had some vocational training in marketable skills in high school. What equipment do the remaining one-and-a-half million have for economic success? Unfortunately, we know very little about what happens in the job market to high school graduates or to high school or college dropouts without vocational skills or work experience. The need for manpower training programs, however, is clear evidence that the schools have not adequately prepared them for work.

The urgent need is for a systematic approach that meshes a number of programs now separated in general education, vocational education, manpower development, adult education, and on-the-job training. Yet, without a backup institution to provide continuing curriculum development, faculty development, articulation with continuing general education programs, youth and job corps programs, etc., very little other than job training, as important a goal as that is, can be accomplished. The community college is ideally suited to provide this backup system.

The first task, then, is to clarify the role of each strand in the web of out-of-school agencies and institutions working in manpower. The role of city, state, and national government is to promote fiscal policies, employment practices, and living, working, and learning conditions that foster employment.

The Department of Commerce is currently sponsoring a program for construction of area vocational schools. The new community colleges could help in designing and developing them. Labor Department manpower development programs are presently the backup system for those outside the central educational system. However, preparing urban youth for open-ended, continuous career development is an educational responsibility.

In the new educational system proposed here, the MDTA programs could have classrooms located in their skill centers but design and operate them jointly with community colleges. The centers could even be empowered to grant high school diplomas and advanced degrees. Any number of students of various ages, interests, and accomplishments, for whom the regular education design has not worked, could attend MDTA-supported classrooms in the cities. Each student would be engaged in an individualized program of studies, and students as a group would share the same classroom only because of its special facilities and services and because they find it pleasant and encouraging to be among other people who are also learning.

A member of the community would be in charge of the special classroom to help students understand the facilities, schedule their assignments, distribute materials, and link the student by visual communication with a specially staffed academic center at the urban community college. The community classroom would be fully supplied with the latest communications equipment. At each study carrel would be cartridge-loading tape machines (visual and sound), closed-circuit television, the appropriate study syllabus, programmed and regular textbooks, and materials for supplementary reading.

The academic center at the community college would provide direction for students in their self-paced study in the classrooms at the skill center. This affiliation with the college would assure the acceptability to employers of the diplomas and degrees and also provide the educational backup work so necessary in manpower skill training.

This cooperation with the Department of Labor's "backup" program would not only serve youngsters enrolled in the main system but also make a variety of goals attainable to many people on their own time in their own community.

Community colleges should also seek cooperative ties with the Office of Economic Opportunity and Department of Housing and Urban Development in their efforts involving human resource development. For example, the community college could act as a backup for HUD's Model Cities program to provide community-run centers.

Redesigning the Community College

In summary, the redesigned community college career program recommended in this chapter would:

(1) Effectively combine general and vocational education for all students, joining in each career program a well-considered mix of general and specialized studies with flexibility of application for students who have differing levels of interest, motivation, and potential.

(2) Provide students who have completed any course with viable options for either full-time employment or further study or a combination of both. This would necessitate improved articulation between community colleges and four-year institutions so that graduates of a qualified two-year program of career education could transfer without handicap.

(3) Design the total community college curriculum in terms of comprehensive career areas such as the arts and communications; business services; engineering, industrial, and science technology; health services; and social, educational, and public services.

(4) Offer sufficient program flexibility so that students can enroll in either specialized career programs or more broadly based studies. Thus, some students might take courses in fields such as data processing, mental hygiene, industrial design, police and fire science, and hotel and restaurant management. Others could direct their career programs toward broader channels—business management, public administration, engineering, or the physical sciences. Students with interests in the arts, be-

havioral sciences, or humanities would be assisted in planning individualized career programs in such curricula as the arts and communications, health services, and the social, educational, and public service areas.

(5) Make cooperative education the focus for enhancing and enriching learning, providing vocational education and guidance, and meeting financial needs of students.

(6) Provide special institutional support for minority groups by developing a partnership program with universities to enhance their capabilities for educating those with diverse learning styles. One-half of all minority undergraduates in predominantly white institutions have attended public two-year colleges, and this trend is likely to continue.

Without the cooperation of senior colleges, today's admissions problems will become tomorrow's transfer problems. One can envision colleges and universities in urban areas committing themselves to admit graduates of special community college programs as upper division students. The substance of the program would be the responsibility of the community college, itself, which could use various combinations of experiences, instruction, work-study, etc., appropriate for individual students.

(7) Introduce new processes of teaching and learning in both the academic and nonacademic phases of experience consonant with the interests and needs of students for their careers.

(8) Mount an adequate staff of highly qualified counselors to advise students in planning and managing their educational and career aspirations. These resources would also be shared with cooperating feeder secondary school programs.

(9) Develop articulated programs in feeder secondary schools which lead to postsecondary career education.

(10) Work in liaison with government agencies as a "backup" institution in the community to implement community programs in adult basic education, entrepreneurial development, civil service and professional licensing, and human service development.

(11) Solicit the participation of all institutions and resources in the community to work with the community college in development of human talent and manpower.

THE AGONY OF CHOICE:
Guidance for Career Decisions

DAVID V. TIEDEMAN

An overwhelming need for extensive change overarches our national destiny in the 1970s. World resources are admittedly finite. Energy conversion proceeds so rapidly that wastes of many kinds become profuse more swiftly than they can be assimilated by natural reconversion. Population mounts, forcing men to dwell in more constricted circumstances than ever dreamed tolerable. Poverty, war, social disorganization, urban and rural blight, hunger, unemployment and underemployment, discrimination, inflation, crime, drug abuse, disease, and overburdened mass transportation, communications, and public utilities—these are just some of the ills which require emergency treatment during this decade.

Dealing with such complex phenomena involves alterations not only in policies and institutions but also in the ways that human beings behave. The ability to change goals, plans, actions, and even feelings and attitudes in light of new information and situations is often a monumental feat. At times, in fact, such an undertaking almost seems impossible. To change, we must commit ourselves to act in the wake of both known and unknown entities, as well as emotions of broad dimension encompassing fear, doubt, anxiety, anger, etc. The necessity for lending self to new orders, and for relinquishing something familiar and comfortable in which we feel a personal stake, is what makes the courage to change such a rare and valued personal trait.

DAVID V. TIEDEMAN holds the rank of Professor in the Harvard Graduate School of Education, where his special field of interest is guidance. He has been director of the Information Systems for Vocational Decisions (ISVD) project.

Education is one particular field which has been sorely pressed to expand its capacity to change and whose response thus far has proved very disappointing. In order to free innovators to carve out enlightened paths for the totality of education, those who want change to evolve rationally rather than through upheaval cannot afford to stand as impervious barriers. They must encourage the injection of new hormones and stand ready to welcome transition, however dramatic, and let change enlarge them without feeling diminished or threatened by it.

The following pages will focus on a new approach to educational guidance, one designed to insure that personal decisions about career are continually reexamined and validated throughout a person's life and one that places him in central control of his own choice mechanisms.

Developing Ego Strength

Erikson [1] has written:

> In youth, ego strength emerges from the mutual confirmation of individual and community, in the sense that society recognizes the young individual as a bearer of fresh energy and that the individual so confirmed recognizes society as a living process which inspires loyalty as it preserves it.

He places the identity crisis in the period of adolescence which brings many physiological changes that find expression in the sociopsychological makeup of the person. During this period the adolescent struggles to delineate and begin acting out a series of roles for his own life, and his identity is ultimately forged in the crucible of action.

The educator occupies a sensitive position in the identity crises; he is a significant figure responsible for facilitating the adolescent's achievement of ego strength. If the teacher can help ease the transition from school to work while keeping his own need for affirmation strictly in the background, then the young person is free to satisfy his own intrinsic need for self-validation as a "bearer of fresh energy." If, however, the educator tries to recreate students in his own image—perhaps as scholar, conformist to the existing social order, or skilled artisan in a given craft or occupational field—then this undermines the very efforts of young people to mature as independent, resourceful, and critical agents with capacity and skill to arrive at their own decisions.

If predictions are accurate, workers of the future will change jobs more frequently than in the past, and this poses a serious problem to guidance education. Such a likelihood makes the actual selection of a specific career a matter of secondary importance, relative to conditions

---

[1] Erik H. Erikson, "Identity and the Life Cycle," *Psychological Issues, 1* (1959).

of the times, rather than a permanent fixture of the person's environment, and places primary emphasis on the process by which justifications for the choice are developed. Training in occupational skills does not automatically guarantee employment either in the present or future. A process of decision making precedes actual entry into any job and must be allocated as much time as skill training in any educational program for employment. Students must be educated for career as well as for occupation. This means more than just communicating information about job opportunities or the nature of particular occupational fields; nor is it sufficient to help students actually choose their jobs. What we must achieve in a lifetime of work is a personal realization of the meaning of career.

Perhaps at this point it would be profitable to clarify a few terms. Vocation, as used here, refers to an individually derived theory of employment which lends continuity to a person's several occupations and many jobs. A person who has mastered the skill of both performance of job tasks and operation in the social and personal environments of work has internalized the theory of vocation.[2] However, there exists a still more individualized form of vocational capacity, namely career competence.

Career, as used here, includes more than a person's present job, occupation or vocation, or even life's work. It is not something pieced together with a number of jobs, although employment is usually a central issue; nor is the definition limited by whatever may be included at the moment.

A career is a sequence of jobs linked by the continuity of the individual personality—a vocation *plus* a sense of one's responsibility and initiative in relation to it; a lifetime achievement, always in the process of emergence. The very feeling that one is in control of his future while changing is a significant part of being a rational human being.

The Process of Deciding

This sense of competence and independence, or "agency," consists of two integral components. One is the series of objects, ideas, or goals being manipulated. They exist within the person as what I. A. Richards has called "feedforward" [3]—that pervading but unarticulated sense of something a person is trying to create or produce. A poem in the mak-

---

[2] See Eileen Morley and David V. Tiedeman, "Confidence: Key to Vocational Competence," *Metals Review*, 2 (1966), 19-20.
[3] See Ivor A. Richards, *Speculative Instruments* (London: Routledge and Kegan Paul, 1955); see also Richards, "The Secret of Feedforward," *Saturday Review* (February 3, 1968), pp. 14-17.

ing, this chapter as it is being written, a vocational choice—all are examples of "feedforward."

The other element is the sense of responsibility and initiative felt by the individual as he works to articulate his vocational choice or "feedforward." This sense of agency is the primary subject of concern to guidance. When it functions effectively in the change process, a student can achieve increased levels of meaningful existence in which his individuality functions for both personal and the common good.

The function of guidance in education is to help students gain self-insights and information about the world outside which can help them reach crucial decisions about their future lives. However, the counselor violates the integrity of his pupils' individual freedom and responsibility if he tries to influence their choices while keeping them ignorant of the basic processes of knowing.

In this chapter career is viewed—and this is not really a new idea—as the time-extended working out of oneself. In the process, the continuity called career is created, and while purposive behavior is central to the process, career is not strictly a chain of activities that leads to some specified predetermined point.

One mechanism for the working out of self is the act of deciding, centered around a problem which has become an obstacle to reaching the decision. Deciding is the key factor. By exercising individual freedom through choice, career becomes the mapping of self instead of just aimless wandering, totally divorced from the individual's own concerns.

There are a number of possible reasons why people have trouble making choices. They may lack a basic rationale for choosing between alternatives. They may not really understand the problem or its implications for the future. Perhaps the most general difficulty—and the one for which help is most needed—is a person's sense of inadequacy about his ability to make sound decisions. At the base of much confusion, ambivalence, or conflict experienced in the decision-making process is the absence of a clear belief on the part of the individual that he can determine what happens to his own life. In the Coleman Report survey, for example, youngsters from low-income families generally believed they could not exercise control over their own destinies; children from middle-income environments were less pessimistic. However, this feeling of powerlessness may be far more widespread throughout the entire population than such statistics would seem to indicate. With the persistence of war, social injustice, inflation, racial tensions, and other social and economic problems of the nation, the average citizen appears to be growing increasingly more convinced that he has little actual control over the crucial decisions that are profoundly affecting his own personal happiness and security.

The Choice Sequence

Landy conceives of knowing in relation to both public and private knowledge,[4] as well as vis-à-vis explicit and tacit knowledge.[5] He proposes that these dimensions be visualized within a Cartesian space as in Table 12.

Table 12   LANDY ON KNOWING

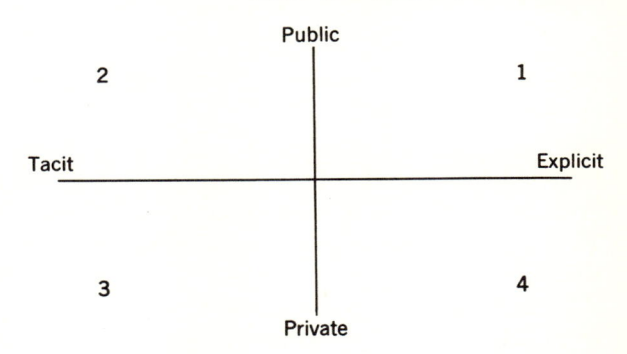

```
                    Public
          2           |           1
                      |
   Tacit ─────────────┼───────────── Explicit
                      |
          3           |           4
                    Private
```

The tacit-and-private-knowledge quadrant generally refers to the assumption that a person is able to know more than he can tell. If he is having difficulty articulating an idea (private knowledge), then the purpose of education is to help him, through the process of communication, to bring it into the public domain. Such knowledge may, for example, come in the form of intuition.

Another way of construing the same process is to focus on the perceptual field in which an idea arises, which includes both the surrounding environment (ground) and the central core of the idea itself (the figure). The student then becomes the integrator of the two, as the idea is moved from tacit to explicit knowledge.

Within this context, guidance becomes more a process of leading out than putting in. The objective is not to pour knowledge into a student as if he were an empty receptacle but to assist the individual who is actor and initiator in bringing his knowledge from the private-tacit quadrant to the stage of explicit-public understanding. The learning process involves trusting one's intuitions sufficiently to risk exposing

---

[4] Stephen Landy, "The known and the measured: a consideration of certain implicit assumptions in testing in the light of some recent additions to the theory of knowledge." Unpublished qualifying paper (Harvard Graduate School of Education, Cambridge, Mass., 1970).

[5] See Michael Polanyi, *The Tacit Dimension* (Garden City, N.Y.: Doubleday, 1966).

them to public testing and examination. Jerome S. Bruner has described intuition as "the act of grasping the meaning or significance or structure of a problem without explicit reliance on the analytical apparatus of one's craft." [6] Bruner places great value on intuition in the process of learning. He writes:

> It is the intuitive mode that yields hypotheses quickly, that produces interesting combinations of ideas before their worth is known. It precedes proof; indeed, it is what the techniques of analysis and proof are designed to test and check. It is founded on a kind of combinatorial playfulness that is only possible when the consequences of error are not overpowering or sinful. Above all, it is a form of activity that depends upon confidence in the worthwhileness of the process . . . rather than upon the importance of right answers at all times.[7]

However, valuing intuition is a radical notion to most educators, who tend to scoff at new ideas grounded on intuition and to demand immediate proof of any hypothesis before it even has a public hearing. They also feel uneasy at the thought of student as independent evaluator and inquisitor rather than passive absorber of new knowledge.

Students themselves are sensitive to this situation. A task force of the National Education Association reported to its annual convention in 1970 that the atmosphere in many schools was unfriendly and repressive, with a feeling of mutual distrust pervading both student body and faculty. Guidance, according to the task force, was often viewed as a tool to control students, rather than an instrument for helping them find their own way, both educationally and personally.[8]

The task of the guidance educator, then, is to help each student bring his knowledge from the third to the first quadrant of the Landy model, from a level of unconscious awareness of a string of issues, events, and concepts to a conscious, deliberate understanding of his own needs and goals. In fact, education should focus on both the explicit and tacit dimensions of knowing; it should encourage the cultivation of tacit understanding of one's inner feelings and help the individual achieve a type of dialogue with himself. In this way, education can encourage a student to come to know and to continue to want to know—powerful motivating agents for a student who is learning about the world of work to reach decisions about his future career. Achieving this synthesis of self and external knowledge, however, requires that he develop the ability to function as decider.

---

[6] Jerome S. Bruner, *On Knowing* (Cambridge, Mass.: The Belknap Press of Harvard University Press, 1964), p. 102.
[7] *Ibid.*
[8] Fred M. Hechinger, "NEA Foresees Greater Student Power," *New York Times* (July 12, 1970), E9. © 1970 by The New York Times Company. Reprinted by permission.

The process of decision making is composed of two major phases, "anticipation" and "accommodation." Anticipation is mainly a thinking-through or reflective period which begins with random exploration of the problem and then moves to a period of rational assessment of alternative solutions. This leads to a choice followed by a clarification. Once a choice is made, action might be expected to follow automatically. In reality, however, doubts often arise, even when the decision seems firm. The waiting period prior to actual implementation of the solution thus provides time for reflection and clarification of the decision, helping to dissipate some of the uncertainty.

Accommodation is the action phase, consisting of three stages. It begins with giving up a part of oneself, in terms of conflicting goals, attitudes, and values to attain the goal at hand (induction). The person then begins to assert himself, perhaps identifying publicly with the choice he has made (reformation). Finally there comes a synthesis of goal and self into a type of "self-system"; and the individual has a feeling of satisfaction and relief as the anticipated action becomes reality.

The ultimate stage of integration is achieved independently of language. Initially, language is used to describe the process and is the medium through which understanding comes about; but language does not actually regulate the process and must be discarded before accommodation is complete in order for action to occur.

The job of the educator is to guide the student through these two phases of anticipation and accommodation until he has mastered the process itself. He must establish the student's proficiency in the language of the process, develop his understanding of this language and its implications, and ultimately facilitate internalization of the process. Then the student is ready to become the significant agent for carving out his own destiny.

Proficiency in application of the process is especially important for students preparing to enter the world of work. Most young people do not have clearly articulated goals as they go through school. Job choice usually remains in the anticipatory stage during this period; hence, skill in applying the decision-making process becomes a significant goal for education and can be the vital link to continued growth and development as adults.

The "Guidance Machine"

Educators are familiar with the overall capabilities of computer-assisted instruction; the computer has ably demonstrated its value for individualized learning which enables students to absorb new material at their own pace and to correct mistakes through instant feedback to their responses.

The computer is also beginning to gain acceptance as a highly valuable support mechanism for occupational guidance. The so-called "guidance machine" has to accomplish at least three goals. First, it must expose the student to language of the decision-making process and lead to the development of skill in its use. Second, the machine must lead to articulation of the process and to self-knowledge in the face of problems that require resolution. The process then becomes a mechanism for manipulation of the relationship between self and predicament to achieve some useful end. Finally, such a machine must bring about a synthesis, one which leads to action and to internalization of the process within the individual. This is knowing, as it relates to decisions.

A model for such a computerized guidance system, called Information System for Vocational Decisions, has been developed at Harvard University in cooperation with New England Educational Data Systems under contract with the U.S. Office of Education.[9] It consists of a computer-based information system that can become part of the vocational and educational guidance efforts of school systems, government employment agencies, trade schools, skill training centers, and even industry.

The task of the system is to enable an individual to transform raw data into information that can be useful to him in making decisions about career. Assuming that the quality of a decision is directly related to the kind, quality, and comprehensiveness of the information considered by the individual during the process of decision making, then a fundamental task of guidance is to identify, evaluate, and classify needed data and make it readily available to students in usable form at needed times and places.

The system teaches a student to interpret data in light of his own knowledge, experience, and intentions; and such organization and utilization of data reflect his own personal relationship to it in the process of decision making. Used in this way, data becomes information and the individual, as a rational human being, is presumed to be capable of acting as a significant agent in control of his own decisions, once he masters the choice process. The incompleteness of the data puts the individual in charge in a two-fold sense—he, not someone or something external to him, makes the decisions; and he is the one who enjoys or suffers the consequences. This educational experience also helps correct the mistaken impression that a person decides something simply by mak-

---

[9] Allan B. Ellis and David V. Tiedeman, "Can a Machine Counsel?" Project Report No. 17 (Cambridge, Mass.: Information System for Vocational Decisions, Harvard Graduate School of Education, 1969).

ing up his mind and that the moment of decision arrives at a free-floating point in time which is uncontrollable by rational reflection.

The computer is particularly valuable for this type of system. It can store large amounts of data; for example, occupational descriptions can be indexed, cross-referenced, and made generally available as the student proceeds through various stages in the decision process. The ISVD project itself contains an extensive collection of data about the world of work, military service, education, personal and family living, and personal characteristics of the student. The prototype occupations data file includes approximately 50 facts on each job category.

At this first level, therefore, the system is essentially a data processing device, performing conventional information-processing tasks faster and more accurately than can be done manually. A second level is more intricate and sophisticated, with the computer system substituting for human counselors in performing certain tasks. The memory of the system is completely available to the student himself, and the computer can interact with him to help ask relevant questions about his understanding of the world of work. Likewise, the student can interrogate the computer without intervention of the counselor, and the machine protects the confidentiality of the dialogue.

Role of the Guidance Educator

The existence of a so-called "guidance machine" would seem on the surface to obviate the need for professional counselors in teaching the process of choice. Presumably, the machine can both dispense data and carry on a dialogue with the student, thus enabling him to become facile in application of the decision-making process within the framework of career selection.

However, human emotions can complicate this otherwise orderly picture. In many instances, students may actually feel blocked in trying to make their way through the process. This could very well stem not from lack of knowledge about decision making but because their own emotional reactions to the problem itself override their desire to decide. Irrational fears and anxieties, anger, ambivalence—these and many other responses to a problem cannot be dealt with in full complexity by a machine. They require the attention of a counselor trained in clinical guidance.

Another way of considering this problem is to distinguish between choice making, which occurs when alternatives are clearly available to the person and he must pick one, and decision making, which involves not knowing what choices exist and having to invent them. Students of today want their independence, but under conditions of choice making rather than decision making, and it is the latter type of problem which critically needs the personal attention of the counselor.

Enumerated on paper, such problems seem to be somewhat extreme and thus applicable only to the proportion of the population with severe neuroses that require prolonged psychological and psychiatric treatment. In reality, however, such emotional problems exist in one form or another and with varying degrees of intensity in almost everyone and are particularly prone to emerge during a crisis in decision making. Becoming increasingly adept in use of the decision process may build sufficient confidence to overcome many of these irrational feelings, but there are no guarantees. Particularly as emotional difficulties relate to factors in the pupil's home environment—parental pressures, sibling rivalries, economic problems, etc.—the need for a more personal approach to counseling becomes apparent, and it is here that the guidance educator has an invaluable role to play.

Alcoholism, drug addiction, and psychological distress are sweeping through the American population. A three-year, federally funded study by child psychologist Olga R. Lurie has concluded, for example, that nearly two-thirds of the children between the ages of 3 and 18 in Westchester County in suburban New York suffer from some degree of emotional impairment.[10] Particularly the young seem to be confronting crises of identification and direction, but Toffler [11] tells us that the adults, as well, are so overcome with the pressures and rapid pace caused by technological invention that the quality of decision making in the occupational world has deteriorated significantly. The agony of choice faces every one of us. Preparing youth to cope with the complexities of choice for career and life will require not only courage but also the intellectual and material resources necessary to help the educational system speed induction into the process of decision making for the seventies and beyond.

---

[10] Linda Greenhouse, "Mental Health Study Concludes . . . ," *New York Times* (June 28, 1970), p. 52. © 1970 by The New York Times Company. Reprinted by permission.

[11] Alvin Toffler, *Future Shock* (New York: Random House, 1970), pp. 311-12.

TEACHING THE TEACHERS:
New Dimensions for Instructional Roles

CARL J. SCHAEFER

It's a classic that's almost cliche—the purpose of American public education is to help each individual develop to the fullest of his abilities and interests. The prevailing pedagogical creed considers each student a unique person, one who learns at his own rate of speed, internalizes knowledge in relation to previous personal experience, and reacts intellectually and emotionally as a very special human being.

Like their students, teachers likewise vary as individuals. They have their own preferences, interests, subject matter expertise, teaching styles, and abilities to establish rapport with students. Unlike most public education rhetoric, however, teacher training programs make no pretensions about individualizing learning for their students. Programs in the nation's 1,200-plus teacher training institutions scarcely take cognizance of variations among their own trainees. Consequently, all teaching apprentices face the same rituals and routines, no matter how poorly these are suited to their previous experience, learning patterns, or professional aspirations. Far too many teacher preparation programs are sterile and uninspiring, and their critics have been numerous and outspoken. One of them, A. H. Yee, has written:

> All facets of modern schools have been significantly improved, but only lip service has been given to the uplifting of teacher quality . . . teacher education centers largely neglect their key social responsibility of supplying

---

CARL J. SCHAEFER is Chairman of the Department of Vocational-Technical Education in the Graduate School of Education of Rutgers University.

schools with well-trained teachers. They help maintain a status quo situation more relevant to the simple, rural society of America's past.[1]

The one-room schoolhouse of yesteryear would have delighted a number of contemporary teachers and teacher trainers. Schooling then was for youngsters who could master it, and teaching was for those who believed that forcing children to ingest knowledge and reproduce it rote was valuable for the intellect. The indifferent or hostile pupil could find instant relief by dropping out of school and finding work as a farmer or laborer.

However, with the advent of compulsory school laws and a diminution in job opportunities for untrained and unskilled workers in an automated economy, the schools found themselves faced with expanded numbers of students who have a wide range of abilities and motivations. The schools responded by devising strategies to deal with this heterogeneous population. For example, almost from day of entry, large numbers of children have been sorted and classified into groups or "tracks" on the basis of test scores. This labelling and shelving system has been understood, either explicitly or implicitly, by all pupils, often with pernicious psychological effects on those classed as sub-brilliant.

Theoretically, tracking was intended to facilitate individualized instruction—but the latter has been more rhetoric than fact. Faced with responsibility for overflowing classrooms, teachers have resorted to planning lessons aimed at an imaginary norm. They have taught everyone approximately the same, which in theory but never in practice provides time for personalized attention. With classes numbering anywhere from 25 to 50 or 60 students, the best of intentions have not produced much individual assistance. Assembly-line education cannot be blamed entirely on teachers, however, for they have had no other models to follow. As students they themselves were instructed in large groups, not as individuals, and their teacher training courses offered no better solutions.

Functional Organization

Anyone who has ever attended or taught school knows that most teachers relate better to some students than others; that is, they are most functional, professionally, within a particular "instructional space," involving a certain type of student population and learning environment. Every teacher has a different set of preferences as he encounters a range of pupil learning styles, personality, characteristics, intellectual skills,

---

[1] A. H. Yee, "Modern Urban Society and Teacher Education," *Education and Urban Society* Vol. 2, No. 3 (May 1970), 277-93. Excerpts reprinted by permission of publisher, Sage Publications, Inc.

and subject matter. Students have long been sensitive to teacher preferences. They are old hands at sizing up the instructor's likes and dislikes, temperament, and expectations, and the more sophisticated students have learned to use this insight to manipulate the learning situation in their favor.

Schools in a democratic society have an obligation to serve all students with equal effectiveness; but it does not necessarily follow that *every* teacher should be expected to reach *every* student with the same skill. This is not a realistic requirement, nor does it reflect an understanding of how human beings interact in a teaching and learning situation. One could argue instead that democracy in education means equal opportunity not only for quality education but also for making choices. As schools are presently organized, students almost *never* have a chance to select their teachers—or vice versa. They are thrown together by other criteria—scheduling mechanics, track systems, or just whim—and the mismatches resulting from random pairings help contribute to the uneven results of educational endeavors.

Of course, not all educators are prepared to accept the premise that interpersonal relationships between teachers and pupils are such an intrinsic part of the learning process. They would contend that subject matter expertise is the paramount and perhaps only significant ingredient for effective teaching. David R. Krathwohl and Benjamin S. Bloom challenge this assumption.

> . . . there still persists an implicit belief that if cognitive objectives are developed, there will be a corresponding development of appropriate affective behaviors. Research . . . raises serious questions about the tenability of this assumption. The evidence suggests that affective behaviors develop when appropriate learning experiences are provided for students much the same as cognitive behaviors develop from appropriate learning experiences.[2]

Without diminishing the value of content as a vital dimension of instruction, Carl Rogers and others have initiated a movement which some call "humanistic" education to make teachers and students more aware of their own feelings and their effects upon others in groups. Their use of techniques such as sensitivity training for this purpose has demonstrated usefulness in bridging the domains of teacher education and curriculum.[3] As Don Davies has stated:

---

[2] David R. Krathwohl, Benjamin S. Bloom, and Bertram B. Masia, *Taxonomy of Educational Objectives, The Affective Domain,* Handbook II (New York: David McKay Co., Inc., 1964).

[3] See Carl Rogers, "Teachers Can Grow . . . ," and Harold Lyon, Jr., "Learning to Feel . . . ," *Educational Needs for the Seventies: A Compendium of Policy Papers,* General Subcommittee on Education, Committee on Education and Labor, U.S. House of Representatives, Sharlene P. Hirsch, ed. (Washington, D.C.: U.S. Government Printing Office, 1970).

Humanizing education, I think, is the central task for all of us whether we are curriculum specialists . . . or specialists in the training of educational personnel. . . . We are coming to understand that when we talk of a relevant curriculum we cannot divorce that from a humane curriculum, for when we try to define relevant curriculum we find that it is one which is related to the way students live and feel and behave.[4]

Humanistic education has considerable promise for helping teachers heighten their own self-awareness and ability to relate to others. It can also sharpen their ability to appraise their own professional strengths in working with various types of students and in making the curriculum a deeper part of the students' own lives.

Functional staffing then becomes an administrative device to assure the appropriate "instructional space" for each learning situation, directed towards differences in both student and teacher populations. *Differentiated staffing*, a term currently in vogue in educational circles, is usually conceived of as placing teachers in specialized instructional roles. One form of differentiation is team teaching, with certain "master" teachers designated as team leaders and appropriately compensated. Teams often include paraprofessional assistants and curriculum specialists as well as teachers. However, such teams are customarily organized around academic areas, e.g., a social studies team might have one teacher working on the American Revolution, another on the Jacksonian period, etc. Little thought, however, has been given to the possibilities for organizing teams according to teaching and learning styles, trying to link up teachers with those students to whom they can relate most positively.

Such a proposal is not without certain difficulties, of course. Functional staffing would require some valid means of identifying teaching and learning styles as well as criteria for joining one with the other, and at present there is no magic formula for doing this. A further complication stems from the probability that pupil learning styles are more fluid than static, and shift with changes in the learning environment, maturation, and experience, etc. For example, it is not uncommon to find a student who appears shy and withdrawn in one classroom acting in an outgoing, effervescent, and even aggressive manner in another. Thus, pupil learning styles have to be approached as products of dynamic, growing organisms rather than fixed labels which stifle change and development. It would be tragic simply to replace one form of compartmentalization or tracking with another.

Hence, this proposal is still in an embryonic stage; but the fact re-

---

[4] Don Davies, "Humanizing the System." Unpublished address before Kimball Wiles Memorial Conference, University of Florida, Gainesville, Florida, 1970.

mains that some teachers reach particular pupils while others do not, and every student deserves a chance to work under inspiring tutelage whenever possible. Functional staffing, if supported by appropriate research and judicious application, has real possibilities for meeting this need. In the absence of hard data to support a model for functional staffing, however, the schools can still take some positive steps in this direction. They might begin by prompting pupils and teachers to examine the whole question of "instructional space" and what it means to them, while stimulating them to try working together in various new combinations.

Implications for Career Education

Ability to convey subject matter, combined with insight into human behavior, constitutes a powerful teaching tool for any educator. Assuring effective learning is especially vital, however, to a program designed to prepare young people for future occupations. Career preparation involves a highly personal and individual response to one's talents and desires, as well as to available opportunities for training and employment. Therefore, knowledge of oneself is basic to career education, and a teacher who combines humanistic skills with content expertise can be a vital asset to such a program.

There is a critical need in particular for teachers interested in and able to work with noncollege-bound students, who comprise about three-fifths of the total student population. According to Dale C. Draper in *Educating for Work*,[5] about 70 percent of all high school students, those remaining after the college bound are skimmed off, constitute a "target" population in need of career education at the secondary level. If such figures even approximate the need, then the staffing of career preparation programs requires concerted attention immediately. The U.S. Office of Education has estimated that by the mid-1970s approximately 345,000 teachers will be needed in vocational fields alone. Yet statistics do not describe the full complexity of the problem. Deciding what type of teacher should be produced is equally important, particularly if some form of functional staffing is to be achieved.

Recruitment and selection of teachers are probably the most significant elements of the teacher preparation process, for as James C. Stone [6] points out, it is fallacious to assume that everyone is capable of teach-

---

[5] Dale C. Draper, *Educating for Work* (Washington, D.C.: © 1967 by the National Association of Secondary School Principals). Reprinted by permission of the National Association of Secondary School Principals.

[6] James C. Stone, *Breakthrough in Teacher Education* (San Francisco: Jossey-Bass Inc., 1968).

ing, even with appropriate training. There is need for a more broadly based screening process focusing on individuals with subject matter expertise and intellectual ability, but also with personal attributes which intensify learning—individuals with, in Stone's words, "the ability to listen, who emphasize inquiry, social sensitivity and self-direction, and who are 'around and about' the classroom, guiding, probing, encouraging." [7]

Career preparation programs must attract a variety of talented people to the teaching profession, including (1) specialists in academic disciplines who are interested in constructing, through experience and independent study, a broad overview of the relationships between the world of work and recurring thematic problems in their fields; (2) persons with sound occupational skills who want to design methods of teaching them effectively; and (3) individuals who can develop human relations and interaction skills through immersion in classroom internship experiences and through such experiences as sensitivity training.

The content of the teacher training program itself must change. In addition to a thorough grounding in the liberal arts, a teacher's preparation should include courses in counseling and psychology; an extensive teaching internship as well as preteaching opportunities for working with children and young people; sensitivity and group process training; and practical experience in the world of work, itself.

Teachers-in-training should spend as much time as possible in supervised experiences in the schools. As dean of Teachers College, Columbia University, Robert J. Schaefer has discussed the fact that there has been general loss of confidence, from the public as well as the education profession, in the relevancy of education today, and he has criticized colleges of education for having too little contact with the public schools. In an initial phase prior to actual practice teaching, trainees should have varied opportunities for contacts with students and they should begin to discover more about pupil learning styles as well as their own skills in working with people. The practice teaching experience should bring the trainee into working relationships with a team of specialists—experts in occupational and academic areas, humanistic education, and guidance.

Another essential ingredient in the training program is actual experience in the world of employment, either prior to or as part of the teacher education sequence. Such exposure should count as credit toward a degree or teaching certificate, with the stipulation that a student be able to demonstrate how this experience relates to his teaching.

---

[7] *Ibid.*

The Regeneration Process

A missing link in the process of preparing education professionals is the lack of in-house opportunities for self-regeneration. Certification, lifelong credentials, and tenure have tended to isolate the profession from normal pressures for continued professional improvement. Those who have sought means for increasing their instructional competence within their own school systems have been offered sporadic short-term workshops. The fact that half the knowledge teachers will need to know ten years from now has not yet been discovered is a powerful force for creation of an ongoing, comprehensive organizational mechanism for inservice education. The principle of continuous renewal must take its place as a foremost precept of the teaching profession, and appropriate structures should be credited to insure its permanence.

Industry should have a key role in any undertaking involving the continuous education of teachers for career preparation programs. One vehicle for institutionalizing such an effort could take the form of a series of regional centers, each housing a physical complex specifically designed to refresh knowledge about industry, for teachers involved in world-of-work programs.[8] Such a center, operated under contract with teacher training institutions and school systems, could provide services for both novice and experienced teachers drawn from the entire spectrum of education. Throughout the program, participants could be exposed to the most recent developments and concepts in the world of work.

Such a center would have three components—a technology function, resource function, and computer center. The technology building would contain a series of laboratories. Each would accommodate a clearly identifiable range of equipment and processes and a central core containing the most modern multimedia presentation facilities and audiovisual recording equipment available. Workshops conducted by industrial personnel, using equipment loaned by industry, would demonstrate a given process or piece of equipment to the teachers. They would then have an opportunity to gain operational experience using it. In addition, they would have use of the recording equipment to document their experiences for subsequent curriculum development. The same center would provide training for multimedia specialists, who would be responsible for recording the demonstrations for a curriculum library.

The resource building would help teachers utilize knowledge produced in the adjacent technology area by translating it into curriculum

---

[8] "The Development of a Technology Resource Center" (New Brunswick, N.J.: Department of Vocational-Technical Education, Rutgers University, 1964).

materials for their classrooms. The curriculum effort would consist of two main units: (1) a developmental laboratory with reference library, single-concept films, motion pictures, still photographs, videotape recordings, and duplicating facilities for production of text materials, manuals, and other training aids developed for a wide range of occupational courses; and (2) an evaluation component staffed by curriculum development specialists and teachers to test the training materials and aids produced in the laboratory.

A computer could be housed in the lower level of the resource building to provide computer-assisted instruction for all educational institutions in the area by means of remote student terminals. Teachers would be able to familiarize themselves with this equipment and the variety of programs available for use with it. In addition, the computer could be used to provide electronic data processing to the same institutions which subscribe to its instructional services, thereby reducing administrative and overhead expenses. The computer facility itself could also be used to train students as operations personnel for the major computers used in business and industry.[9]

The Externship

Experienced teachers in career preparation courses should be encouraged and even required to return to the world of work periodically to revitalize their understanding of its demands, constraints, and opportunities. Through arrangements with business and industry, universities ought to arrange externships, for credit, enabling teachers to spend a semester or year in actual jobs similar to those for which they are preparing their students. School systems should also grant incremental credit on their salary schedules for such experience. The currency of experience has been overlooked far too long. As Roy L. Woolridge has written, "Even the generalist in liberal arts can enhance his education through periods of guided employment in the world beyond the campus." [10] Besides actually holding jobs, teachers should be enabled to spend time in the world of work following up on the effectiveness of their courses. They should be encouraged to interview former students and their employers, feeding back such information into the system to update and redesign the curriculum.

---

[9] John G. Nealon and Carl J. Schaefer, "The Development of Professional Staff Personnel for Post-Secondary Vocational-Technical Education." Unpublished paper presented at the National Conference on Post-Secondary Vocational-Technical Education, Dallas, Texas, 1969.

[10] Roy L. Woolridge, *Cooperative Education and the Community Colleges in New Jersey* (New York: National Commission for Cooperative Education, Inc., in cooperation with the New Jersey Governor's Conference on Education, 1966).

Summary

One of the most positive forces for change in the teaching profession has been the Education Professions Development Act. As Associate Commissioner for Educational Personnel Development in the U.S. Office of Education, which administers this legislation, Don Davies has stated:

> I see a basic strategy in the provisions of the Education Professions Development Act. It says, in effect, that the kind of educational change we are seeking requires one thing—changing people. It means reeducating the education professions in the kinds of attitudes and skills and knowledge they need to perform effectively in a new setting and under new conditions. That means changing ourselves and everyone else who has anything to do with running or serving the schools—teachers, aides, counselors, superintendents, teachers of teachers. It means recruiting and training new kinds of people.[11]

Changes in the training and utilization of education professionals have been suggested throughout this chapter. In summary:

- The profession must devise ways of differentiating teacher styles and pupil learning characteristics to facilitate the functional matching of instructors and learners.
- The education profession must recognize that attitudes, interests, appreciations, values—or what is called "affective" behavior—are as important as the acquisition of knowledge in the career preparation process, and teachers must be prepared to help their students with these behaviors.
- Work experience should serve as a currency for acquiring academic and salary credit.
- A new breed of educator, prepared to teach about broad clusters of occupations, is needed. At the same time, the need for teachers of specific vocational courses continues.
- Because lack of self-regeneration has plagued the education profession, steps must be taken to provide for continuing education to keep teachers abreast of technological developments which will affect their students' preparation for the world of work and appropriate pedagogical methods which can be used to convey this information.

To bring about such changes will require courage on the part of many and the devotion of *all* who are engaged in the education profession.

---

[11] Don Davies, "Getting Into the EPDA Act," *American Vocational Journal, 44* (September 1969), 51-53.

COLLABORATION AT THE CROSSROADS:
Business and Education

SAMUEL M. BURT

Employers Look at Schools

It took considerable strength of character for the vocational education supervisory staff of the New York public schools to release findings of a two-year self-study in 1969 in which they indicted their own stewardship during much of the previous decade. The study charged, among other things, that equipment and curriculum used in New York schools were meaningless, that enrollments in vocational education courses were far too low, and that the programs had no ties with the world of work.[1]

The information supplied by New York and 19 other city school systems as baseline data for the investigation indicates how little the schools are now doing to ready our nation's youth for the working world. For example, Chicago—in the heart of the Midwest industrial complex—had a lower proportion of students in trade and industrial courses than any of the cities studied. New York, the business center of the world, enrolled a smaller percentage of high school students in these areas than four other cities. Although a well-established need exists for workers in health occupations, none of the cities had a substantial program in this

---

SAMUEL M. BURT is Director of the Business Council for International Understanding program of American University. He was formerly Senior Project Director of W. E. Upjohn Institute for Employment Research, Washington, D.C.

[1] Martin Hamburger and Harry E. Wolfson, *1000 Employers Look at Occupational Education* (New York: Board of Education of the City of New York, 1969).

140

area. The absence of close ties between the school systems and state employment services was also widespread.

That the world of work has rated only marginal attention from the education community is reflected in the fact that formally organized school relationships with corporate management, organized labor, and related community groups were practically nonexistent in half the cities surveyed. Most school people interviewed expressed a need for citywide educational advisory committees to create such ties, but only four of 18 systems had even bothered to organize them. Apparently, however, school people are reluctant to extend invitations to the business community to help assess the effectiveness of education for work and to chart new directions for school programs. Their ambivalence is reflected, for example, in the report's recommendation that employers "engage themselves in occupational education by visiting and learning what is done in the schools," without prescribing any formal role for them in the policy-making process. It seems almost ludicrous to suggest that leaders of the economic community engage in empty exercises which can have no genuine impact on the educational program. Thus, a major problem is that educators have cloistered themselves from counsel by outsiders; they have been unwilling to accept members of the business world or the community in general either as participants in the process of analyzing educational issues and considering alternative policies, or as actors in the instructional process.

Industry has for many years tried to make inroads into the phalanx of resistance by offering specific services, staff, and funds to help improve public education (see Table 13, pp. 142-43). Generally, however, school administrators have responded with less than wholehearted enthusiasm. As the National Association of Manufacturers' education committee reported:

> Because of the organization structure of the formal educational system, it is difficult for a representative of industry to identify the proper person with whom he should discuss an educational issue of concern. . . . An industrialist may have concerns over curricula content, vocational education programs (or their lack), educational philosophy, or the operational procedure of one or more school districts within a given state. In the absence of knowing the proper authority to contact within a school system, an industrialist either takes no action or takes considerable time discussing his concern with well-intentioned officials who do not have the interest, intent, or authorization to bring about needed changes.[2]

The NAM committee recommended that state and local public school officials appoint special liaison staff to develop lines of communication

---

[2] "Handbook for Education Committee Members" (New York: National Association of Manufacturers, 1969).

Table 13 CHECKLIST OF ACTIVITIES AND SERVICES PROVIDED BY LOCAL INDUSTRY-EDUCATION ADVISORY COMMITTEES

Student Recruitment, Selection, and Placement

(1) Encouraging young people (and parents) to consider vocational and technical education and training through visits to "feeder schools," speeches to civic clubs, career day meetings, etc;
(2) assisting in the screening of students applying for admission to the courses;
(3) participating in the development of aptitude tests for selection of students;
(4) providing information concerning desirable aptitudes, education, and experience background which applicants for entry level jobs should have so that educators may properly plan their student recruitment, as well as educational and training programs;
(5) arranging plant or field trip visits for students and counselors;
(6) providing vocational guidance literature to teachers, counselors, and students;
(7) assisting and participating in surveys of local industry manpower needs;
(8) assisting in the development of aptitude tests, achievement tests, and certification and licensing tests concerned with initial employment of school graduates;
(9) placing students in part-time work during school year or summer vacations;
(10) placing school graduates in jobs.

Instructional Program

(1) Assisting in the preparation and review of budget requests for laboratory and shop equipment and supplies;
(2) evaluating physical conditions, adequacy of equipment, and layout of laboratory or shop;
(3) assisting in the development and review of course content to assure its currency in meeting the changing skill and knowledge needs of the industry;
(4) obtaining needed school equipment and supplies on loan, as gifts, or at special prices;
(5) assisting in the establishment of standards of proficiency to be met by students;
(6) assisting in the development of school policy concerning the kinds and volume of production work or "live jobs" to be produced by students so that this work will be of instructional value in the educational program;
(7) establishing and maintaining a library of visual aids, magazines, and books concerning industry;
(8) assisting in the development of special educational and training programs conducted with funds made available by the Manpower Development and Training Act, the Economic Opportunity Act, etc.;
(9) assisting in the development of evening school skill improvement and technical courses for employed plant personnel;
(10) assisting in the development of apprenticeship and on-the-job training related courses;
(11) arranging plant or field trip visits for teachers;
(12) providing sample kits of raw materials, finished products, charts, posters, etc., for exhibit and instructional purposes in classrooms and shops;
(13) assisting in the establishment of student fees and charges for courses and programs.

Table 13 (Continued)

Teacher Assistance

(1) Providing funds to assist local teachers to attend regional and national meetings of industry and teacher organizations;
(2) arranging meetings of teachers to establish cooperative relationships between the schools and industry;
(3) arranging summer employment for teachers;
(4) assisting in the establishment of teacher qualification requirements;
(5) conducting clinics and in-service and out-service training programs for teachers;
(6) arranging for substitute or resource instructors from industry to assist regular teachers;
(7) subsidizing teacher salaries in such unusual cases as may be necessary to obtain qualified instructors.
(8) paying industry organization membership dues for teachers;
(9) providing awards and prizes to outstanding teachers.

Student Recognition

(1) Providing scholarships and other financial assistance for outstanding graduates who wish to continue their education and training;
(2) providing prizes to outstanding students.

Public Relations

(1) Providing speakers to address trade and civic groups concerning the industry's education and training program in the school;
(2) providing news stories concerning school programs to magazines published for specific industry groups;
(3) providing news stories concerning school programs to local news media;
(4) attending meetings in support of vocational and technical education which may be called by local and state school officials, boards, and legislative groups;
(5) participating in radio and television programs designed to "sell" vocational and technical education to the public;
(6) contributing funds to advertise specific school occupational education and training programs;
(7) advising employees and their families concerning school programs by posting the information on bulletin boards, news stories in company publications, and enclosures in pay envelopes.

Source: Samuel M. Burt, *INDUSTRY AND VOCATIONAL-TECHNICAL EDUCATION* (New York: McGraw-Hill Book Company, 1967), Chapter 3.

between industry and education. A number of local and national corporations and professional associations have retained former educators as heads of their school relations programs, but only the larger organizations have felt they could justify the expense, particularly if the schools themselves have not made a similar commitment of staff resources.

Employers are not alone in having been overlooked by the educational planners. State and local labor union leaders have been excluded, as well. Lieberthal reports:

While the trade and industrial occupations [educators] have developed apprenticeship programs in close cooperation with many building trades unions, they have involved too few of the large basic industry unions. The United Automobile Workers, the United Steel Workers of America, and the International Association of Machinists have seldom been consulted in program planning and implementation. Yet, in many communities, the leaders of these unions are influential, intelligent, and very much interested in education and occupation training programs. They suffer from lack of contact with T & I program administrators.

One of the fastest-growing unions in the country is the Retail Clerks International Association. Many local leaders in this organization have a deep-seated concern about the development of distributive education programs at the high school and post-high school levels. Other unions in the distributive services field include the Retail, Wholesale, and Department Store Union, and the Hotel and Restaurant Employees Union.

DE program people rarely involve these people, despite the fact that they could help plan programs that would serve students more realistically and could enlist the support of other union representatives in the community. The same holds true for business and office educators. They could profit in the same way by seeking the cooperation of unions that represent business and office employees and federal, state, and local government employees.[3]

This writer's studies [4] of industry-education cooperation in vocational education have documented instances of distrust and defensiveness on the part of many school administrators in response to overtures from the business community to serve as volunteers in public school programs. State licensing systems are a formal barrier to hiring persons from the business community as classroom teachers. The rebuffs in this instance were more subtle, however, for no transfer of employees was involved. The message was clear. Outsiders, no matter how well qualified in the business world, were not welcome on any basis other than as visiting observers, and perhaps not even then. Today, however, the overwhelming need to prepare young people effectively for working roles demands that every available resource be tapped, and particularly that the business community be attracted into a genuine partnership with education to improve schooling. Once this principle has been clearly established, then a number of management alternatives are open to the schools, the most immediate being the appointment of a liaison staff.

---

[3] M. Lieberthal, "Labor: Neglected Source of Support," *American Vocational Journal* (December 1967), pp. 49-52. See also Trudy W. Banta, "Why Aren't More Schools Involved in NAB Programs?" *American Vocational Journal* (October 1969); Banta and Douglas C. Towne, *Interpretive Study of Cooperative Efforts of Private Industry and the Schools to Provide Job-Oriented Education Programs for the Disadvantaged* (Knoxville: University of Kentucky, 1969).

[4] See Samuel M. Burt, *Industry and Vocational-Technical Education* (New York: McGraw-Hill, 1967); Burt and Leon M. Lessinger, *Volunteer Industry Involvement in Public Education* (Lexington, Mass.: D.C. Heath and Company, 1970).

The NAM, among others, has recommended creation of industry liaison staff in at least the larger school systems offering vocational-technical education programs, as well as in state departments of education and the U.S. Office of Education. As one example of what a school with this type of staff can accomplish, the Los Angeles Trade-Technical College has received over $1 million in donated or loaned equipment and annually gets many thousands of dollars' worth of supplies from industry. Over 600 industry representatives serve on its advisory committees. A number of other schools report the growth of equally positive relationships with industry as a result of effective liaison staff work (see Table 13).

Business has consistently expressed interest in the development of quality education, and indications are that the level of concern is growing. For example, in a study of participation in public affairs by over 1,000 companies the National Industrial Conference Board found most active involvement concentrated in the field of education. The companies were involved in upgrading and expanding local school facilities, improving local school curriculum, developing programs for school dropouts, and creating expanded career opportunities for minority groups. In 1969 *Fortune* surveyed the 500 largest American corporations regarding what should be the role of business in resolution of social problems. The most frequent response was that business should support education.

Such involvement has elements of self-interest, of course. Companies need a continuing supply of properly trained and well-educated manpower and hope to rely on the public and private educational systems whenever possible as a major source of supply for their plants, offices, and stores. Their concern about education has been further augmented, at least in recent times, by the upsurge of activism on college campuses and in public schools for its potential effects on the stability of the nation's business climate. As a Chicago banker put it, private property is an esteemed value only as long as the majority of American people respect it;[5] hence corporations have to keep their lines of communication open with the society as a whole. The schools, in turn, have a stake of their own in perpetuating and strengthening the participation of business, for the private sector has always had considerable influence on the destiny of local school bond issues as well as passage of education legislation at the state, federal, and local levels.

The problem, therefore, is not whether schools can interest employers in education. The desire already exists. However, school people must be moved to build upon this interest and make more appropriate responses

---

[5] "The Executive As Social Activist," *Time* (July 20, 1970), pp. 62-68. Reprinted by permission from *Time*, The Weekly News magazine; copyright by Time, Inc., 1970.

to offers of help from the business world and devise means for optimum utilization of these talents and resources.

Joint Business-Education Ventures

Texas. One level of cooperative effort occurs when the business community assists educators in designing new school programs. An outstanding example of such joint industry-education efforts has developed in an innovative curriculum designed by the Texas construction industry and Texas Education Agency. A shortage of skilled manpower in construction led the Texas Mechanical Contractor Association and allied industry groups to form the Texas Construction Industry Council for Manpower, Education and Research in January 1968. Six months later, with support of the state's commissioner of education, a construction industry-education cooperative program was designed to involve, in the first year, over 1,000 ninth grade students in 16 pilot schools.

Plans called for students in the first year to study a one-unit "Introduction to Vocation," providing a broad look at industry. The tenth and eleventh grade courses were to consist of two-hour laboratories on the basics of plumbing—pipefitting and heating-cooling. Twelfth grade students could choose among construction, repair, estimating, and distributing, spending three to five hours a day in on-the-job training and related classroom instruction in their areas of specialty. The Construction Industry Council of the state has arranged through member companies of its affiliates for job placement of students in the program, who take Construction Industry Council tests to determine credit towards journeymanship for previous experience and education.

In reporting on this program, an industry magazine concluded:

> For the industry it means a new potential trained manpower source that could add thousands of men every year at all levels from the warehousemen through apprentice through middle and upper management. For society as a whole, it means a new approach to the problem of school dropouts and, obviously, a reorganization of the total educational process.[6]

Commenting on the program, the executive director of the Texas Advisory Council for Vocational-Technical Education stated:

> We think it is a bright spot from many aspects. . . . (1) students are involved in the program for four years beginning in an exploratory manner, going through the skill development and on-the-job training, through cooperative training in the senior year; (2) the close working relationship between the school and industry will assure the validity and continuing of the program; (3) industry has been organized and motivated to support the program

---

[6] "Manpower Shortage: A Texas-Sized Solution," *Mechanical Contractor* (September 1969).

during the training process and to provide jobs for those trained in the program.[7]

Connecticut. The utilization of volunteer business executives to advise school systems on management-related problems constitutes another dimension of industry-education cooperation. An example of this is found in a series of experiences centering around the New Haven, Connecticut, public school system. In 1966 the newly appointed school superintendent addressed the local Chamber of Commerce education committee on problems facing the schools in areas of administration and communications. The committee chairman, an executive in Olin's Westchester group—the largest employer in the area—suggested that his company could render assistance by undertaking an organizational study of the school system. Consequently, Olin made available one of its management consultants on a full-time basis for six months.

Following this period of investigation, the consultant's findings were reported to the superintendent. The "Price Report," as it came to be called, offered 45 recommendations, most of which had been prepared in conjunction with the school's professional staff. It served to generate considerable discussion within the system and among citizens' groups.

About the same time, the Southern New England Telephone Company, which had sponsored a number of programs in cooperation with local schools, asked the superintendent how the company might assist the New Haven system. The superintendent requested a task force to implement recommendations of the "Price Report." Three executives were assigned to assist the superintendent and his staff in improving the system's procedures for contract administration, data processing, record keeping, internal and external communications, and office management.

Among the accomplishments which can be attributed to this industry-school cooperative effort are the following:

(1) production of a policies and procedures manual applicable to all phases of school administration;
(2) creation of a series of monthly inservice management training sessions for educational leaders, conducted by Southern, Olin, and other firms in the community;
(3) construction of organization charts for the entire school system;
(4) implementation of an ambitious public relations program for the school system;
(5) development of a plan to organize citizens advisory councils for each school in the system.[8]

---

[7] Letter to Samuel M. Burt from Alton Ice, November 6, 1969.
[8] See *Decentralization and Community Involvement* (Washington, D.C.: American Association of School Administrators, 1969); see also *Industry and Education*, Study No. 1 (New York: Institute for Educational Development, 1969).

Companies involved in these efforts handled themselves in a statesmanlike manner. They sought no publicity for their efforts, nor did they attempt to impose advice on school people. An important added benefit of the experience came in the form of better relations between business and the schools. The corporations developed a deeper understanding of school problems, and the educators felt more confident, because they had gained allies in the community.

Louisiana. A third type of business participation in public education involves providing actual job training. The Adult Education Center, Inc., of New Orleans, conducted two successful demonstration programs in 1966-67 under sponsorship of the Manpower Development Training Act to train young women from minority groups for office careers. The project gave instruction in the use of correct business English as well as office practice. When local and state authorities refused to extend funding of the project, a group of employers in New Orleans, who had hired and were pleased with the performance of project graduates, raised almost $39,000 to meet conditions under which the U.S. Labor Department would grant an additional $20,000. The total contributions of the business community far exceeded finances, however. Businessmen of New Orleans became involved in the administrative, instructional, and placement phases, as well. They helped refine and further develop the curriculum, acted as resource persons in the classroom, and assisted in the purchase of necessary equipment and furniture.

Illustrative of other equally important directions in industry-education cooperation are:

(1) Cleveland's factory-school, Woodland Enterprises, which is headquartered in a four-story building donated by General Electric Company. Students have been able to attend classes operated by the school system part of the day and work at jobs provided by companies which lease the remainder of the building. Individual jobs have varied from simple, unskilled work to running drill presses and turret lathes. This educational program has been designed to serve a student population which includes potential high school dropouts and unemployed and underemployed adults.
(2) Philadelphia's Parkway School, a "school without walls" for high school students. Students have attended classes in over two dozen different public and private institutions located along or near the mile-and-a-half Benjamin Franklin Parkway in downtown Philadelphia. The program has involved approximately 75 cooperating agencies, including business and industry, government, and cultural and educational institutions.

Sharing the Financial Burden

Education for the world of work is a very expensive undertaking. The Labor Department uses $3,500 as an estimated investment per person to train persons for jobs, but costs often run much higher. As the direct benefactors of school programs which prepare pupils for the world of work, employers should rightfully assume a special obligation to participate financially as partners in the educational process. As president of Eastern Michigan University, Harold E. Sponberg told the American Management Association: "If industry expects to get productivity out of an employee, it must invest in the preemployment preparation in a more direct manner than paying taxes and contributing physical facilities." [9] Support from business is crucial to the vitality of public school effort to educate for work.

Long-range commitments are needed from the business community in such efforts as the following: financial assistance to public schools for equipping and staffing specialized skill training programs; training for teachers in occupational fields offering apprenticeship and internship experiences for all students as a regular part of their schooling; guaranteed employment for graduates of specialized programs; linkages between company training programs and education and training offered in the schools; and appropriate compensation for graduates of school training programs. Many employer and industry groups have assumed these responsibilities on a casual basis, but they must now be made standard policy by the business community as a whole.

The business community can also be helpful in other efforts to expand education for the world of work. This includes creation of teaching units on the following: introduction to work in the early grades; prevocational training which exposes students to a wide range of occupational choices in junior high school; pursuit of still tentative occupational fields in high school; an interdisciplinary fusion of such subjects as English, mathematics, and science with career-oriented programs; organization and effective utilization of industry advisory committees; incorporation of relevant part-time work experiences in all educational programs at the secondary school level; job placement services; follow-up assessments of the effectiveness of career education programs; and in-service professional education of teachers through experiences in the business community.

Thus, both educators and businessmen must exercise new levels of courage in their efforts to prepare young people for effective participation in the world of work; but the educationists in particular must cast away fears of interference with their domain and realize that education, as Francis Keppel, Peter Drucker, and others have said, is too important a task to leave solely to the educators.

---

[9] Douglas W. Cray, "Latest Teaching 'Hardware' Shown," *New York Times* (August 5, 1970), pp. 45-46. © 1970 by The New York Times Company. Reprinted by permission.

MARRIAGE OF VITAL SKILLS:
Vocational Education and Manpower Training

LOWELL A. BURKETT

A Matter of Understanding

When the United States government spends $2,000 to $7,000 per student to train dropouts for entry-level jobs, an obvious lack of common purpose exists between those who set national manpower policy and those who command the resources of public education.

When a community college duplicates courses taught for the past decade in a vocational school 12 blocks away, coordination within the education community may be lacking.

When a local employer tells a vocational teacher who is trying to organize a cooperative vocational education program, "I wouldn't take a student employee if you paid me, let alone me pay him," the purposes of vocational education have failed to be understood at the community level.

From this and other evidence, one must conclude that links in communication, coordination, and understanding are missing in the chain of vocational education and manpower development.

If this country intends to confront its problem of human resources and manpower development—the problem of filling employment demands of industry and fulfilling aspirations of people—it must forge a chain that will link, not duplicate, the efforts of vocational educators and manpower trainers. And if that chain is to have the tensile strength

---

LOWELL A. BURKETT is Executive Director of the American Vocational Association, Washington, D.C.

to withstand the pulling and hauling it is certain to get, the links between education and industry have to be frequent and sturdy.

Vocational education, business, and industry have been on speaking terms for years. They have been communicating with each other in manpower councils and advisory committees, on special commissions, and at conferences and conventions. Some of this dialogue has resulted in cooperative action—in cooperative vocational education programs, in industry-sponsored seminars for vocational teachers, sharing of facilities, and other instances. But such interface is easier to achieve in isolated instances at local levels than on regional or statewide, much less national, bases. In the whole manpower fabric, they add up to little more than a patchwork. Piecemeal and fragmentary, they are not likely to produce any measurable change unless cemented at the top where policy decisions are made.

From the vocational educator's standpoint, the most unattainable objective appears to be public understanding of vocational education. This historical problem is now compounded. The terms *vocational education* and *manpower training* are used as two distinct, unrelated segments of national and state manpower efforts. This confusion is an aftermath of the passage of the Manpower Development and Training Act of 1962. Since that time, *manpower* has gained currency as a term to designate the nation's work force. The word is a U.S. Labor Department coinage, and thus *manpower training* has come to be associated with employment training programs supported by government funds but carried on outside the public schools.

Actually, vocational education *is* manpower training and development in its most comprehensive sense. These are interchangeable terms. Not all vocational education programs—maybe not even half—reach the standard we call "total vocational education." The limitations are largely a result of missing linkages.

The Educators and the Trainers

Who are vocational educators and manpower trainers? We do not usually think of a corporate-level executive as a manpower trainer. But very likely he has definite views on manpower development and utilization—and he probably makes those views known to the governor's manpower commission and the state house.

The superintendent of a metropolitan school district is not usually considered a vocational educator, nor is it likely that he came through the ranks of vocational education. Yet, his thinking about vocational education's purpose and place in the school system will directly affect the kind of budgetary and other support that such a program receives.

The head of training activities in a big company might be compared to the vocational education director in a city school system; trainers in industry might find their counterparts in the vocational education department of a teacher training institution. The closest parallel, however, is the classroom vocational teacher and the shop foreman or supervisor in business and industry. (In a small shop, the latter might be the employer himself.)

Because of wide diversification in job roles, however, such comparisons are meaningless. It seems more useful to consider manpower trainer and vocational educator as generic terms and examine their characteristics as they affect various programs.

Both have one outstanding characteristic in common: they believe it is best "to learn by doing" rather than through irrelevant abstractions. The main difference between them is expressed in their respective occupational titles. One is an educator, the other, a trainer.

The vocational educator is usually a professionally prepared teacher, a product of the nation's teacher education institutions. Therefore, he is grounded in the principles of teaching and learning. He subscribes to the philosophy of American education which is concerned with transmittal of occupational skills and knowledge but also with full development of students as human beings.

The teacher's role is to guide and lead, but he respects individual prerogatives and is careful not to trespass on students' creativity and right to freedom of choice. This requires sensitivity and skill that come essentially from the kinds of experiences the teacher is given in his program of preparation. Thus, every vocational teacher becomes a counselor to his students. He must be concerned with them as persons—with their emotional problems, home environments, and any other personal or social obstructions to learning and growth, which for vocational students include occupational choice and vocational development.

In comparison, the role of the industry trainer is more narrowly and specifically defined. His assignment is to teach a certain set of skills required for the job for which the trainee has already been hired. He may be a skillful teacher and he probably knows how to work with people. Most likely, he offers trainees useful advice on how to get along on the job and also on matters not related to skill training.

But his central responsibility is different. He may have his students' interests at heart, but his first duty is to the company that pays him. Evaluation of his teaching and supervisory performance is translated immediately into profit and loss columns of a ledger. Therefore, the industry trainer has every reason to place more emphasis on skill training and productivity than on total human development.

The effectiveness of the vocational teacher is more difficult to gauge. He is not so close to the point of evaluation; his performance gets mixed in with many other factors and shows up much later in placement figures and follow-up studies. His motivation takes the form of dedication to his mission, and that mission is a broad one. He is expected to turn out not only productive workers but also responsible members of society. When young people go on a rampage of rioting, pot-smoking, and campus sit-ins, the public schools share the blame with parents. No one points a finger at the industry trainer.

This is not to say that business and industry do not share a special concern about public welfare. The National Alliance of Businessmen, for example, resulted from a desire of business and industry to rehabilitate the urban hard core unemployed. Organized in 1968, the NAB reported an impressive number of such workers placed in jobs during its first year and an expansion of operations from 50 to 125 cities. However, according to a seven-month survey of 247 urban-based companies by a management consulting firm, corporate officials found programs much more costly than anticipated and in need of far greater planning and management than expected.[1]

No one would blame NAB companies for having second thoughts about commitments made in the wake of the ghetto riots in the summer of 1967. Their business in the long run is to show profits, not to train dropouts.

Leadership from Public Schools

By public consignment, training and education of youth rest with the schools. If there is a high incidence of dropouts, the schools have failed in their mission, and it is their responsibility to make restitution to society and to the youth they let fall by the wayside.

The major thesis of this chapter is that, from any long-range viewpoint, preemployment training which gives the worker entry-level skills along with well-rounded education is the best way to build up a sound work force and eliminate the need for high-cost remedial programs. If this argument is valid, it follows that the primary program of manpower development should be placed in the public schools and the main thrust of the national manpower training effort should be in support of a total vocational education program.

Linkages to Career Education

Vocational education cannot be carried on entirely within school walls. It must go out into the community to use facilities and human resources of business, industry, and public services.

---

[1] See "The Ghetto: A Loss of Zeal . . . And a Touch of Pride," *Newsweek* (March 23, 1970), pp. 83-84. Copyright Newsweek, Inc., 1970.

School programs. A total program of vocational education presupposes linkages between educators and manpower trainers at every level. In the early grades, it relies on contacts with local employers to help young children view their world as a realistic but exciting domain where man's occupations take their place along with the arts and sciences. This is the first step in the child's career development, which adds an entirely new dimension to his traditional program of education.

As the child progresses through the grades, he is offered exploratory experiences. While still too young for skill training, he is allowed to try his hand at different kinds of simple work skills along with his general education and introduction to the arts and sciences. By the time he must make decisions about the future, a young person has some idea of the world of work and his own aptitudes and limitations. In short, he has acquired a framework for choice and further exploration.

The high school student who chooses a vocational education program to learn skills for an entry-level job needs help in making the right occupational selection. High school students often have some notion of what they want to do and may show strong aptitude for certain kinds of work. But these vague directions need refining.

To help them in this undertaking, vocational counselors need the closest kind of working relationship with manpower experts in the local U.S. Employment Services as well as personnel staffs of community industries, businesses, and public service agencies. From the standpoint of vocational education, this linkage between public school and manpower trainer is extremely important, because of the emphasis placed by public schools on the individual's right to free choice.

Work of one sort or another, whether occupational or professional, consumes the better part of a lifetime. There is nothing so tragic as the captive worker who stays on the job year in and out, tied by family responsibilities to work that neither suits nor interests him.

The student in a vocational education program must be taught skills and content relevant to the entry-level job he is aiming for. But linkages with manpower trainers are required to insure that relevance. They may take a number of forms, such as craft advisory committees, exchange of personnel between industry and education, summer work experiences for teachers, and cooperative work-study programs.

The most effective and immediate linkage—one which can scarcely be improved—is the cooperative vocational education program. Cooperative education contains elements of apprenticeship training; it is on-the-job experience coupled with related subject matter and is perhaps the best example of linkage between vocational educator and manpower trainer.

In this closely coordinated program they are, in effect, a teaching team. Such a relationship has spin-off value, as well. The workshop supervisor gains new insights from his association with a professional educator; the educator, in turn, derives a realistic picture of what is currently required in the world of work. The student profits from an in-depth work experience and frequently finds a direct route to a full-time job.

Data needs. Schools need information on graduates for evaluation and planning purposes. They must know the number of students placed on jobs, relationship of those jobs to their vocational training, length of stay on one job, etc. While the schools should conduct their own surveys, they also need cooperation of manpower trainers as well as employers and community agencies.

Even more critical to the success of vocational education programs is data on labor market demands. For this purpose schools must rely almost entirely on manpower agencies and business and industry sources. If schools are to plan training programs to meet employers' needs, then manpower agencies must accept a responsibility to make sound data on current and predicted labor demands available to schools.

Adult programs. The retraining of workers whose job skills have been rendered obsolete—or workers who wish to change occupations—should be an integral part of the total program of vocational education. A flexible vocational education program can plan and offer adult courses from two weeks to two years in length, preservice or inservice, daytime or evening, at very low cost.

Programs are needed to train employees, for example, in new job techniques or new procedures to be installed in a company. Where school and industry linkages are well cemented, a company's training director will frequently ask the vocational director in the school system to design and operate such a program. This kind of cooperation makes good sense, because the school has a valuable community resource in its learning facilities and professional staff skills.

Vocational education has never pretended that it can do the manpower training job alone. As this chapter has tried to point out, vocational education needs the cooperation and support of all segments of the nation's manpower effort. Vocational educators claim no more than the ability to train entry-level workers, whether they are high school students beginning their careers or adults wanting to change jobs or upgrade their skills or positions.

The argument here is that the public school is the one institution in the national manpower structure that can reach the great mass of society and serve it at lowest cost. Its doors are open to all.

This has great implications for adult education and consequently for the national manpower effort. The concept of education and training as a lifetime pursuit is gaining acceptance not only in the United States, but internationally as well. One of the objectives of International Education Year, sponsored by UNESCO and celebrated in 1970, was that continuing education is a concept worthy of worldwide promotion. One can conceive, then, of a future in which the adult worker is not isolated from education. He is part and parcel of it.

Within the American public school system, vocational educators have without doubt the longest experience in adult education. The adult, either seeking to upgrade himself or to change occupations, is highly motivated. But he may have some drawbacks that a youngster does not have—a certain slowing down of reflexes, sensitivity about his adulthood, lack of confidence, increased family responsibilities, etc. The vocational educator, because of his professional preparation and experience, understands these strengths and weaknesses. His professional teaching and human relations skills can make a unique contribution.

Teacher Education and Manpower Training. Aside from professional teaching techniques, the vocational educator brings to his job technical skills and knowledge comparable to those of the industry trainer. But in an accelerating technology such as ours, technical skills can become outdated as rapidly in an instructor as a worker. Among valuable linkages, then, are those that permit vocational teachers to move back into their occupational fields at regular intervals. A number of cooperative arrangements are possible to give teachers this necessary refresher and inservice stimulation.

When a teacher goes back into employment while his industry counterpart takes over his vocational classes for a semester, the vocational teacher has an opportunity to brush up on new techniques, materials, and processes. He also gains new insights into conditions that will confront his students and firsthand knowledge of what industry supervisors, employers, and organized labor will expect of them. The strengths and limitations of his teaching performance are likely to become more apparent there than in his own teaching shop or classroom. At the same time the industry supervisor learns something of the broad role of the vocational teacher, better understands what to expect from an entry-level worker, and perhaps gains some appreciation of the strengths of preemployment training.

Many of these same benefits accrue when a vocational educator uses the summer to return to industry. He reexperiences some of the trials of an entry-level worker and goes back to his classroom or laboratory better equipped to teach both skills and attitudes.

Programs conducted by teacher trainers for industry and business supervisors are among the most valuable services of vocational education to the private sector. Their worth was proved during World War II when industry had to reach a high level of production under acute manpower shortages. Industry was faced with on-the-job training of inexperienced employees, and instructional techniques taught by vocational educators to line supervisors contributed greatly to this effort.

Connectors to Public Policy

Advisoryship, a practice of vocational education since its inception, is now recognized in the federal vocational acts and education in general, as well as in manpower training supported at the national level. The still persistent problem, however, is achieving full implementation of the concept. Often the advisory committee is tolerated rather than really utilized. The role of the advisory committee is to counsel and not to assume an administrative function—but advice that contravenes cherished myths and standardized ways of doing things can still be nettlesome to the routine-oriented educator. Advisory committee members, moreover, sometimes accept such assignments as a civic duty with no real comprehension of the commitment necessary.

Manpower councils, when broadly constituted to represent every element of manpower development, have great merit in planning comprehensive programs. Again, theirs is not an administrative function. They are advisory bodies whose objective is to keep every element in a comprehensive manpower development program in focus.

At the national level, the respective advisory councils for vocational education and manpower programs should be brought together for more frequent interaction. Their combined reservoirs of knowledge and talent could have a tremendous impact on efforts to establish national manpower training priorities, evaluate educational and training programs already in existence, and make recommendations to the various government agencies involved in preparing people for employment. This linking of human resources should also be achieved at the state level.

Legislatively, changes should be made in several ways. To prevent fragmentation, comprehensive manpower legislation should include specific provisions for national, state, and local planning and coordination. Comprehensive manpower plans on all levels should include the vocational education resources of the nation; advisory, planning, evaluating, and coordinating bodies should include official representatives of vocational education.

In addition, vocational education should have initial responsibility for development and delivery of the educational component of manpower programs, including basic education, communication and computation skills, high school equivalence, prevocational orientation, institutional training, cooperative occupational training, upgrading of employed workers, retraining, and work-study programs such as the Neighborhood Youth Corps.

In the administration of such a program there should be clear delineation of responsibility between the U.S. Department of Labor and Department of Health, Education, and Welfare. Interdepartmental rivalries in the past have been responsible for much of the overlap and lack of coordination that have characterized manpower policies. The Department of HEW should have administrative authority for the educational component. There should also be a coordinating interdepartmental council representative of operating departments and agencies and the public, appointed by and reporting to the President. In addition, the President should have on his staff a liaison between that advisory group and all agencies of the federal government which conduct manpower development programs.

Serving the Nation's Needs

A comprehensive program based on the public schools, such as that outlined here, is not in evidence today. But neither is it a utopian dream. It is subscribed to by a vocational education profession numbering some 50,000 members throughout the United States, and there is scarcely a component of it that is not being researched, developed, pilot tested, or refined somewhere in the 50 states. Career development, career choice, curriculum relevance, cooperative education, adult education, teacher education and updating, program planning, evaluation, and follow-up—the groundwork is being laid. An undertaking of such vast proportions, however dedicated its proponents, cannot succeed without adequate support, which implies linkages of another type, including a voice at the highest policy-making levels.

Through an evolutionary process, and in large part prompted by federal legislation, the philosophy of vocational education has become—simply stated—education for all. Vocational educators are now bound by responsibility to segments of the population that have heretofore been alien to their concerns—the dropouts, the disadvantaged, and the physically and mentally handicapped.

To discharge this responsibility effectively, vocational educators will need linkages with the professional community, including specialists in remedial education, learning disabilities, and the social sciences and ties in the public sector with manpower trainers in the Rehabilitation Services and personnel in public health agencies.

Inherent and inescapable in comprehensive vocational education are the premises that every individual has the basic right to as much education as he wants and is intellectually capable of absorbing, the right to employment in a job for which he is qualified, and the right to participate in the democratic processes of his society. Any attempt to solve the nation's manpower problem, then, must be viewed in a dual perspective—taking into account aspirations of people and job slots to be filled.

The worker who finds satisfaction in his job because he is in the career of his choice is the most productive worker. The public school program whose doors are open to all, whose philosophy is based on career choice and full development of the individual, and whose offerings are enhanced through a network of linkages with industry and the community should be in the best position to produce a maximum number of intelligent and adaptable entry-level workers and to provide those workers an opportunity to recycle through public educational institutions for a lifetime of learning.

Industry will benefit from a work force that is continually being retrained and reeducated and that constantly seeks opportunity to improve its own condition and its contribution to the economic and civic processes of society.

SPARKING STATE INITIATIVE:
An Education Bureaucracy Innovates

SHERWOOD DEES

The states run education by default, it might be said, for nowhere does the federal constitution mention public schools. Consequently, major responsibility for educational policy rests with the states, and throughout history they have fought to guard this prerogative. Most state constitutions specifically address this obligation. For example, the Illinois Constitution mandates its state government to "provide a thorough and efficient system of free schools, whereby all the children of this State may receive a good common school education."

The Founding Fathers' reserved power clause has resulted in the emergence of 50 somewhat different state educational complexes. They range from a single school district covering one state (Hawaii) to a pattern of well over a thousand districts in another (Illinois). Organizational arrangements also vary from state to state, ranging from complete decentralization of authority, with local school districts enjoying almost total autonomy, to highly centralized control from the state level.

The amount of supervision exercised by a state department of education is related in part to its financial support for local education. When the state contribution comprises a very small percentage of the total local educational budget, then decision making almost invariably reverts to the local school board. Where, however, the level of state support increases to 60 per cent or more of total operating costs, closer state regulation

---

Sherwood Dees is Director of the Vocational Education Division of the Illinois Board of Vocational Education and Rehabilitation.

naturally tends to ensue. This takes the form of requirements for course offerings, building and safety standards, teacher certification, etc.

Action and Inaction

Roald F. Campbell and Gerald E. Sroufe [1] have identified four classifications of functions performed by a state department of education:

(1) service activities—advising, consulting, preparation of curriculum guides, and dissemination of statistical and other information possessed by the department;
(2) planning and development activities—setting goals, establishing procedures to attain them more efficiently, and continued evaluation of programs in terms of original goals and new situations;
(3) public support and cooperative activities—seeking public support and working in liaison with other agencies;
(4) regulatory activities—providing a set of minimum standards for all public school systems in the state.

A delicate balance must constantly be struck between applying pressure for change in local districts and protecting the initiative and integrity of local control of education as a viable entity. In general, however, it can be said that state departments of education have been far less active in the reform of education programs than in any other aspect of public education.

New developments in curriculum and pedagogy have originated in colleges and universities and more recently in regional educational laboratories or independent innovative schools, usually without either state support or stimulus from the state level. New approaches have been disseminated through these same channels and by the education industry, again independent of state action.

State education agencies have typically confined their interests to personnel and facilities standards, and only incidentally have they endeavored to modify curriculum content or instruction. Yet, the greatest unmet need in American education today lies precisely in the improvement of the instructional program; specifically, the educational challenge of the seventies is preparing youth for the world of work.

Historically, schooling in the United States tried to emulate Western European designs; hence, the emphasis on formal academic subjects, with highest value on verbal skills, has evolved into a hallmark of American

---

[1] Roald F. Campbell and Gerald E. Sroufe, "The Emerging Role of State Departments of Education," *Strengthening State Departments of Education*, R. F. Campbell, G. E. Sroufe, and Donald H. Layton, eds. (Chicago: University of Chicago Midwest Administration Center, 1967), pp. 76-101.

pedagogy. For example, the public has come to rank its high schools on the basis of how many graduates they send to college. In view of this dominant criterion, most state departments of education have not felt encouraged or been organized or authorized to refocus educational programs toward developing youth for future occupations, and hence they have not made significant inroads into school curriculum matters.

With passage of the Vocational Education Amendments of 1968 by the Congress, federal legislation has finally given substance to state leadership in this field, authorizing a total of almost $4 million for vocational education over a four-year period. Emphasis now is on meeting the training needs of individuals, particularly the disadvantaged and handicapped, rather than on specific occupational programs. The Act, among other features, strengthens such existing programs as work-study, consumer and homemaking education, and demonstration residential vocational schools. Additional funds can be expended on new efforts in teacher education; curriculum development; exemplary, innovative guidance and counseling; and other special vocational programs for the disadvantaged and handicapped. For the first time, financial motivation of a substantial breadth can stand behind leadership from the state level to stimulate a metamorphosis from primarily academic education, in the traditional sense, to an education broadly inclusive of every student, including relevant instruction for occupational entry for the 80 percent of the student population which never finishes college. Finally, this legislation provides opportunity for realization of what has been called "creative federalism" —a partnership involving federal, state, and local agencies in a joint effort, a shared sense of responsibility for developing new activities.[2]

New Staffing Requirements

Gearing up for this leadership role requires both new blood and special administrative mechanisms at the state level. As Lloyd N. Morrisett, Sr., told the Education Commission of the States:

> Like de Tocqueville's ships, many state departments of education, in their structure and organization, have become obsolete in light of the rapid progress being made in the art of management. They are not structured, organized, nor provided with appropriate manpower to do the job. What is the job? It is to provide enlightened, forward-looking leadership and educational

---

[2] See Ewald B. Nyquist, "State Organization and Responsibilities for Education," *Emerging Designs for Education*, eds. Edgar L. Morphet and David L. Jesser, eds. (New York: Citation Press, 1968), pp. 133-91.

statesmanship; to extend services to the schools and the state; and to administer, at the state level, the state's system of public education.[3]

One such new mechanism is a separate state board of vocational education representative of state agencies involved in career education, such as executive departments dealing with public instruction, labor, business and economic development, manpower development, etc. The function of such a board, which is created under the Vocational Education Act to be separate from and independent of a state board of education, is to administer federal and state funds for vocational-technical programs and to establish priorities for such programs in the state. Many states use such a board as an administrative agency, technically meeting the requirement under the law, but they spend time and effort in other crises and problems rather than in career education. Education cannot operate in a vacuum, whether political, philosophical, or social; hence, a state board of vocational-technical education must develop a close working relationship with both the governor and chief state school officer if its work is to have statewide impact.

State departments of education have long been criticized for their failure to plan adequately. However, the Vocational Education Amendments provide for this need, in the form of state advisory councils for vocational education in every state. In order to receive its allotment of federal funds under this law in any fiscal year, a state must submit a plan to the U.S. Commissioner of Education. The state board of vocational education draws up such a plan in consultation with the council. A state plan has three essential parts:

(1) an administrative framework for organization of the vocational program;
(2) a long-range five-year program plan in terms of state manpower needs, anticipated enrollment, etc.;
(3) an annual program plan defining priorities, allocating funds in terms of manpower needs and enrollments, and providing for evaluation.

The primary function of the advisory council is to evaluate the progress of vocational education in meeting the needs of the state and to recommend changes for future state plans.

Staffing of a state vocational education agency also constitutes a key element for change. As governor of North Carolina, Terry Sanford wrote in *Storm Over the States:*

---

[3] Lloyd N. Morrisett, Sr., "Change and Development in State Departments of Education," *Power Play for Control of Education.* Proceedings of the 1967 Annual Meeting of the Education Commission of the States (Denver, May 1967), pp. 59-69.

. . . structure and organization alone are not enough. The states, more than anything else, need leaders strong and unafraid, willing to try new ideas and seek new paths, determined to make their states worthy of the name, to arouse the people to their opportunities, and to fulfill the role of the states in the American federal system.[4]

Since their founding, most departments or divisions at the state educational level have been filled with older occupational specialists waiting to retire. As a result, they have demonstrated little interest in taking the necessary steps to institute reforms. Instead, occupational education, under their supervision, has grown outdated in many states. As New York Commissioner of Education Ewald B. Nyquist has written:

Some state education departments are poorly staffed, too highly bureaucratized, and politically dominated. Some are characterized by intellectual incest: the personnel, in training and experience, seem to have come from the state's own educational system, and often from small school systems. Their qualifications show little outbreeding with business and industry, subject matter disciplines, and diversified provenance.[5]

Reversing this picture requires, first of all, attracting talented professionals in the prime of their careers who have the courage to change education through state leadership. Finding and holding these creative leaders will depend in part on the ability of state government to offer suitable compensation—competitive with business, industry, or distinguished educational institutions for positions of comparable responsibility—as well as paths of vertical mobility within the department of education.

In addition, such a staff will require inspired stewardship from above to encourage new ideas, support staff members on the firing line, and develop both professional and political ties to help reinforce the goals of change. This directive applies to the state director of vocational education, as well as the chief state school officer, the state board of vocational education, and the governor. As a final measure for change, the state vocational education agency must encourage initiative. Its professional staff should not have tenure or civil service status. Instead, performance should be subject to regular review under administration supervision of the state board of vocational education.

Revamping the Structure

The process of modernizing educational programs to prepare youth for future occupations involves, first, development of an eclectic phi-

---

[4] Terry Sanford, *Storm Over the States* (New York: McGraw-Hill Book Co., 1967).
[5] Nyquist, "State Organization and Responsibilities for Education," p. 147.

losophy of education, one which integrates all phases of the educational program into a common framework. As the various components interact, they hopefully will develop responses which contribute towards the student's preparedness for an adult world of work. Such a philosophy should apply to schooling from a very young age until leaving time and beyond that to the point of return for further training.

Updating the occupational education curriculum should also be examined in light of structural changes in the economy and the manpower requirements of the state and nation. A current need, for example, is for creation of new programs in such fields as the health occupations and personal and public service. Leadership at the state level must encourage —even require—schools to offer effective programs in career education in order to be eligible for state and federal funds. Continued high-level support of training which has lost its relevance to today's and tomorrow's family of occupations must be discouraged and terminated. In Illinois, for example, all school districts and community colleges are required to demonstrate continued progress in the expansion of career education to serve all youth and adults in their respective geographic areas as a condition of further funding. Such a directive might be carried out in a number of ways, including full utilization of the facilities of business and industry. Schools should also be prepared to subcontract with established private training institutions when they can provide such education more economically and effectively than the public education system.

The vocational education agency itself must be organized to provide for continuous interaction among all levels and facets of education and between vocational education and manpower programs. Such a structure must also give emphasis to the administration of the various titles of the Vocational Education Amendments of 1968. The administrative organization of the Illinois Division of Vocational and Technical Education can serve as one model (see Table 14). For example, the Special Programs Unit has responsibility for administering programs which are included in Title I of the Vocational Education Amendments—guidance, the handicapped and disadvantaged, cooperative education, work-study, consumer and homemaking education, and residential and area center planning. The Research and Experimentation Unit oversees research and development and exemplary programs, also included in Title I.

Within this division, occupational education consultants serve solely in the role of advisors to improve programs in their areas of specialization. The approval of programs for funding is authorized by a separate administrative division, the Program Approval and Evaluation Unit, which is separate from and independent of occupational education consultants. In most other states, such consultants have influence on both the qualitative aspects of programs and on funding, which is detrimental because

Table 14 ORGANIZATION CHART, DIVISION OF VOCATIONAL AND TECHNICAL EDUCATION, ILLINOIS BOARD OF VOCATIONAL EDUCATION AND REHABILITATION

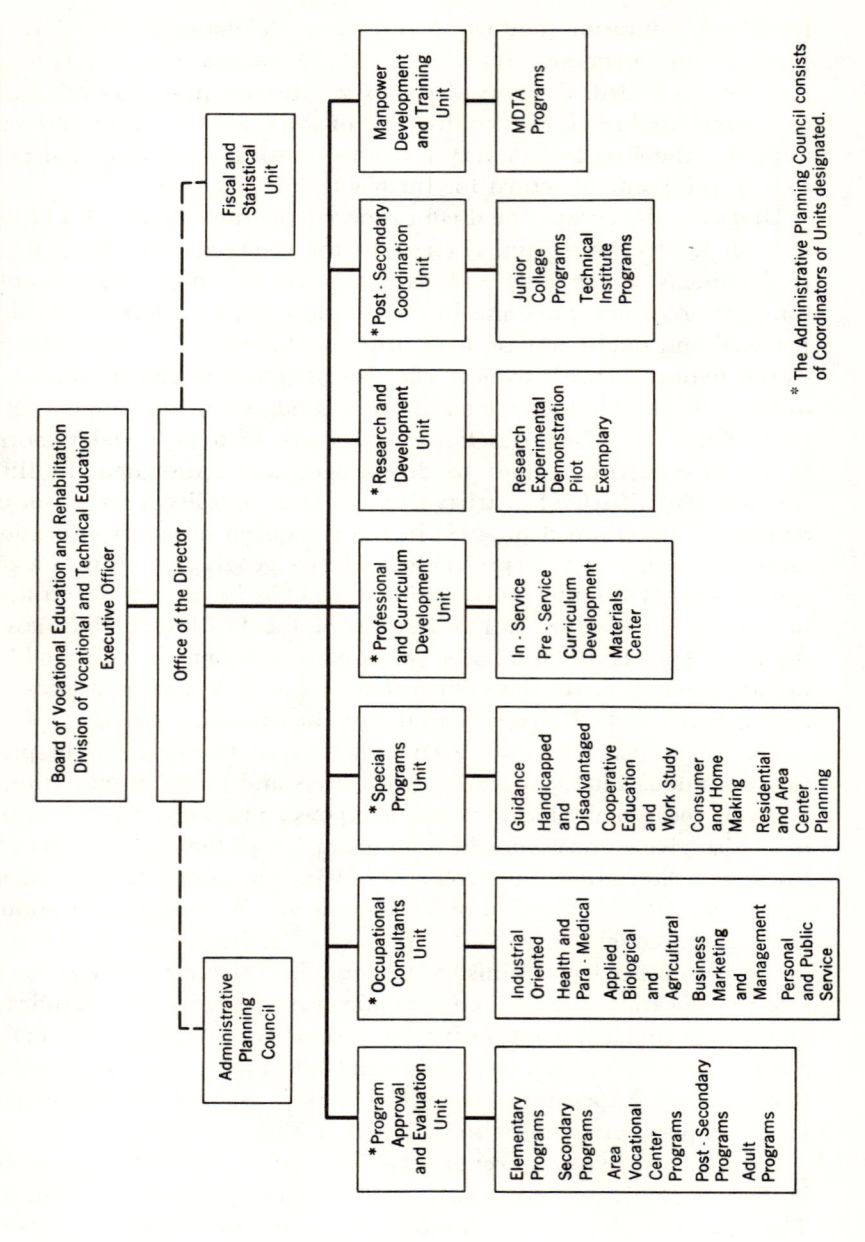

```
                    Board of Vocational Education and Rehabilitation
                    Division of Vocational and Technical Education
                                  Executive Officer
                                          │
      ┌───────────────────────────────────┼───────────────────────────────────┐
 Administrative                    Office of the Director                Fiscal and
 Planning                                                                Statistical
 Council                                                                    Unit
                                          │
   ┌──────────┬──────────┬──────────┬─────┴────┬──────────┬──────────┬──────────┐
 *Program   *Occupational *Special  *Professional *Research  *Post-     Manpower
 Approval   Consultants  Programs   and Curriculum and       Secondary  Development
 and        Unit         Unit       Development   Development Coordination and Training
 Evaluation                         Unit          Unit       Unit       Unit
 Unit
```

*Program Approval and Evaluation Unit	*Occupational Consultants Unit	*Special Programs Unit	*Professional and Curriculum Development Unit	*Research and Development Unit	*Post-Secondary Coordination Unit	Manpower Development and Training Unit
Elementary Programs	Industrial Oriented	Guidance	In-Service	Research	Junior College Programs	MDTA Programs
Secondary Programs	Health and Para-Medical	Handicapped and Disadvantaged	Pre-Service	Experimental	Technical Institute Programs	
Area Vocational Center Programs	Applied Biological and Agricultural	Cooperative Education and Work Study	Curriculum Development	Demonstration		
Post-Secondary Programs	Business Marketing and Management	Consumer and Home Making	Materials Center	Pilot		
Adult Programs	Personal and Public Service	Residential and Area Center Planning		Exemplary		

* The Administrative Planning Council consists of Coordinators of Units designated.

they tend to follow the programs of the past. In Illinois, on the other hand, the Program Approval and Evaluation Unit makes use of outside experts from business, industry, and labor to visit programs and examine the whole area of vocational education.

Responsibility for manpower training has been assumed by most state governors to be separate from the educational functions supervised by chief state school officers. However, education for the world of work is actually a hybrid undertaking, bridging the specialized knowledge of both manpower and school programs. Therefore, it is strongly advisable for a vocational education agency to have supervisory authority over the administration of manpower development and training programs at the state level.

Most state education agencies have been weak in the areas of research and experimentation in vocational education. Their usual practice has been to fund new programs as research without careful attention to research design, provision for evaluation of results, mechanisms for recycling feedback to modify projects, or dissemination of results. Therefore, a separate unit in the state agency should be devoted to research and development, with significant financial support from the state level for funding experimentation, demonstration, pilot, and exemplary programs to improve career education.

Finally, a state division of vocational education must bring together all educational interests which participate in providing youth with opportunities for future career preparation. Programs in the public elementary and secondary schools, community colleges, universities, and private training agencies, along with the business and industrial community, must be united in a team effort so that every school makes an equal effort to train and place students for employment. In addition, a state education agency should bring in young people to advise on programs. Their idealism, imagination, and energy must be utilized in helping to strengthen and broaden public education for the world of employment.

If they are to retain the mantle, states must exercise new courage and leadership for change in American education. Courage comes in many forms—moral, personal, organizational—but whatever the shape or size, the substance must be the same, for the future of every young person in each local school district in the nation depends on it.

IV

THUNDER FROM ABOVE

CAPTAINS AT THE HELM:
New Directions for Educational Leadership

SHARLENE PEARLMAN HIRSCH

WHO LEADS?

The Experts

"We have amply eloquent expressions of the directions in which we ought to go. We just haven't gone there."[1] John W. Gardner's astute observation reflects much of the frustration experienced by Americans everywhere in assessing the deficiencies of their public education systems.

Studies continue to multiply and diagnoses and prescriptions mount; yet the blemishes grow more profuse and abscessed. Charles Silberman's analysis, *Crisis in the Classroom*,[2] offered potent examples of recent successes in experimental school programs and cost the Carnegie Corporation of New York $300,000 to produce. This document is now on the shelves next to such well-known and expensive predecessors as the Havighurst report (on the Chicago schools), Passow report (Washington, D.C.), Bundy report (New York), recommendations of the National Advisory Council on the Education of Disadvantaged Children (on Title I of the Elementary and Secondary Education Act), reports of such university service stations as the Harvard Center for Field Studies (on St. Paul and other cities), recommendations of private consulting firms, and

---

[1] "Living Up To Professed Values," *The Christian Science Monitor* (September 30, 1969), p. 9. Quoted by permission from *The Christian Science Monitor*. © The Christian Science Publishing Society. All Rights Reserved.

[2] See Charles E. Silberman, *Crisis in the Classroom* (New York: Random House, 1970).

171

countless other investigations liberally financed by school boards, federal legislation, foundations, and private donors.

The analysts have, for the most part, done their jobs well; many excellent, workable recommendations have been offered to clients. Yet, although some have been implemented, the proliferation of quality ideas and suggestions continues to outdistance any tangible results. This illustrates historian Andrew Hacker's observation that mere articulation of social problems does not seem to ensure their solution. Hacker has written:

> More and more of us are now part-time sociologists; we have no difficulty in dilating on all manner of crises from poverty and civil liberties to pollution and violent crime. Whether in conferences, committee meetings, or cocktail parties, we talk endlessly about . . . generation gaps, . . . bad bureaucratic bungling, the need for community and the demise of the American spirit. We are literate, knowledgeable, and as correct as any society has ever been in its assessment of its dislocations. . . . [But] sociological sophistication seldom prompts individuals to eschew personal pleasures so as to make society a better place.[3]

Those in Charge

Reformation of American education will necessitate more than new formulae for change. It will demand an unparalleled depth of commitment from all citizens—from the general public as well as the education profession—to achieve anything of lasting value. Inspiring the necessary measures of altruism and dedication will, in turn, depend on the quality of leadership which guides the functioning of the education enterprise —and today this includes a surprisingly large group of executives. Each of the approximately 21,000 public school districts is headed by a superintendent. A total of about 30,000 principals head public and nonpublic secondary and junior high schools. There are over 73,000 public and 15,000 nonpublic elementary schools, each with its own principal. Within these systems, in addition, assistant principals, department chairmen, curriculum directors, and team leaders all share responsibility for innovation. The growing number of small experimental schools being founded by parents, community groups, and educators offers additional leadership possibilities.

The range of titular and actual leadership positions extends far beyond schoolmen, however. Officials in state and federal education bureaucracies with titles such as commissioner and branch, division, and bureau chiefs and directors often have significant influence on shaping policy. Professional organizations and associations, some of which maintain effective

---

[3] Andrew Hacker, "We Will Meet As Enemies," *Newsweek* (July 6, 1970), pp. 24-25. Copyright Newsweek, Inc., 1970.

political lobbies for education, have their officers and directors. Members of the "education industry" also can claim an impact on the quality of instruction. Task forces and advisory councils on education have their chairmen and staff directors. Governors, mayors, Presidents, and Congressional and state legislative committees have their education assistants and consultants. Community action, model cities, and job training programs and day care centers have directors for their educational activities. At the university level, faculty and administration influence policy in their roles as trainers, researchers, and advisors (through speeches, publications, appearances before legislative committees, etc.).

Courage To Change

Clearly, however, as the present status of American education—including vocational training—has demonstrated, "courage to change" does not automatically develop with accession to positions of authority. "This enormous complex is no better than the people in it," Edward J. Meade, Jr., has written, "and American education, unfortunately, has no surplus of able, enlightened, creative, knowledgeable, and effective leaders." [4] Thus, Meade views the executive role in education as more than just competent administration of educational policy, with emphasis on management and organization. The distinctive characteristic of leadership is the added dimension of courage exercised through the initiation and implementation of educational policies which may not be universally appealing at first but hold high promise of paying off in sound education. Leadership in this sense entails the audacity to move from the status quo toward improvement of education at a time when uncertainties exist about outcome, resistance from some constituents is inevitable, and all the problems normally accompanying change are practically guaranteed.

Too many educational leaders, though well-intentioned, have been unwilling or unable to make the difficult decisions which could move education forward, because this might risk their own good will with the profession and community interests or threaten their job security and advancement. Such ambivalence is not peculiar to education, of course. It seems to abound in government, business, and the society at large. While self-protection is justified by some as a necessary measure for survival, the most powerful values in this instance argue that institutions *must be reformed* when they fail to serve the public interest and that this can occur only if strong, wise, and skillful leadership presides at the helm of public trusts such as education.

---

[4] Edward J. Meade, Jr., *Foundations, Schools, and the Public Good* (New York: The Ford Foundation, 1965), p. 9.

How does an individual develop the capacity for such leadership? Unfortunately, too little is known about personal and environmental processes and events which endow a person with high ideals and the determination to persevere despite actual or potential threats to professional security and which give him sufficient breadth of insight, perspective, and knowledge of education to make a genuine difference in the lives of its consumers. Research into educational leadership has been superficial and generally inconsequential; and speculation on the subject has hardly proved more productive. In the interest of probing the problem further and of offering some possible new direction, let us begin with these working assumptions:

(1) the identification and selection of future leaders has critical implications for the health of American education;
(2) the types of training experiences provided for educational leaders can further influence their capacities to function with courage as agents of change; and
(3) promising new environments must be created to help leaders implement reforms.

What efforts are being made at present to improve the quality of executive practice in the field?

THE TALENT HUNT

Self-Perpetuating Profession

The education fraternity is infamous for its inbreeding. Most of its executives have advanced in a typical pattern that begins with a degree from a college of education and moves on to teaching positions and ultimately to administrative assignments, probably with a break to pursue further education. Professional incest is, of course, practiced widely and perhaps prima facie does not constitute an automatic evil. However, if this practice operates to exclude capable, talented individuals just because they lack the requisite in-house training and experience, then the entire field is threatened with loss of able and gifted manpower.

James B. Conant, former U.S. Commissioner of Education, was a physicist prior to assuming the presidency of Harvard. Horace Mann was trained in the law. Engineers, urban planners, ecologists, clergymen, attorneys, architects, medical doctors, community action leaders—they and others might qualify as potential candidates for educational leadership, but almost none is currently serving in such a capacity. Powerful professional cliques of education associations and schools of education, coupled with state education bureaucracies, have prevented the reform of state credentialing systems which in turn eliminate noneducators from most leadership positions.

A few of the more advanced doctoral programs in educational administration, such as that of Stanford University, have made some effort to attract noneducators, but even those outposts continue to be dominated by the education fraternity. The program at Ohio State University received a generous federal grant to attract experienced executives from other fields to educational administration; however, their program is separate from the regular doctoral path, and no degree options will be offered to them.

If education were a strong, self-sufficient profession with a substantial body of tested knowledge and a solid record of service to the nation's youth, then perhaps this narrow perspective could be tolerated more comfortably. However, education, despite some of its ancient ivy trappings, remains a very young, fragile, and incomplete discipline which has just begun to offer some new hypotheses. As such, it could only stand to suffer at this critical juncture from perpetuating homogeneity and superficial exclusivity at the expense of encouraging cross-fertilization—or what Donald P. Mitchell has called the "necessary mix"—which could well provide the transfusion needed to suggest new directions. While still in its infancy, therefore, education has a unique opportunity to resist the dogmatism which has plagued so many other fields and invite a broadly based group of talented people to take charge of major educational endeavors.

Conducting the Search

Identifying men and women with the potential courage for reforming American education is not simple, particularly if ordinary assessment criteria are employed. Intelligence and aptitude tests currently in use—the Graduate Record Examination or Miller Analogies Test is typically required for entrance to graduate schools—tell little about leadership ability as defined here; nor do college academic records measure these attributes any more satisfactorily.

The real test should be previous performance in leadership situations, as evaluated by the individual himself and others capable of judging his accomplishments. The search should therefore center on recruiting those who have shown a strong commitment to quality education, are willing to risk self for higher goals, and have demonstrated hard skills or aptitudes for creating educationally sound alternatives.

STRENGTHENING EDUCATIONAL LEADERSHIP

The Degree Hassle

In education the tangible symbol of competence for leadership has been the advanced degree—perhaps a master's but preferably the doctorate —most often in educational administration. A few writers, such as David Hapgood and, in Chapter 2, Hugh Calkins, have challenged the assumption that diplomas and credentials insure quality performance in teaching; their skepticism can also apply to educational leadership.

Acquisition of any academic degree seems to have little relationship to possession of the ability to exercise effective leadership. Americans have made important contributions to education without benefit of the earned doctorate. Such a list includes two former U.S. Commissioners of Education, Francis Keppel and Harold Howe II; former Secretary of Health, Education and Welfare John W. Gardner; Cleveland Superintendent of Schools Paul W. Briggs; New York State Commissioner of Education Ewald B. Nyquist; and the late Mrs. Agnes Meyer, founder of the National Committee for Support of the Public Schools. But there are also effective leaders, such as Detroit Superintendent of Schools Norman W. Drachler and former head of the Newton, Massachusetts, schools Charles Brown, who have the doctorate. As many who hold the Ph.D. or Ed.D. in education would readily admit, earning the degree is probably not a significant factor in one's ability to exercise sound leadership. Furthermore, as many have confided in private conversations, they would not choose the doctoral route again if the pressures to do so were lifted.

Even more persuasive evidence of the deficiencies in most administration programs is found in the legacy of rapidly deteriorating public education which now confronts us. Education's leaders must bear a major responsibility for this impoverished state, and consequently, programs charged with training these standard bearers must also accept their share of the blame for ineffective performance in executive development.

University programs in educational administration have suffered from a number of shortcomings, a primary complaint being that their orientations and expectations are usually remote from the vital issues facing contemporary leaders. While graduates move almost immediately from their studies to decision-oriented settings, programmatic emphasis, in contrast, dwells on the designing and conducting of research, compelling participants to meet performance standards appropriate for scholarly vocations in the academic world rather than high-powered executive positions.

If such criticisms are justified, why do these programs ordinarily attract so many applicants? Educators can answer this one rather quickly: the road to key positions in this field has traditionally required a doctorate. This requirement takes the form of state credentialing laws and local salary schedules, both of which reward the pursuit of further education. It is also reflected in the influence of doctoral programs on professional placement. Higher educational institutions have long exercised substantial influence on the selection of leaders, particularly in public school systems but also in government and the private sector. Faculty members regularly serve as consultants to communities, organizations, and institutions searching for executives, and they are naturally inclined to recommend their own graduates. Consequently, the advanced degree syndrome is reinforced through personal and institutional networks of communication, and those without the credential are simply unable to compete.

Research Versus Performance

In recent years some institutions have tried to improve their offerings, primarily by building a performance component into otherwise academic curricula, usually through off-campus internship arrangements. These include Teachers College of Columbia University, the University of Pennsylvania, University of Wisconsin, Stanford University, University of Chicago, Claremont, Harvard, and the University of Massachusetts. Nevertheless, their research biases remain intact through requiring a whole series of traditional courses in education and related areas, and by staunchly maintaining the standard thesis.

The University of Massachusetts has experimented with making requirements somewhat more flexible and performance-based. A candidate may substitute prior job or related experience for particular courses and receive university credit in "modules" for undertaking projects such as the development and evaluation of programs. Despite these positive efforts, however, the research thesis survives. The School of Education has proposed replacing it with on-the-job performance which would be evaluated by a committee, but this awaits approval by the university.

Hence, no matter what the particular program or school, a candidate for the doctorate in administration who aspires to revamp the education scene through effective decision making is judged not by his actions in a natural executive setting but on his skill in reviewing literature, however irrelevant; designing a research project, however contrived; and demonstrating results measured according to the orientations of faculty committee members, however inexperienced in the effective implementation of educational change. Over time, these criteria can tend to affect the whole selection process, as well. If research becomes the primary goal of a program, then it naturally follows that persons with high potential for succeeding in this area should be recruited, but typically their values, orientation, strengths, and interests are far removed from those needed in decision-centered environments. Under the circumstances, it does not take long for an entire leadership training effort to become transformed into another academic exercise with low output of courageous educational executives.

Educational leadership development programs are needed to expose trainees to the range of vital educational issues confronting the nation, to equip them with management tools and techniques, to develop their intellectual ability to analyze problems, to deepen their capacity to relate to others—especially young people—and to provide broad, long-term experiences in real-life situations which can enable them to test out various leadership behaviors. Such programs, as Alvin Toffler has emphasized, should be future oriented, not just historical in their approach.[5]

Equally necessary is a programmatic commitment to lifelong professional development of educational leaders. Leadership can be a lonely, isolated existence in a world where acceptance and belonging are important to most people. Taking risks in order to achieve results requires support in such forms as access to current information about successful change strategies and the nature of national and state priorities; new insights into one's own behavior as a leader; and encouragement from other professionals. Leadership development programs should therefore assume a continuing sense of obligation for their offspring, beyond conferral of the degree or organization of alumni reunions and encompassing a person's entire professional career.

Not all directors of leadership training efforts are short-sighted or unaware of these needs. Many have tried to introduce more performance elements into their plans, only to collide with negative reactions from faculty or face threats of takeover by the traditional academic mold. The Administrative Career Program at Harvard began with a strong experiential base and even introduced the project as an alternative to the thesis requirement. Through the years, however, research and course requirements have been added under various faculty pressures and the project itself is now expected to include a considerable chunk of research evidence.

Antiperformance attitudes are deeply rooted in the university ethic, which rewards scholarship and research and tends to look askance at any proposed departure from the research doctorate. They forget that music students customarily give recitals to win their degrees or that painters and sculptors are expected to display their products as a test of com-

---

[5] See Alvin Toffler, *Future Shock* (New York: © Random House, 1970).

petence. However ingrained this may be in an arts curriculum, the traditionalists fail to see the analogy to educational leadership. Because faculty members have power of approval over changes in academic policy, most reformers have found their goals thwarted before they are even tested.

Some scholars such as Jacques Barzun are genuinely concerned about what they consider the threatened debasement of the university's role in advancing inquiry and scientific investigation. To them, a performance-based degree is vocational and has no place in an environment devoted to intellectual pursuits. Others take the narrower and more personal position that because they "came up the hard way" via the traditional route, it should be preserved for all time.

This dialogue is part of the larger debate focused on the role of the university in society and its relationship to contemporary issues and events. The range of prevailing sentiments was rather clearly reflected in discussion of the question of legitimacy of student participation in the election campaigns of 1970 for academic credit. Princeton had developed a proposal whereby students could spend the first few months of the 1970-71 academic year working on election campaigns and receive university credit by meeting certain requirements (this was later modified when the U.S. Treasury Department began questioning the tax-exempt status of institutions which supported participation in partisan political campaigns). Almost every other university faculty which considered the Princeton plan, including Harvard, voted it down by sizeable majorities as inappropriate to the intellectual objectives of the university.

Whatever might have been the merits of this particular situation, it seems increasingly evident that any attempts to institute performance-based academic programs at any level, but especially for doctoral candidates, can expect considerable resistance from academicians and, if initiated, will probably be subject to constant scrutiny and critique before they have had an opportunity to mature.

The Lone Dissenter

Perhaps the only genuinely hopeful sign on the academic horizon is the Union Graduate School, a relatively new consortium of approximately 18 institutions which provides doctoral programs tailored to individual career goals and centers on the integration of performance and knowledge with the student himself as synthesizer. The substance of each candidate's work is developed with his committee, whom he chooses from among leaders (not necessarily academicians) in his special area. The program focuses on the student's project, which is undertaken in an experiential setting such as a job or internship. Committee and candidate decide what knowledge is needed to complete the project and the individual may then obtain it through any means at his disposal—course work, independent study, consultation with experts, etc. Performance is evaluated on the basis of criteria established mutually by committee members and the candidate.

Hence, Union is the only American institution to date which has made a firm commitment to a performance-based doctorate. To exist, it must still overcome certain traditional obstacles, such as accreditation. Moreover, its graduates at this early stage run the risk that their degree will be considered inferior to those from more established institutions. But the long-range possibility that Union could serve as a model for programs of the future more than justifies these short-term sacrifices.

Internships

In recent years some innovators have begun to doubt whether performance-based programs stand a chance of survival in the university. Concurrently, they have legitimately questioned whether the doctorate is necessary for anointing their chieftains. The degree requirement has become a particularly salient issue to those concerned about increasing the number of black, Spanish-speaking, and other minority group leaders in education. Lack of advanced degrees has prevented many otherwise able and experienced persons from applying for such positions, thus pointing to the need for reexamination of these requirements. Thus, the case has been made that participation in significant leadership development experiences should constitute a valid criterion for the selection of educational executives and should even be considered an acceptable substitute for the doctorate.

A number of nondegree internship programs have been created, all looking toward identification of potential leaders and the design of appropriate activities to develop and strengthen their particular abilities. Some, such as the Congressional Fellows program of the American Political Science Association and the Academic Administration Internship Program of the American Council on Education, expect candidates to have the doctorate or to be in final stages of doctoral study. Others, however, have seen the internship as an alternative to traditional study.

Perhaps the largest effort towards the development of local leadership in education is the Leadership Development Program operated by The Ford Foundation on a regional basis throughout the United States. Fellows have a commitment to the improvement of education at the local level. They take a year off from their regular assignments to spend in internship experiences, travel, and various types of meetings developed according to their individual professional goals. Many return to their previous employment at the end of the program. As a follow-up, the program offers small grants to ex-Fellows to pursue special projects while on the job.

At the national level perhaps the largest programs in education (excluding the White House Fellows, who may be in a wide variety of fields including education) are the Office of Education Fellows and Washington Internships in Education. Concern about development of a performance degree has been of particular concern to the latter.

Established in 1964, Washington Internships in Education annually brings to Washington a group of approximately 18 potential leaders in education, based on nationwide recruitment. Fundamental to the WIE concept is the belief that future educational executives should have an opportunity to gain realistic experience in positions of substantive responsibility under the tutelage of existing leaders and should also have the chance to broaden their understanding of educational policy through exposure to various governmental and national agencies and organizations, travel to educational programs, meetings with key policy makers, etc.

The program has two basic parts, the agency assignment and educational component. Each intern spends three-fourths time in a position with an agency, organization, or institution in Washington which has a major commitment to the improvement of American education. Sponsors of interns are at a sufficiently high level to afford them a broad overview of leadership responsibilities. The educational component fills the final quarter of an intern's time. It provides resources for interns as a group to explore educational issues of mutual interest, to travel, to meet significant leaders, to observe programs in action, etc.

One problem common to internship programs is lack of involvement of interns in substantive assignments. Very often they become merely observers or are totally excluded. With a few exceptions, WIE has succeeded in overcoming this problem by a combination of strategies. The agency itself is required to provide compensation to the program for three-fourths of the intern's time, whereas most internship programs provide their manpower free of charge. The agencies also have final selection of those assigned to them. Having made these commitments, therefore, most sponsors are careful to include their interns as an integral part of the staff, often with a special title and set of responsibilities.

The WIE selection process emphasizes past performance. As part of the application form, the potential intern describes a project or program in which his participation has made an important contribution. The program also recruits widely to include both noneducators and those with background and experience in the field. Interns' major fields have included law, economics, political science, mathematics, biology, theology, and public administration.

While most academic programs have concentrated on filling school superintendencies and principalships, WIE graduates have ranged widely in their choice of professional positions. Several are, in fact, school superintendents or headmasters of independent schools. Others have had key staff roles as assistants to university presidents, governors, and congressmen or have held line positions such as director of model cities education, associate commissioner in the U.S. Office of Education, and division head in the Department of Labor. A few have become directors of educational organizations, and many are middle managers in education bureaucracies.

For those without the doctorate, participation in WIE has not always been sufficient to qualify for key leadership positions. This has been particularly true for minority group members. Therefore, WIE sought out a number of higher educational institutions to explore ways in which the program might become the vehicle for a performance doctorate. Except for Union, however, each program insisted on retaining course or thesis requirements, or both. Hence, the degree hurdle still remains a very real one for those who want to move into responsible executive assignments, even when they have had a stimulating training experience in WIE.

NEW ENVIRONMENTS FOR CHANGE

No matter what the calibre of existing leadership, the environment has a strong effect on possibilities for reform. A former associate commissioner in the U.S. Office of Education was asked how he liked his new job outside government. "At last I'm in charge," he said with obvious satisfaction. A staff member close to an Assistant Secretary's office, and rumored to be influential, left the Department of Health, Education, and Welfare to head a nongovernment program. "What will I do with this money?" he pondered, staring at his new budget, which was only a small fraction of the funds he had budgeted in his old job. "I'm used to dealing with billions, it's true, but this is the first time I've ever really been able to decide how to spend it."

Unwieldy organizational arrangements have stifled creativity, imagination, and drive, making valuable leadership talent swiftly come to feel paralyzed by the distant chains of command. Some have suggested the need for "self-destruct organizations" or autonomous modules of talent which could be mobilized for particular functions and then dismantled. Others have foreseen the expansion of computerized decision making. The intelligent application of group process techniques could help to create a more open, sensitive working environment, whether or not basic structures are altered.

Any realistic projection of human resources indicates that the pool of available talent for leadership with the characteristics discussed in this chapter will always be smaller than the demand. With scarce resources for training, one possibility is to invest in those with greatest potential, in hope of creating a multiplier effect. Another is to reexamine the entire spectrum of leadership roles, particularly in public school systems. Are 20,000 school superintendencies necessary or even viable today? Donald P. Mitchell, for example, has suggested that schools might be run by "executive teams" composed of economists, social workers, architects, etc., as well as educators.

It seems apparent that new means of organizing human resources to provide new roles and relationships, better opportunities for impact and involvement, and a sense of closeness to problems and decisions must be found. Their creation must parallel the appearance of more effective training programs and better means of identifying potential leaders. The vitality for change must clearly come from "captains at the helm," but also needed are arrangements in which people of value can work with satisfaction and even become inspired to expand their skills, knowledge, and productivity. Patterns and structures must be changed along with the people in them.

LEADERSHIP AND PROFESSIONAL VALUES

Too many educational leaders today spend substantial segments of their professional time pursuing outside consulting, building private businesses, serving on the boards of various companies and organizations, and otherwise increasing their own personal reservoirs of influence with only marginal if any benefits for the institutions they serve. An executive with constant public exposure receives numerous invitations for speaking engagements, writing assignments, consulting, etc., offering anywhere from $200 or $500 to $1000 or more per appearance. It is not uncommon for such leaders to be listed on the boards of directors of 10 or 15 outside enterprises, and James Ridgeway has documented some of the ties between university leaders and major companies in *The Closed Corporation*.[6]

Conflict of interest as a legal entity is not involved here. Instead, there is a relevant ethical question concerning the extent to which educational leaders responsible for public trusts should use their positions for bla-

---

[6] See James Ridgeway, *The Closed Corporation* (New York: Random House, 1968).

tantly self-entrepreneurial purposes. A leader with outside interests can easily increase his annual income by $10,000 or more. But for many the plum is not just financial—it is the opportunity for expanded personal contacts and potential power. Were they required to forego honoraria and fees, the issue would still remain unresolved.

Nor is the problem simply one of time usage. Most leadership positions are not simply eight-hour-a-day, five-day-a-week jobs. The more important the assignment and demanding the task, the less possible it is to separate one's private and public lives. Given the situation, an educational leader is not in a position to justify his extracurricular pursuits as part of his own private time, because his role is such that he is always considered part of the public payroll and a public servant.

Educational leadership positions must be filled by extraordinary men with the highest integrity and regard for the nature of the educational enterprise as a public responsibility demanding full professional attention. New models of appropriate executive behavior in public service are urgently needed, but these examples must be set by the educational leaders themselves.

The problem of outside involvement can be approached from several directions. The most positive course of action is to identify and train potential leaders who can devote themselves entirely to public service. In turn, the people should be prepared to compensate their educational stewards for the financial sacrifices they make in assuming such positions. As a parallel measure, professional organizations such as the American Association of School Superintendents, American Association of Junior Colleges, American Council on Education, etc., should look into this question and recommend full public disclosure of noninstitutional activities, indicating approval of only those commitments which have a direct relationship to the immediate concerns of their respective institutions. Such professional accountability is clearly justifiable where public funds are involved, and it is long overdue from the education community.

IN PERSPECTIVE

The main theme of this book has centered on the need for an eclectic approach to career education, a union of intellectual and practical exercises which can build a solid foundation for entire working lifetimes. Without courageous leadership, however, these will remain paper goals. The identification and development of potential leaders, creation of new professional environments for accomplishment of change, and the renovation of public service values are the instrumental vehicles for the reform of American education.

V

THE COURAGE TO CHANGE RECONSIDERED

EPILOGUE:
Prospects for the Future

ROMAN C. PUCINSKI

Debut of a Decade

The 1970s are upon us. Deep within the cosmic aggregate of our economic, social, political, physical, cultural, and even spiritual souls throb the wheels of change, hurling the nation's seemingly formidable but nonetheless fragile institutions into the tumultuous currents of controversy and challenge—probably for the rest of the twentieth century. The great problems of the seventies cannot be ignored. And surely one of the most persistent issues for the nation's educational system is this: Can American education measure up to the broad mandates for reform and, in particular, confront the overwhelming need for effective career preparation?

It is hardly news that our work-oriented society creates extraordinary dependence on job satisfaction for personal happiness or that deep psychological distress often results from unemployment, underemployment, or lack of a suitable job. Given these conditions, and assuming the work ethic will continue to dominate our value system in the final third of the twentieth century—albeit the nature of employment may change with new developments in technology, fluctuations in the economy, shifts in the social milieu, etc.—the contributors to this book have expressed their astonishment at the marginal attention, if not total neglect, accorded the problem of career development by the nation's schools.

As noted, education in its present form prepares people primarily for more education. The fact that almost all pupils will eventually join the world of work merits only peripheral acknowledgment, at best, from any school curriculum. Instead, education programs are buried in a maze of perhaps individually worthy but nonetheless disconnected undertakings, highly uneven in quality, which have pushed the schools beyond their basic institutional capacities to respond to the needs of children and youth and have ignored the fundamental question about what should be the central concern of American education.

Schools must be judged *first* and *foremost* on the basis of how they affect young people—not on their ability to serve the interests of teachers, principals, the education industry, government bureaucrats, or vested interests in the community. The cold, insensitive, even inhumane treatment of learners in many of our schools has been vividly documented in books by a number of ardent educational reformers, and their powerful appeals can speak for themselves. One might add the suggestion that the schools' lack of humanity may be linked in some inextricable way to their preoccupation with expansion and power, at the expense of their clients. Therefore, a moral imperative of the seventies must be to reinfuse the schools with sensitivity toward their learners and rededication to making lives richer and more productive.

Looking Ahead

The legacy of the sixties has already begun to plague the nation's schools in the new decade. Continuing fiscal constraints, mounting student demands for greater flexibility and more relevance in their instruction, and growing community disaffection with the quality of American education are going to force America's educational institutions to achieve a new dimension of tough-mindedness in setting priorities. It takes little clairvoyance to foresee some of the calamities that may well force American education to reconsider its directions for the remainder of the decade.

1. *Per-pupil expenditures, though rising nominally, will probably fail to meet the growing demands for expanded educational services.* Nationwide, investment per student ranges from $430 to $1350. Increased pressures from teachers' unions, plus mounting inflation, will most likely cause these figures to rise, but growing public resentment over tax increases will generally keep such increases to a minimum. In fiscal 1969, for example, the public approved less than 44 per cent of $3.9 billion in bond issues, the lowest rate of approval in seven years. Moreover, as President, Richard M. Nixon made clear that he intended to hold the lid on federal spending for education, despite the protests of a majority of both houses of the Congress.

Faced with such limitations, the schools will have several alternatives. For one, they can simply create a holding pattern for their operations, eliminating proposed new programs and trying to maintain their existing empires intact, in the hope that financial restrictions will eventually ease. For those school executives without the courage to change, this path is particularly appealing. It promises to offend very few of those already established in the school system, and it places the leader in a position to plead poverty to the community when questions are raised concerning the quality of schooling being produced.

The other alternative—far more risky, politically, but sounder professionally—is to undertake a thorough appraisal of present commitments, relative to the benefits consumers have a right to expect from education and the role schools can reasonably be expected to play in achieving such goals. This will require abandonment of the notion that schools can continue as the everyman of social institutions, firmness with educational constituencies which have established fiefdoms in the form of ongoing school programs, and complete candor with the public regarding the capacity of the schools to perform various functions.

2. *Student defiance against schooling as presently constituted will probably continue to mount in the seventies.* Expressions of discontent from young people were voiced long before they began resorting to overt forms of social protest in the nation's high schools and junior highs. Dropping out, truancy, delinquency, and underachievement were early warning signals of the need for broad educational reform. Regrettably, however, these harbingers were ignored by most of the academic community—and adults in general.

Today, virtually all students, no matter what their geographical location, socioeconomic bracket, or age, seem to share a common sense of frustration that most of what confronts them in school is useless. During the seventies, they can be expected to augment their level of defiance, overtly or covertly, against business as usual in education, against the authoritarianism and rigidity which characterize much of the learning process, and against absorbing a curriculum which they deem remote from their concerns about adult issues and their aspirations for their own future lives.

3. *Public dissatisfaction with the quality of American education will probably continue to spread rapidly.* A special 1970 Gallup poll of the public's attitudes toward public schools indicated that adults were rapidly losing confidence in the claims of educators that American schools are doing an effective job. As the schools persist in failing to meet their traditional educational responsibilities—such as teaching youngsters to read and compute—and as the education profession's resistance to public accountability grows more obvious, parents and concerned citizens can be expected to raise their growing collective and individual voices to demand results.

Concerns about school discipline and drugs, as well as learning achievement, may well pit the community against its schools. Of course, the most extreme forms of social deviance can be dealt with by stringent measures. Nevertheless, a social disease cannot be eradicated by use of force, or by spawning new programs requiring extra funds. Dealing with the phenomenon of alienation—of both students and community—from the schools will require a total redirection of the educational effort.

The Collective Wisdom

Contributors to this book have expressed the belief that one of the primary missions of public education is to help prepare pupils for the world of employment, and to this end they have offered a number of specific recommendations. Comprehending their full meaning, however, requires that there should first be some clarification of what these suggestions do *not* mean.

1. *Neither replication nor replacement of vocational education is being proposed.* Career preparation must be conceived as a broad social process, one which includes educators and adults not connected with the education community, and one which draws on wide areas of knowledge as well as job skill training. The constant interaction of student with larger environment is an essential ingredient in his orientation to employment, as is equipping him with those marketable skills which schools themselves can teach efficiently and effectively. To the extent that vocational education can contribute to occupational training for this technological era, it should become an integral element of the total concept, which legitimately includes a number of other components.

2. *The value of more traditional academic subjects—the humanities, natural and social sciences, and mathematics—should not be discounted.* Rather, the issue is one of focus. The main contention here is that priority must be placed on the student's preparation for adult roles and that this type of education is most effectively imparted when he can place the concepts and information from various disciplines within some type of common, integral framework which has personal, experiential meaning and future value to him.

Educators have already learned through sad experience that most of the so-called "important knowledge" they transmit is never retained beyond the tests for which it was memorized. Earliest findings of the National Assessment project tend to confirm the theory that the most powerful learning occurs when abstractions can be tied to concrete experiences of the individual learner.

At a time of mounting teenage unemployment and dissatisfaction with schools throughout the country, we cannot afford to waste pupils' time ingesting knowledge as a mere abstract exercise. Rather, learning must be made real, vital, and significant for an adult world which will require all available talent and resources to solve its pressing problems, and which has enormous potential to provide personal happiness for its citizens.

3. *That pupils must master basic learning skills (reading, computational skills, etc.) is not to be overlooked.* These skills should be taught early in a child's life, using the most efficient and effective methods available. Such instruction might occur in school or could be concentrated through learning laboratories in the private sector on a performance contract basis.

With these parameters clearly in mind, it becomes possible to summarize briefly some of the major changes recommended by the contributors to this book and then to search for ways in which they might be implemented:

- A school diploma should carry a performance index, stating precisely what marketable skills the student can be expected to produce as a result of his education. (Hugh Calkins)
- The schools should be held accountable by parents, students, and the economic community for preparing pupils for work. (Grant Venn)
- In light of projected needs for manpower during the rest of the seventies, career preparation programs should focus more broadly on an orientation to employment as well as more specifically on many of the newer technical occupations. (Garth L. Mangum)
- Teacher preparation programs should focus on human interaction, helping to match up trainees' teaching styles with pupils' learning protocols in order to maximize the utilization of available human resources. (Carl J. Schaefer)
- Guidance and counseling programs should center on the process of rational decision making for careers, and help students use vocational information to make rational choices. (David V. Tiedeman)
- The educational system should mobilize both vocational educators and manpower trainers in a common effort to provide occupational training through the public schools, and should expand national and state advisory councils to include both groups. (Lowell A. Burkett)
- The community college should play a central role in coordinating career education from first grade through four-year higher education, beginning with a general orientation to work in the younger grades and progressing to specific marketable skills. (Marvin J. Feldman)
- Educators should welcome the participation of businessmen in career development programs and not feel threatened by the presence of "outsiders." (Samuel M. Burt)
- To make job training relevant to the needs of the black community, there should be a national policy of full employment and a "Marshall Plan" for America's inner cities. (Cleveland L. Dennard)

- Career education in city schools should be linked directly to job opportunities which exist in the metropolis and strengthen students' insights into the urban environment in which they will live and work. (Paul W. Briggs)
- The states must exercise more active leadership in the reform of vocational education programs through reorganization of the state education bureaucracy, stripping state education bureaucrats of civil service protection and attracting talent through increased salaries and opportunities for promotion, and a strong, independent state board of vocational education. (Sherwood Dees)
- Vocational education for women can be strengthened through curriculum reform to include more realistic understanding of women in employment situations, inclusion of more women in policy making for vocational education and in leadership of professional education associations, and further research into various aspects of women in the working world. (Elizabeth J. Simpson)
- The key to changing education lies in its leadership, and the quality of educational decision making by executives in various positions in public and private school systems, government, and the private sector depends on their ability not only to make sound judgments but also to exercise courage in difficult situations. Present programs to train educational leaders are too strongly immersed in research techniques and traditional classroom work and too little related to on-the-job performance. They should be replaced with action-oriented programs which stress the ability to make and execute decisions. (Sharlene Pearlman Hirsch)
- Career education should reserve large blocks of time for students to spend in the real world of work under supervision of adults in tutorial types of arrangements. This might be accomplished through the "three-and-two-day week" in which students would spend three schools days in classes dealing with basic subjects and participate in field work the other two days. This would free teachers for inservice training and professional preparation. (Roman C. Pucinski)

The National Response

Coming to terms with these and other needed changes will not be easy. Yet, Americans have never been known to turn their backs on difficult educational problems, even in the face of opposition.

When Horace Mann called for free elementary schools for the poor in the early 1800s, there were public outcries that the working class did not need formal education.

When concerned parents brought action in the Kalamazoo Case for universal education at the secondary level, the critics charged that the principle of high school for everyone created needless expense.

When John Dewey fought for more humane treatment of students and development of the "whole individual" in schools during the twenties and thirties, opponents retorted that "training the mental faculties" through rote memorization and harsh discipline was far more beneficial.

When B. F. Skinner demonstrated through rat and bird experiments that learning could be effected by operant conditioning, he was labeled a far-out laboratory scientist—until programmed instruction through application of computer technology was developed from his findings.

When the Brown Case was prosecuted in 1954, the policy of separate-but-equal de jure educational systems was long entrenched and seemed immovable in many states throughout the nation. Today, such systems are being broken up under court orders.

And when, in 1958, the National Defense Education Act was passed by the Congress—the first significant piece of legislation in this field since the Morrill Act of 1862 creating land-grant colleges—total federal spending for education was only $21 billion. Today, that figure has reached over $60 billion.

The present list of federal legislative accomplishments in education is lengthy. Besides NDEA it includes provisions for such purposes as vocational education, school libraries, curriculum innovations, research and development, school construction, school lunches, training of teachers and administrators, education of the handicapped and the educationally disadvantaged, preschool education, adult basic education, bilingual education, higher education program and facilities, guidance and counseling, strengthening state departments of education, and a number of other purposes.

The lingering problem, as many critics have pointed out, lies in the fragmented nature of these various approaches. The resulting state of legislative disarray, in turn, has tended to reinforce the divisive, contradictory, and piecemeal state which permeates a large proportion of existing educational efforts at the local level. The Congress cannot expect major movement towards broad-scale renovation if its education laws move in scores of different directions, with each "speck" funded by a different part of the U.S. Office of Education or state education agency, each having its own guidelines and priorities.

Now that recent legislative history has firmly established the principle of strong federal support for education, the next step must be consolidation of many of these provisions based on the central thrust of *universal, lifetime, comprehensive career education for all Americans*. From early years until retirement, the nation must guarantee every individual the opportunity to develop his capacities, skills, knowledge, and personal attitudes in continuous preparation for changing roles of his adult working life.

But this goal can only be achieved if mandated through the laws which provide federal support for American education—and if those laws are fully funded by the Congress and supported by the President.

Economic growth, personal security and satisfaction, the vitality of our social fabric and durability of the democratic system—all will depend on the effectiveness of a strong, successful public educational system and, most of all, on our own national "courage to change."

INDEX

INDEX

A

Abortion laws, 62
Accommodation, 127
Accountability of educators, 34-35, 193
   community control and, 37
   computers and, 38-39
   distrust of social institutions and, 39
   National Assessment of Education and, 36-37
   performance contracting and, 39
   program effectiveness evalutions and, 35-36
   recommendations about, 40-42
   student protests and, 37-38
Administrative Career Program (Harvard), 178
Adult education, 155
Adult Education Center, Inc. (New Orleans), 148
Advertising for workers, 73
Advisory mechanisms about women, 75
Advisoryship, 157, 163
Aeronautical engineering programs, 12
Age Discrimination in Unemployment Act (1967), 70
Agriculture programs, 12-13
Air pollution, 45
Aircraft repairmen, 99, 101
Alcoholism, 44
Alienation from schools, 109-11
American Association of Junior Colleges, 77
American Council on Education, 180
American Political Science Association, 180
American Technical Education Association, 77
American Vocational Association, 77

Apprenticeship programs, 12, 99-101, 111
Area Redevelopment Act (1960), 55
Area Redevelopment Act (1962), 13
Area vocational schools, 13
Armour family, 11
Arson in schools, 46
Assistant principals, 172
Auto body and fender repairmen, 101
Automation, 111
Automobile mechanics, 95, 101
Automotive sales, 101

Bureau of Work Training Programs, 56
Burkett, Lowell A., 84, 150-59, 193
Burt, Samuel M., 84, 140-49, 193
Business
　minority, 56
　role of, in vocational education, 137, 141-46, 150-53, 193
　　Connecticut, 147-48
　　financial, 148-49
　　Louisiana, 148
　　Texas, 146-47
Buying, consumer, 78

B

Banta, Trudy W., 142n
Barbers, 101
Barnard, Henry, 3
Bartending by women, 71
Barzun, Jacques, 179
Basic skills, 50, 193
Bean, Orson, 7
Beauvoir, Simone de, 76
Berg, Ivar, 10, 24
Bestor, Arthur, 4
Black studies, 49
Black Americans, 22
　career preparation and, 53-58, 193
　in community colleges, 112-13
　leave South, 44
　women, 72
Blacksmiths, 101
Bloom, Benjamin S., 133
Blue-collar workers
　discrimination against, 32-33
　See also specific occupations
Bond issues, 190
Bookkeeping, 95
Brick masons, 99
Briggs, Paul W., 22, 42-51, 194
Brown, Charles, 176
Bruner, Jerome, 3, 126
Budget, national, for education, 34, 110, 190
Budget analysis, 107
Building trades, 101
Bundy report, 171
Burchinal, Lee G., 63

C

California, 112
Calkins, Hugh, 21-33, 176, 193
Campbell, Roald F., 161
Capital expansion of schools, 45
Career
　children, marriage and, 62-64, 71-72
　definition of, 123
　job, home, family, and, 69-72
Carnegie, Andrew, 3
Carnegie family, 11
Carpenters, 99
Center for Priority Analysis, 55
Certification, teaching, 137
Chambermaids, 66
Chemical engineering programs, 12
Chicago, 5, 112, 140, 171
Child care, 63, 77-78
Child care aide, 70
Childbirth, time off for, 71, 73
Children and marriage and career, 62-64, 71-72
Children's Community Workshop (New York), 7
Cities
　disparities of, 43-45
　education in, 45-46, 194
　　Cleveland, 46-48, 50-51
　　work preparation, 48-51
Citizenship, 9
Civil disorders, 37-38, 109, 191
Civilian Conservation Corps, 55
Civil Rights Act (1955), 55

Civil Rights Act, Title VII of, 70
Civil Service Act (1883), 70
Claremont College, 179
Clark, Kenneth B., 5, 40
Classification Act (1923), 71
Cleaners, 66
Clerical jobs, 65, 67
Clerical workers, 9, 90, 95-100
Cleveland, 45-48, 50-51, 113, 148
Clothing service worker, 70
Clothing services, 77
Coleman Report, 36, 124
College of Human Services, 30
Colleges of education, 136
Color, discrimination based on, 70
Commercial art, 101
Communal living, 62
Communications, 45
Community, 18, 141
Community colleges, 111-15, 193
   connecting with four-year institutions by, 116-17
   interlocking educational systems and, 115-16, 150-51
   manpower training and, 117-19
   redesigning, 119-20
Community control of education, 37, 161
Compensatory education, 36
Competence, 123-24
   job, education and, 10
Compositors, 99
Computer programming programs, 12, 101
Computers
   educators and, 38-39, 138
   guidance and, 127-29
Conant, James B., 174
Congress, 57
Congressional Fellows program, 180
Connecticut, 147-48
Construction, 86, 90, 95
Construction Industry Council, 146
Consumer buying and ethics, 78
Consumer education, 15
Contraception, 62
Contractors, federal, 70, 73
Control over one's life, 124
Cooks, 66
Cooperative education, 14

Corporations
   leave cities, 44
   See also Business
Craftsmen, 9, 67, 99
Cray, Douglas W., 149*n*
"Creative federalism," 162
Credit, 101
Crime, 44-45
Current Occupation and Past Training of Adult Workers, 95*n*, 99*n*
Curriculum, 161
   development of, 15, 137-38, 162
   obsolescence of, 111
Curriculum directors, 172

D

Data processing programs, 12, 101
Davies, Don, 133-34, 139
Day-care facilities, 63, 77-78
Decentralization of school systems, 37
Decision making
   guidance and, 123-27
   in terms of goals, 78
Dees, Sherwood, 84, 160-67
Degrees, 21-22, 176-77, 193
   alternatives to
      blue-collar discrimination, 32-33
      education as preparation for work, 28-29
      educators reform, 31-32
      occupations redesigned, 29-30
      performance standards, 27-28
      tests, 26-27
   minority groups and, 180
   quest for, 23-26
Dennard, Cleveland C., 22, 52-58, 193
Dennison, George, 7
Denonn, L., 6*n*
Department chairmen, 172
Department of Health, Education and Welfare, 158
Department Store Union, 142
"Desegregation Report," *Congressional Quarterly*, 49*n*
Dewey, John, 3, 21, 195
Die-making, 101
Differentiated staffing, 134
Diplomas. *See* Degrees

Domestic servants, 66
Double sessions, 45
Drachler, Norman W., 176
Drafting, 101
Draftsmen, 95
Draper, Dale C., 135
Dropouts, 150, 153
Drucker, Peter, 32, 33n, 149
Drugs
  addiction, 44-45
  in schools, 46

E

East St. Louis, 46
Economic Opportunity Act (1964), 13
Education Professions Development Act, 139
Educators, 18, 107
  accountability of, 34-35, 193
    community control, 37
    computers, 38-39
    distrust of social institutions, 39
    National Assessment of Education, 36-37
    performance contracting, 39
    program effectiveness evaluations, 35-36
    recommendations, 40-42
    student protests, 37-38
  externship of, 138-39
  functional organization for, 132-35, 139
  reform of, 31-32
  regeneration process of, 137-39
  training programs for, 131-32, 136, 151, 156-57, 162, 193
  in vocational programs, 135-36, 151-52, 156-57
Effectiveness evaluations and educators, 35-36
Egner, R., 6n
Ego strength and guidance, 122-23
Eight-Year Study of progressive schools, 35
Eisenhower, Dwight D., 54
Electrical engineering programs, 12
Electricians, 99-101

Electronic technologists, 106
Electronics programs, 12
Elementary schools, 75-76, 115, 154
Elementary and Secondary Education Act, 16, 38, 171
Ellis, Allan B., 128
Employment
  national policy of, 54-56, 58
  nature of, 189
  occupations, 90-108
  projections, 86-90
  of women, 60-61
Employment Act (1946), 54
Engineering technologists, 106
English teachers, 76
Environmental health occupations, 107
Equal Employment Opportunity Commission, 57
Equal Pay Act, 70
Erikson, Erik H., 122
Ethics, consumer, 78
Ethnic studies, 49-50
Executive Order 11246, as amended by 11375, 70
Executives, educational, 172-73
Exemplary programs and projects, 14
Experts as educational leadership, 171-72
Explicit knowledge, 125-26
Externship, 138-39
Extinction of school systems, 5-6

F

Factory jobs, 67
Fallaci, Oriana, 76
Family
  career, job, home and, 69-72
  forms of, 62
Farber, M. A., 9n
Fayerwether School (Cambridge), 7
Featherstone, Joseph, 30n
Federal contractors, 70, 73
Federal employees, 90
  salary of, 71
Federal guidelines about women, 73
Federally Employed Women (FEW), 71-72, 75

"Feedforward," 123-24
Feldman, Marvin J., 83, 109-20, 193
FEW (Federally Employed Women), 71-72, 75
Fifteenth Street School, 7
Figure and ground, 125
Finance, 90, 93, 101
Financial management, 78
Finch, Robert H., 4
Firemen, 101
First Street School, 7
Fishery programs, 12
Florida, 112
Floristry, 107
Folger, John K., 24
Food management, 77
Food service worker, 70, 101
Ford family, 11
Ford Foundation, 180
Foremen, 67, 99
Fortitude, personal, 4
Fortune, 143
France, 65
Francis Parker School (Chicago), 7
Freedom, 9
Friedenberg, Edgar, 4
Froomkin, Joseph, 24
Functional organization for educators, 132-35, 139
Functional staffing, 134-35

G

Gardner, John, 6, 171, 176
Gary, Indiana, 39
General Electric Company, 50-51
George-Barden Act, 12
George-Deene Act, 12
George-Ellzay Act, 12
George-Read Act, 12
Goals, decision-making in terms of, 78
Gooding, Judson, 11
Goodman, Paul, 4, 7
Goods producing industries, 90, 93
Graduate Record Examination, 175
Grants, state, 13-14
Graphic artists, 101
Graves, Robert, 76

Greenhouse, Linda, 130*n*
Ground and figure, 125
Group care worker, 70
Group process training, 136
Guidance, 136, 162, 193
  computers and, 127-29
  counselors, 76, 129-30
  decision-making process and, 123-27
  ego strength developed and, 122-23
  services, 77

H

Hacker, Andrew, 172
Hamburger, Martin, 140*n*
Handicapped people, 162
Hansen, Lorraine, 79
Hapgood, David, 24*n*, 31, 32*n*, 176
Harman, David, 25
Harriman family, 11
Harvard Center for Field Studies, 171
Harvard University, 177, 179
Havighurst report, 171
Hawaii, 160
Health occupations, 106, 140, 165
Hechinger, Fred M., 126*n*
Henry, Jules, 11
Hentoff, Nat, 4
Herndon, James, 4
Hill family, 11
Hirsch, Sharlene Pearlman, 171-84
Hofstadter, Richard, 10
Holt, John, 4
Home and career, job, and family, 69-72
Home economics programs, 12-13, 15, 63, 77-78, 162
Home services, 77
Horn, Marilyn J., 69
Horowitz, Elinor Lander, 71
Hotel occupations, 101
Hotel and Restaurant Employees Union, 142
Hough area (Cleveland), 47-48
Housing, 44-45
Howe, Harold, II, 176
Humanistic education, 7, 133-34, 136
Humanities, 192

I

Identity crisis, 122
Illich, Ivan, 4, 7
Illinois, 160, 165
Illinois Division of Vocational and Technical Education, 165-67
Illiterates, 25
Inadequacy, 124
Income and education, 10
Independence, 123-24
Induction, 127
Industrial workers, 93
Industry
  career preparation programs and, 137, 141-46, 150-53, 193
  Connecticut, 147-48
  financial, 148-49
  Louisiana, 148
  Texas, 146-47
  goods producing, 90, 93
Information System for Vocational Decisions, 128-29
Initiative, 124
Instinct and intellect, 7
Instructional space, 134-35
Insurance, 90, 93
Intellect and instinct, 7
Interior decorator's aide, 70
Interlocking educational systems, 115-16
International Association of Machinists, 142
International Education Year, 155-56
Internships, 136, 180-82
Interpersonal relationships between students and teachers, 132-36
Intuition, 125-26

J

Jackson, Andrew, 21
Jaffe, 24
Jefferson, Thomas, 11, 21, 52
Jencks, Christopher, 7, 114-15
Jesser, David L., 162n
Job and career, home, and family, 69-72
Job competence and education, 10
Job Corps, 13, 26, 56
Job performance and education, 10, 24-25, 27-28
John Adams High School (Portland), 7
Johnson, Lyndon B., 13
Johnston, David F., 10n

K

K-16 system, 115
Kalamazoo Case, 194
Kaufman, Jacob J., *Role of the Secondary Schools in the Preparation of Youth for Employment, The*, 67-68
Kennedy, John F., 13
Keppel, Francis, 149, 176
Kindergarten, 75-76
Klaurens, Mary, 79
Knowledge, 125
Koerner, James D., 31
Kohl, Herbert, 4
Koontz, Elizabeth, 72
Kozol, Jonathan, 4
Krathwohl, David R., 133

L

Labor force, 9-10
  employment predictions for, 86-90
  occupations, 90-108
Laborers, 100
Landy, Stephen, 125
Language, 127
Layton, Donald H., 161n
Leadership, educational, 194
  climate for change and, 182-83
  courage of, 173-74
  executives as, 172-73
  experts as, 171-72
  professional values and, 183-84
  search for
    conducting, 175
    self-perpetuating profession, 174-75
  strengthening
    degrees, 176-77
    internships, 180-82
    research versus performance, 177-79
    Union Graduate School, 179-80

Leadership Development Program, 180
Learning styles, 134
Lecht, Leonard, 55
Legislation for women, 70-71
Leonard, George, 17

M

Maccoby, Eleanor E., *Work in the Lives of Married Women*, 63
McComb, Mississippi, 38
Machine shop, 101
Machinists, 99
McLuhan, Marshall, 17
Male, Raymond F., 31-32
Managers, 9, 67, 93, 95
Mangum, Garth L., 83, 85-108, 193
Mann, Horace, 3, 21, 174, 194
Manpower development
  community colleges and, 117-19
  programs, 54-56
  vocational education and, 150-59, 193
Manpower Development and Training Act, 13, 55, 148, 151
Manpower Report of the President, 90n, 100n
Manufacturing, 86, 90, 93-94
Marriage and children and career, 62-64, 71-72
Masia, Bertram B., 133n
Mass transportation, 44-45
Materialistic values, 62
Mathematics, 192
Mead, Margaret, 17
Meade, Edward J., Jr., 173
Mechanical engineering programs, 12
Media, 5
Medical care, 44
Medical technologists, 101
Memorization, 4
Merchandise clerks, 101
Meyer, Agnes, 176
Miami, 46, 113
Middle class, 44
  children of, 45
Midjaas, Ruth E., 77
Millay, Edna St. Vincent, 59
Miller, S. M., 28-29
Miller Analogies Test, 175

Mining, 86, 90
  by women, 71
Minority groups
  degrees and, 180
  industry and, 143
  in labor force, 86-90
Mississippi, 38
Mitchell, Donald P., 175
Model Cities program, 119
Morgan family, 11
Morley, Eileen, 123n
Morphet, Edgar L., 162n
Morrill Act (1862), 195
Morrisett, Lloyd N., Sr., 162-63
Mort, Paul, 35
Mueller, Kate H., 79
Muggings, 44

N

Nam, Charles B., 24
National Advisory Council on the Education of Disadvantaged Children, 171
National Alliance of Businessmen, 153
National Assessment of Education, 36-37, 192
National Association of Manufacturers, 141, 143
National budget for education, 34, 110, 190
National Defense Education Act (1958), 12, 195
National Education Association, 37-38, 126
National Industrial Conference Board, 143
National Labor Relations Act, 70
National Organization of Women (NOW), 71-72, 75
National origin, discrimination based on, 70
National Planning Association, 55
National Vocational Student Loan Insurance Act (1965), 13
National Youth Administration, 55
Natural science, 192
Neal, Gaston, 52
Nealon, John G., 138n

Neighborhood Youth Corps, 13, 56, 158
Neill, A. S., 7
New Careers program, 30
New Haven, 147
New Orleans, 46
New York, 5, 46, 112, 140, 171
New York City, 37-38
Nixon, Richard, 190
NOW (National Organization of Women), 71-72, 75
Nursery school, 76
Nurses, 95, 101
Nursing assistants, 101
Nyquist, Ewald B., 162n, 164, 176

O

Obsolescence of curriculum, 111
Occupations, 90-108
  redesigned, 29-30
Ocean Hill-Brownsville district, 37
Office of Economic Opportunity Act (1965), 55
Office of Education, 72
Office of Education Fellows, 181
Officials, 9, 90, 95
Ohio State University, 175
Origin, national, discrimination based on, 70
Ott, Herbert A., 5
Overcrowding in schools, 45

P

Painters, 99
Paraprofessionals, 30
Parkway School (Philadelphia), 7, 148
Passow report, 171
Pearl, Arthur, 30
Pedagogy, 161
Performance
  job, education and, 10, 24-25, 27-28
  research and, 177-79
Performance contracting and educators, 39
Per-pupil expenditures, 190
Personal development, 78
Personal fortitude, 4

Philadelphia, 40, 44, 46, 113
Phillips, Charles, 79-80
Photography, 101
Planning and advising, 15-16, 18
Plumbers, 99
Polanyi, Michael, 125n
Police, 101
  cost of protection by, 44
  inside schools, 46-47
Pollution, 45
Poor people, 44
  children of, 45
Population explosion, 62
Postman, Neil, 4
Powerlessness, 124
Practical nursing programs, 12, 101
Practice teaching, 136
Pregnancy, time off for, 71
President of United States, 57, 158
President's Task Force on Women's Rights and Responsibilities, 73-74
Price Report, 147
Princeton University, 179
Principals, 6, 172
Private knowledge, 125
Private property, 143
Private sector of economy, 57
Professional jobs, 9, 67, 90-93, 95
Professional values and educational leadership, 183-84
Program auditing, 36
Program effectiveness evaluations and educators, 35-36
Project 100,000, 26
Promotions and education, 10
Property, private, 143
Proprietors, 9, 67, 90, 95
Protective laws for women, 71, 73
Protests, student, and educators, 37-38
Psychology, 136
Public attitude toward schools, 191-92
Public knowledge, 125
Public utilities, 44, 90, 94
Pucinski, Roman C., 3-19, 189-96
Purse snatchings, 44

Q

Quality control clerks, 107

R

Race, discrimination based on, 70
Radio repairmen, 99
Real estate, 90, 107
Recall in test situation, 27
Reformation, 127
Registered nurses, 107
Religion, discrimination based on, 70
Research, 93
 performance and, 177-79
 training and, 15
 on women, 74-75
Residential schools, 15, 162
Resources, management of, 78
Responsibility, 124
Reston, James, 39
Retail Clerks International Association, 142
Retail Store Union, 142
Retail trade, 90
Retirement age, 73
Rhodes, James A., 40-41
Richards, I. A., 123
Rickover, Hyman G., 4
Ridgeway, James, *The Closed Corporation*, 183
Riesman, David, *The Academic Revolution*, 114-15
Riessman, Frank, 30
Riots in school, 46
Robberies, 44
Rockefeller family, 11
Rogers, Carl, 133
Rogers, David, *110 Livingston Street*, 3
Role conflict for women, 60-62, 71-72
Rossman, Jack E., "Relations Among Maternal Employment Indices and Development Characteristics of Children," 63
Russell, Bertrand, 6

S

St. Louis, Mo., 44, 113
St. Paul, Minn., 171
Salaries
 of federal employees, 71
Salaries *(cont.)*
 gaps between men and women in, 66-67, 70
 increase of, education and, 10
Sales jobs, 5, 67, 99
Sales workers, 9
Sandler, Bernice, 67
Sanford, Terry, *Storm Over the States*, 163-64
San Francisco, Calif., 113
Schaefer, Carl S., 84, 131-39, 193
Schaefer, Robert J., 136
Schrag, Peter, 4, 28
Seay, Donna, 79
Secretarial occupations, 101
Semiskilled work, 65
Seniority lines, 73
Sensitivity training, 133, 136
Service jobs, 9, 65, 67, 70, 77, 90, 93-94
Sex, discrimination based on, 70
Sexual mores, 62
Sheet metal, 101
Shoe repair, 95, 101
Silberman, Charles, 4, 171
Simpson, Elizabeth J., 22, 59-81, 194
Skinner, B. F., 3, 195
Slater, Philip E., 69-70
Smith-Hughes Act, 12
Social institutions, distrust of, 39
Social science, 192
Social studies teachers, 76
Southern New England Telephone Company, 147
Special education, 13
Specialists, 136
Sponberg, Harold E., 149
Sroufe, Gerald E., 161
Staffing
 differentiated, 134
 functional, 134-35
 of vocational programs, 162-64
Stanford University, 175, 177
State government, 90, 118
State grants, 13-14
States and education, 160-61, 194
 action and inaction and, 161-62
 revamping structure of, 164-67
 staffing, 162-64
Status quo in education, 3-8
Stone, James C., 135-36
Strikes, 44-45

Index 206

Student protests, 37-38, 109, 191
Sub-contractors, federal, 70
Suburbs, population move to, 44-45
Summerhill, 7
Superintendents, 6, 172
Systems analysis, 107

T

Tacit knowledge, 125-26
Taxes, 45
Teachers, 18, 104
    accountability of, 34-35, 193
        community control, 37
        computers, 38-39
        distrust of social institutions, 39
        National Assessment of Education, 36-37
        performance contracting, 39
        program effectiveness evaluations, 36-37
        recommendations, 40-42
        student protests, 37-38
    externship of, 138-39
    functional organization for, 132-35, 139
    reform of, 31-32
    regeneration process of, 137-39
    training programs for, 15, 131-32, 136, 156-57, 162, 193
    in vocational programs, 135-36, 151-52, 156-57
Teachers College of Columbia University, 177
Teacher training programs, 15, 131-32, 136, 156-57, 162, 193
Teaching certification, 137
Teaching internship, 136
Team leaders, 172
Team teaching, 134
Technical jobs, 9, 67, 90-93, 95, 106
Technicians, 95
Tennyson, Wes, 79
Tenure, 134
Tests, as alternative to diploma, 76-77
Texarkana, Texas, 39
Texas, 146-47
Texas Construction Industry Council for Manpower, Education and Research, 146

Texas Education Agency, 146
Texas Mechanical Contractor Association, 146
Textbooks, 76
Thesis, 177
Thoni, Richard J., 79
Tiedeman, David V., 84, 121-30, 193
Tinsmiths, 99
Title VII of Civil Rights Act, 70
Toffler, Alvin, 130, 178
Towne, Douglas C., 142n
Tracking, 132
Trade programs, 12
Traffic rate clerks, 104
Training, college as, 94-108
Transportation, 44-45, 90, 101
TV repairmen, 99
Typesetters, 99

U

Unemployment, 11, 192
    of blacks, 53-54, 56
    women, 66
Unemployment Act (1967), age discrimination in, 70
Union Graduate School, 179-80
Unions, 111
    role of, in vocational education, 142
    teachers', 37
United Automobile Workers, 142
United Steel Workers of America, 142
University of Chicago, 177
University of Massachusetts, 30, 177
University of Pennsylvania, 177
University of Wisconsin, 177
Unskilled labor, 10, 85, 110
Upward Bound, 26
Urban studies, 50
Utilities, public, 44, 90, 94

V

Values, decision making in terms of, 78
Vandalism in schools, 46
Venn, Grant, 22, 34-42, 193
Viorst, Judith, 60, 76
Vocation, definition of, 123
Vocational Education Act (1917), 12

Vocational Education Act (1946), 12
Vocational Education Act (1963), 13
Vocational Education Amendments (1968), 13-14, 77, 84, 162-63, 165

W

Washington, D.C., 5, 40, 46, 171
Washington Internships in Education, 181-82
Water pollution, 45
WEAL (Women's Equity Action League), 71-72, 75
Weight-lifting by women, 71
Welding, 101
Welfare roles, 45
White-collar workers, 90, 93
White House Fellows, 181
White people leave cities, 44
Wholesale Store Union, 142
Wholesale trade, 90
Wolfson, Harry E., 140n
Women, 22, 30, 59-60, 90, 194
   abortion laws, 62
   career education of, 60-61, 63-64, 66-69, 71-72, 74-77
   child rearing, marriage, career and, 62-64, 71-72
   federal guidelines about, 73
   job, career, home, family and, 69-72
   legislation for, 70-71

Women (*cont.*)
   President's Task Force on Women's Rights and Responsibilities and, 73-74
   recommendations about
     advisory mechanism, 75
     education, 75-77
     higher education, 79
     home economics, 77-78
     new programs, 79-81
     organizations, 75
     research, 74-75
     special programs, 79
   role conflict situations and, 60-62, 71-72
Women's Equity Action League (WEAL), 71-72, 75
Women's Talent Corps of New York, 30
Woodland Enterprises, 148
Woolridge, Roy L., 138
Work ethic, 189
Works Progress Administration, 55
Writing, 5
Written instructions, responsiveness to, 27

Y

Yee, A. H., 131-32
Youth Conservation Corps, 13
Youth in labor force, 86
Youth revolution, 18